*For all boys and girls
who love to help things grow*

Jane Eayre Fryer

A GARDEN WHICH MARY FRANCES AND BILLY PLANTED

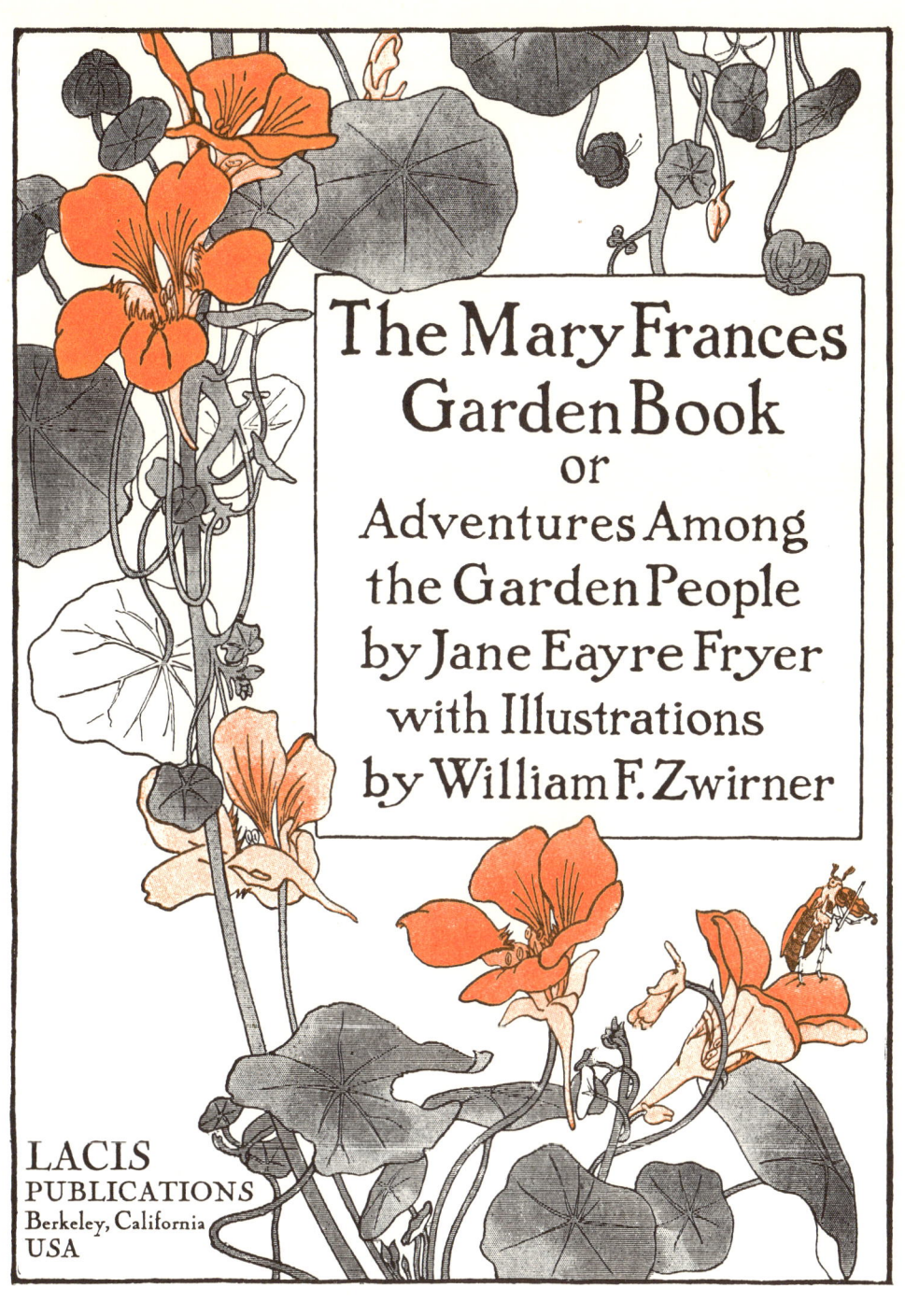

This book has been reprinted in response to the requests from the many friends of Mary Frances who have shared the joys of her world of imagination and who find the understanding of nature's wonders of utmost importance for all generations.

Originally published in 1916 under the same title; published by the John C. Winston Co. Original copyright 1916 by Jane Eayre Fryer

This book was the fourth of the Mary Frances instructional/story books which were designed to teach useful things in an entertaining way. The complete series includes:

THE MARY FRANCES COOK BOOK or
Adventures Among the Kitchen People (1912)

THE MARY FRANCES SEWING BOOK or
Adventures Among the Thimble People (1913)

THE MARY FRANCES HOUSEKEEPER or
Adventures Among the Doll People (1914)

THE MARY FRANCES GARDEN BOOK or
Adventures Among the Garden People (1916)

THE MARY FRANCES KNITTING & CROCHETING BOOK or
Adventures Among the Knitting People (1918)

THE MARY FRANCES FIRST AID BOOK (1916)

Most of these are available in similar heirloom quality editions from this publisher.

LACIS
PUBLICATIONS
3163 Adeline Street
Berkeley, CA 94703

© 1998, LACIS
ISBN 1-891656-01-5

PREFACE

Dear Boys and Girls:

Mary Frances and Billy have been growing up, and with their growing, they have learned to love the great out-of-doors.

No, they haven't outgrown fairy folk, at least Mary Frances hasn't, for that is a part of this story—how Feather Flop, the rooster, and Jack-in-the-Pulpit and Bouncing Bet, the fairies of the wood, helped teach her to garden.

But in their study and work, Mary Frances and Billy learned more than that—they learned to appreciate what a wonderful amount of energy is expended by Mother Nature in growing one little plant from a seed; how careful she is that nothing be wasted; and what pleasure there is in tilling the soil, and helping things grow!

Everything else in the Mary Frances stories had

to do with indoors: in cooking, feeding the body; in sewing, clothing the body; in housekeeping, sheltering the body. In gardening, which took them out-of-doors, the children had so much fun and had so much to learn, that the whole story cannot be put down here—you must finish it out for yourselves in your own gardens.

That you, too, may learn to help things grow, and share the pleasure which Mary Frances and Billy, and their friends, Eleanor and Bob, had in making a garden, is the wish of

THE AUTHOR.

MERCHANTVILLE, N. J.

ONTENTS

CHAPTER		PAGE
I.	Feather Flop, the Garden Boss	17
II.	Feather Flop Oversleeps	22
III.	Billy Plans the Garden	26
IV.	Feather Flop's Argument	31
V.	Gardens for Little Folks	34
VI.	Gardens for Big Boys and Girls	46
VII.	Early Spring Garden	51
VIII.	Early Summer Garden	54
IX.	Mid-Summer Garden	56
X.	Autumn Garden	61
XI.	Some Favorite Annuals	63
XII.	Window Boxes	69
XIII.	Billy Tests the Soil	74
XIV.	How to Plant	79
XV.	The Outdoor Seed-Bed	84
XVI.	Seed Babies and Their Nurses	89
XVII.	Names of Parts of Flowers	96

Contents

CHAPTER		PAGE
XVIII.	Good Mrs. Bee	102
XIX.	The Story of Fertilization	106
XX.	The Story of the Honey Bee	113
XXI.	How the Bees Work	119
XXII.	The Children's Money-making Plans	126
XXIII.	Mr. Hop Toad Hops In	131
XXIV.	Mr. Cutworm, the Villain	142
XXV.	Birds as Plants' Friends	145
XXVI.	Little Ladybird	153
XXVII.	Curly Dock	157
XXVIII.	The Stupid Honey Drops	161
XXIX.	Some Sprays for Garden Pests	165
XXX.	Early Vegetables	170
XXXI.	Feather Flop's Temptation	175
XXXII.	Feather Flop Gets Angry	178
XXXIII.	Father and Mother's Surprise	183
XXXIV.	Feather Flop Makes Up	188
XXXV.	Roses	192
XXXVI.	The Best Roses to Plant	199

Contents

CHAPTER		PAGE
XXXVII.	The Wicked Rose Bugs	211
XXXVIII.	The Fairy Wood Nymphs	217
XXXIX.	Good and Bad Weeds	225
XL.	Bouncing Bet and Her Friends	233
XLI.	Buttercup and Daisy Families	242
XLII.	Water Babies	249
XLIII.	How Plants Grow	257
XLIV.	A Wicked Innkeeper	262
XLV.	Uninvited Guests	267
XLVI.	How Seed Babies Travel	270
XLVII.	Have a Seat on a Toad Stool	274
XLVIII.	Some Ways to Rid of Weeds	280
XLIX.	Queen's Lace Trims Well	287
L.	The Wild Flower Garden	292
LI.	Growing Perennials from Seed	298
LII.	The Money the Children Made	303
LIII.	Mary Frances' Garden Party	310
LIV.	Feather Flop's Conceit	323
LV.	Bob and Billy's Vacation	328
LVI.	Daffodil and Other Bulbs	334

CONTENTS

CHAPTER		PAGE
LVII.	Billy Builds a Hotbed	344
LVIII.	Some Hints on Growing Vegetables	348
LIX.	The City Garden	360
LX.	Garden Color-Pictures	364
LXI.	Patterns for Paper Flowers	367
LXII.	The Mary Frances Garden Cut-Outs	371
LXIII.	Little Gardeners' Calendar	373
LXIV.	Budding and Grafting	376
LXV.	Prizes at the County Fair	377

THE MARY FRANCES GARDENS

To be Cut Out and Mounted by the Reader

(For Instructions, See Chapter LXII)

		INSERTS
1.	MARY FRANCES' PLAY HOUSE	I, II
2.	MARY FRANCES' EARLY SPRING GARDEN . . .	III
3.	MARY FRANCES' EARLY SUMMER GARDEN .	IV
4.	MARY FRANCES' MID-SUMMER GARDEN . . .	V
5.	MARY FRANCES' AUTUMN GARDEN	VI

These cut-outs will familiarize the child with the plants shown, and their season of bloom, and inspire a love for practical out-of-door gardening.

The Plant Families

Cherry

Rose

Blackberry

Strawberry

Peach

Apple

Potato

Egg Plant

Tomato

Instructions — GARDENING

CHAPTER
1. To Prepare the Soil . . . . XIII, XIV
2. How to Plant Seeds . . . . XIV, XV
3. Names of Parts of Flowers . . . XVII, LXI
4. Fertilization or Reproduction . . XIX–XXI
5. Insect Enemies and Remedies XXIX
6. How to Plant Bulbs LVI
7. Concerning Vegetables LVIII
8. Roses: How to Plant and Tend XXXV–XXXVII
9. The Best Roses to Grow XXXVI
10. Annuals: When and How to Plant . . . XI
11. Perennials: When and How to Plant . . . LI
12. How to Tell the Common Wild Flowers . . . . XXXIX–XLVIII
13. How Plants Grow XLIII
14. How to Make a Hotbed LVII

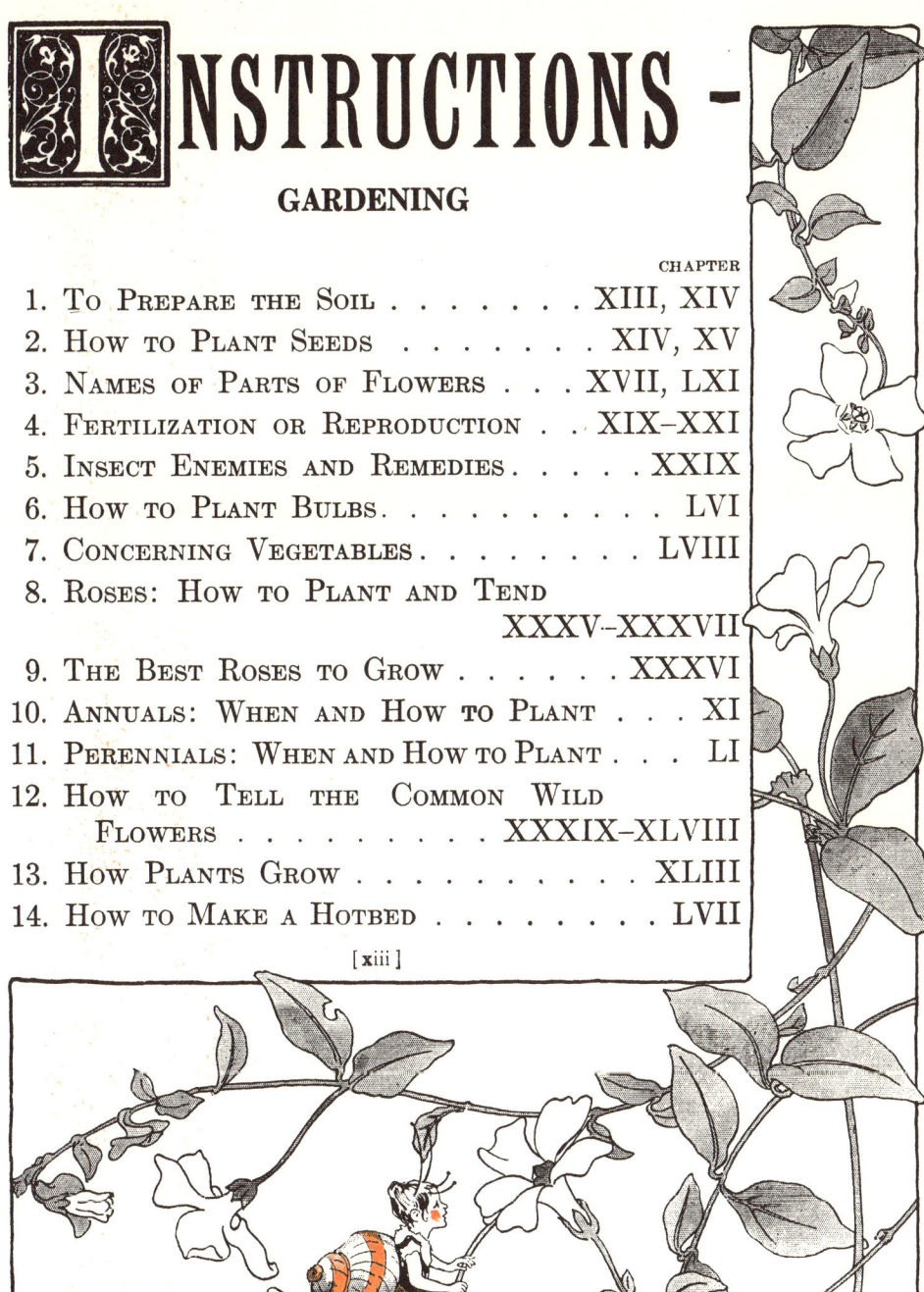

	CHAPTER
15. Best List for Children's Flower Gardens	V
16. Best List for Children's Vegetable Gardens	V
17. Outline of Each Month's Work for a Year	LXIII

THE GARDEN PEOPLE

Good Mrs. Bee

Feather Flop

Little Lady Bird

Beauty Butterfly

Mr. Hop Toad

Mr. Cut Worm

The Wicked
Rose Bugs

CHAPTER I

FEATHER FLOP, THE GARDEN BOSS

"OH, dear, I can't understand a word this book says," sighed Mary Frances, who was sitting on the garden bench, looking over a seed catalogue. "I can't understand it!"

"Of course you can't," said a strange voice. "Not without help."

Mary Frances was startled; she looked about, but saw no one.

"Why, who can it be?" she exclaimed.

"You can't without help, I said."

Feather Flop, the big Rhode Island Red rooster, came strutting around the corner of the bench.

"Why, is it you?" cried Mary Frances. "What do you know about gardening?"

"I ought to know a lot about gardening. I've lived in a garden most of the time ever since I was hatched," shrilled Feather Flop.

"Yes, you have," laughed Mary Frances, "and you've eaten up what you oughtn't to, too."

"That was when I was bad. I'm going to be good now."

"Oh, well, that is different," replied Mary Frances. "What's the first thing to do?"

"Let me see," said Feather Flop, scratching his head with **one** foot. "Let me see—why, the first thing—**the first** thing is to get the ground ready!"

"What do you do to get it ready?" asked Mary Frances.

"Why, dig, of course," answered Feather Flop. "I can dig."

"Well, well," replied Mary Frances, "I see you really want to help me, so we'll plan out what we're going to do. I want all kinds of flowers and vegetables."

"Did you start the seeds in the house in March so that some would be ready to set out now?" asked Feather Flop anxiously.

"Oh, no," said Mary Frances, "but Billy did. He has a lot of little seedlings growing."

"Can't you steal some?" asked Feather Flop.

"Oh, I wouldn't do that, Feather Flop," said Mary

Frances. "Would you? I'd rather ask Billy for them."

"Don't say anything about me when you do," begged the rooster.

"Why?" queried Mary Frances.

"I'm afraid of him. He's chased me out of the——"

"Vegetable garden several times this Spring, already," laughed Mary Frances. "Maybe if he knew how much you wanted to help with this surprise garden of mine, he would be kinder to you."

"He's kind enough," said Feather Flop, "but I'm not anxious to know him much better yet a while. So I'll ask you not to mention me."

"All right," agreed Mary Frances, "I think I understand. But Billy wouldn't hurt you."

"Do you really wish me to help you, Miss Mary Frances?" asked the rooster.

"I certainly do, Feather Flop," said the little girl; "if you will be so kind."

She could scarcely keep from laughing at how pleased and proud he looked.

"Then, let us take a look at the garden plot," he

said, leading the way to the front of Mary Frances' play house.

"I'll set right to work," said Feather Flop, beginning to scratch, "right to work, and dig the whole afternoon, and early to-morrow morning, too."

"Don't work too hard," said the little girl. "I think I ought to help you."

"Oh, no, little Miss," answered Feather Flop. "Why, see what's done already."

Mary Frances put her hand over her mouth to keep from laughing aloud as she looked at the little round hole the rooster had made.

"You do splendidly," she said, "and to-morrow morning I'll be here bright and early."

"Just one question," called Feather Flop. "Is the garden a secret?"

Mary Frances turned back. "In a way," she explained. "You see, Father gave Billy a part of our big garden for his camp and garden——"

"I know," said Feather Flop, nodding. "I was down there one day—and I don't care to go again."

"I wanted to ask Father for a garden plot of my own," went on Mary Frances, "but Billy said, 'Why

Feather Flop, the Garden Boss

don't you have a flower garden in front of your play house, and a vegetable garden back of it and surprise all the folks?' You can't imagine, Feather Flop, how delighted I was with that idea."

"Fine idea!" agreed Feather Flop, scratching again. "Won't it be splendid when the things grow!"

"And won't it be a perfectly lovely surprise!" cried Mary Frances.

"I won't tell anybody," volunteered Feather Flop. "It will be grand to have a real secret with someone."

"Oh, thank you, good old Feather Flop," answered Mary Frances. "Are you certain you don't want me to help spade up the garden?"

"Claws were made before spades," said Feather Flop, scratching away. "I'd like to do this myself, please. Come bright and early in the morning when you hear me crow."

CHAPTER II

FEATHER FLOP OVERSLEEPS

VERY early in the morning Mary Frances awoke and listened a long time for Feather Flop's signal, but not a sound was to be heard except the faint crowing of a distant rooster at the far end of the village.

"I expect he crowed before I was awake," concluded Mary Frances, as she quickly dressed and went down-stairs on tiptoe.

The sun was just getting up as she ran out into the garden.

"Hello, Feather Flop," she called softly as she hurried along, but there was not a sight or sound of Mr. Rooster.

"Mercy," she thought, "I hope nothing's happened to him. Where can he be? Oh, see, he's dug—let me count," (counting them off) "eighteen holes! My, it must have tired him out."

"But where can he be?" she went on, and called again and again as loudly as she dared:

Feather Flop Oversleeps

"Feather Flop!"

"Feather Flop!"

"FEATHER FLOP!"

"Oh, maybe he's in my play house!" she suddenly thought and ran to look. And there he was—where do you think? Fast asleep in one of the doll's beds with the covers tucked close up under his bill!

"Well, you're a funny kind of a gardener," laughed Mary Frances as soon as she recovered from her astonishment. "Here it is long past crowing time."

Feather Flop turned over. Then he began to mutter sleepily:

"I don't care what people say,
 I shan't get up and crow to-day;
 I've never laid in bed—so then!
 I shall not crow till half-past ten—to-night!"

"Oh, Feather Flop!" cried Mary Frances. "Oh, Feather Flop! How you disappoint me! Why, I've gotten up early because you promised to help in my garden! Come, get up!" going toward the bed.

"Excuse me!" exclaimed Feather Flop, hopping out of bed. "Excuse my bad manners, dear Miss,"

and away he ran out the door and into the garden before Mary Frances could catch up.

"My, but you can dress quickly, Feather Flop," she called.

"Oh, nothing like having your clothes grow on you," answered Feather Flop, lifting his wings, "especially if they are pretty."

Mary Frances laughed. "Come, come, no conceited remarks, please," she chided; "and now to work."

"It takes longer than you'd think," said Feather Flop, beginning to scratch, "especially with an empty stomach."

"How dreadful of me not to think of your breakfast, Feather Flop," she said, and ran to get some corn.

"Thanks, thanks," said Feather Flop, hungrily eating. "If they only didn't keep the food locked up, I could help myself, and not have to trouble anybody."

"Well, this is not gardening," he went on; "and besides, I want my dessert. I had splendid luck yesterday—four hundred and fifty-one grubs I ate, and several score of nice long worms. Besides, I let Robin Redbreast have a hundred or so."

"Oh, my," shuddered Mary Frances.

"What's the matter?" asked Feather Flop, looking up. "You didn't want any, did you? I'd have been delighted to have saved some for you."

"Oh, my, no!" cried Mary Frances. "Oh, no, thank you! No!"

"You're sure?" inquired Feather Flop. "Well, you must certainly be glad they are not left here in the garden to eat up your plants, I know."

"Indeed! I'm much obliged, Feather Flop," said Mary Frances. "While you dig, I'm going into the house to get some seeds, and to plan out my garden."

"All right!" said Feather Flop. "Don't mention me, please, to——you know."

CHAPTER III

BILLY PLANS THE GARDEN

"MARY FRANCES," called Billy, as she came into the house, "I say, let's start work in your garden to-day. The first thing to do is to dig and spade it."

"Oh, Billy, it looks as though it had been done," answered Mary Frances. "I guess I can plant it right away."

"Ha! Ha!" laughed Billy. "Why, it has to be dug deep; the earth has to be turned under, and compost mixed with it and all pulverized before little seeds or plants can take hold with their roots."

"How deep?" asked Mary Frances.

"Oh, about a foot, I guess," said Billy; "but don't let's talk too loud if you want to keep this garden a secret. Let's go out and have a look at it."

"You needn't mind—" began Mary Frances, but Billy was well on the way.

"That old Rhode Island Red! See what he's done!" exclaimed Billy, throwing a stone at the rooster.

[26]

Billy Plans the Garden

"Oh, Billy," begged Mary Frances. "Poor old Feather Flop! Don't scare him! Maybe he thought he was helping!"

"Helping?" laughed Billy. "Helping! If he tries to help that way when things come up, I'll wring his neck!"

"Oh, you wouldn't do that, Billy," cried Mary Frances. "He'll be good, I know."

"Well," said Billy, "you're responsible for his behavior then—he's your rooster. I'd like to clip his wings and cut his tail off right up next his ears—maybe."

"He will be good, Billy, I feel sure," answered Mary Frances. "But you are very kind to dig my garden up."

"Well," answered Billy with a very grown-up air, "I know what sort of an undertaking this is. How're you going to lay the garden out?"

"Oh, I don't know yet," answered Mary Frances. "Won't you help me plan it?"

"Yes, but it's best to begin with pencil and paper; that's the first thing Miss Gardener told us in our 'Home Garden Course.'"

"Well, here they are," laughed Mary Frances, throwing open the play house door.

"Fine," said Billy, seating himself at Mary Frances' little desk and helping himself to the articles needed.

"But wait," he continued. "If I show you how to plan this surprise garden you must carry out my directions. I don't get caught with any promise to do all the work."

"Oh, no! No-indeedy! Of course not; I'm just crazy to start and I promise not to trouble you a bit."

"Well then," said Billy, "here goes for the—

Garden Lesson No. 1
Planning a Garden

First: How much ground have you to work in?

Let us say 15 x 25 ft. in front of the play house for the Flower Garden, and 15 x 15 ft. in the rear for the Vegetable Garden."

He rapidly drew an outline of the two gardens with a pretty sketch of the play house between.

BILLY PLANS THE GARDEN

"Now," he went on, "you will wish to leave a walk down the center with a border of flowers on each side," sketching them in.

"You see, the beauty of a garden depends so much on the way it is laid out that garden planning has become a profession, and the man who studies it is known as a landscape gardener."

"My," laughed Mary Frances, "how much you learned at the garden school; you're lots better than a seed catalogue."

"Much obliged," replied Billy, "that'll do for bouquets. Now listen: the way to grow early Spring flowers is to plant bulbs in the Autumn—about the first of November. Then, early in March, sometimes even in February, tiny snowdrops will pop up and, a little later, beautiful crocuses."

"Won't that be grand!" cried Mary Frances.

"Yes, in the next lesson perhaps, I'll give you a list of bulbs and plants which you can set out at the proper time.

"The best scheme for the vegetable garden is to work it out into small rectangular beds between well-kept walks," said Billy, finishing the—

Lay-out of the Gardens

"How perfect!" exclaimed Mary Frances examining the sheet of paper which Billy handed her. "I can just imagine how beautiful my gardens will look. Isn't it a lovely idea to have that circle in the walk!"

"It would look fine if it had a sun-dial built in the

THE MARY FRANCES PLAY HOUSE GARDEN

center," said Billy, much pleased with his sister's praise.

"Oh, Billy, Billy," laughed Mary Frances, "I believe, I do believe you are going to surprise me!"

"What are you talking about?" cried Billy. "I must be going—another lesson to-morrow, if you say so, because you didn't interrupt more than twice while I was talking."

"It pays to be good," he teased as he went off.

CHAPTER IV

Feather Flop's Argument

NEITHER of the children had noticed the head of the big rooster as he peered curiously through the curtained window of the play house while they were talking.

As Mary Frances came out of the door, Feather Flop walked around the corner of the house. The little girl was so absorbed in looking at the plan that she did not see the rooster.

"Caw-caw!" Feather Flop cleared his throat. "Caw-caw!"

"Why, Feather Flop," cried Mary Frances, "How you surprised me! I was so busy studying out Billy's plan for the garden——"

"Is he anywhere about?" inquired Feather Flop, looking around anxiously. "I thought I saw him go."

"Yes, he's gone, Feather Flop," laughed Mary Frances. "But let me show you—he has been planning such a delightful garden for me."

"Delightful!" shrilled Feather Flop. "Delightful! I don't think so."

"Why, what makes you say that? How do you know what he planned?" inquired Mary Frances.

"I heard every word, every word," said the rooster. "Of course you didn't see me—I was peeping in the window."

"Oh, Feather Flop!" cried Mary Frances. "Were you eaves-dropping?"

"I was listening," acknowledged Feather Flop, "and I don't approve of the plan at all."

"Why, what's wrong with it?" asked Mary Frances. "I think it's beautiful."

"It's not sensible!" said Feather Flop. "It's not useful!"

"But it seems perfect to me. How would you change it, Feather Flop?"

"Nobody can eat flowers!" exclaimed Feather Flop. "See here," he looked over Mary Frances' shoulder as she sat down on the bench, and pointed with his claw, "that plan fills the entire front yard with bloomin' plants and gives only the little back yard for such things as taste good!"

PICTURE OF MARY FRANCES PLAY HOUSE BEFORE THE CHILDREN PLANTED THE GARDENS
For Directions for Garden Cut-Outs, see Chapter LXII

NOTE ON THE GARDEN CUT-OUTS

DEAR GIRL OR BOY:

No doubt you will wish, just as Mary Frances did, to be able to cut flowers every few days from your garden for your mother to use as a "centerpiece" on the dining table, or for your father's desk, or for your grandmother's dresser, or to give to some dear friend.

Now, anyone can have a few plants which will bloom at some time or other, but the garden you and Mary Frances have in mind is one which will have flowers blooming from March, through April, May, June, July, August, September, October, and on into November, until killed by frost.

Flowers nearly nine months of the year! Yes, that is quite possible in almost every part of our country—if you study carefully the outlines given on pages 51–62, inclusive.

The *first* outline gives a list of plants which bloom in the Early Spring. (See Garden Cut-Out No. 1.)

The *second* names the plants which bloom in the Early Summer. (See Garden Cut-Out No. 2.)

The *third*, the plants which bloom in Mid-Summer. (See Garden Cut-Out No. 3.)

The *fourth*, those blooming in Late Summer or Early Autumn. (See Garden Cut-Out No. 4.)

For instructions for making the Garden Cut-Outs, see Chapter LXII, page 373.

"Dearie me! Dearie me!" laughed Mary Frances. "Is that it, Feather Flop? Why, don't you love to see beautiful flowers?"

"Not half as much as I do to eat beautiful lettuce and beet tops and other beautiful vegetables," declared Feather Flop, shaking his head sadly.

"It's too bad, Feather Flop," said Mary Frances, smoothing his fine feathers, "but I'll see that you get plenty of such green things as you like."

"Oh, thank you, little Miss," said the rooster. "If you will do that, I'm ready to help with your silly— I mean your brother's, plan."

"Thank you, Feather Flop, for all your help," said the little girl, "and good-bye for now. I must go or maybe mother will send Billy to look for me."

"Good-bye! good-bye!" cried Feather Flop, jumping off the bench and running away as fast as possible.

CHAPTER V

GARDENS FOR LITTLE FOLKS

"HOW would you like another lesson on gardening to-day, Mary Frances?" asked Billy the next morning as he appeared at the door of the play house.

"Oh, Billy, you know I'd just love to have one!" said Mary Frances, getting the desk ready.

"This time we are to make a list of what to plant, if I remember correctly," said Billy, taking a seat.

"Let me see: we will try to plant the garden so that we will have flowers in bloom from early Spring till late Fall.

In order to have flowering plants continuously in the garden, we must use the class of flowers called Per-en-ni-als,* *the roots of which live from year to year*.

If we depend on An-nu-als,† the seeds of which must

---

* See Chapter LI on Perennials.
† See Chapter XI on Annuals.

be planted every Spring, we will not have blooms until Summer or early Fall.

So you see, in order to plan wisely, our next lesson is very important, and it is our—

GARDEN LESSON No. 2
What to Plant

Now, Mary Frances, I have really planned a delightful landscape flower garden for you to plant in front of your play house, and a wonderfully useful vegetable garden for the back of the play house; but before I give you that outline, I am going to pretend that you are a very little girl, and I will give you a list, just as our teacher handed it to us. I have it here:

Garden for Little Folks

1. Plan out the garden; that is, make a list of what you wish to plant.
2. Draw a picture map of your garden, marking the space where each different kind of flower or vegetable is to be planted.
3. Remember that low-growing plants should be placed in the foreground (front part) of the garden, and tall-growing plants in the background.
4. Order the plants or seeds.
5. Get the ground ready. (See Chapter XIV.)
6. Now begin to plant, following instructions in Chapter XV.

If space for your garden is about 10 x 15 ft. it would be delightful to plant it as shown by the picture-map drawn here.

Garden for Little Folks—10 x 15 Feet

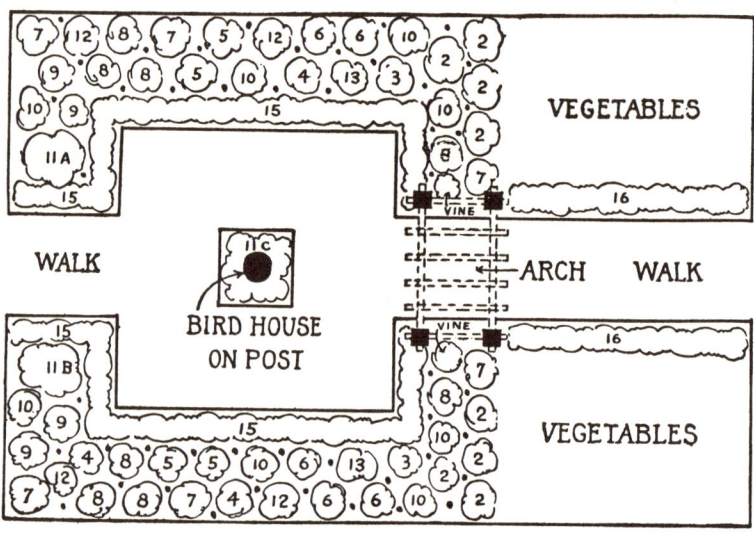

(.) Bulbs. 2. Iris (blue). 3. Bleeding Hearts. 4. Pyrethrums. 5. Sweet William. 6. Phlox. 7. Eupatorium. 8. Coreopsis. 9. Gaillardia. 10. Chrysanthemums. 11A, 11B, 11C. Roses. 12. Hardy Asters. 13. Iceland Poppies. 14. Cosmos (not to be given a permanent place in garden; it may be used, however, as a filler between Hardy Perennials. 15. Alyssum. 16. Nasturtiums.

Plant Daffodils and Tulips between Hardy Perennials as indicated on plan with dots.

Gardens for Little Folks

Now, for an—

Explanation
of
THE LITTLE FOLKS FLOWER GARDEN

Four Hardy Bulbs for Little Folks Garden

These bulbs should be planted in late October or early November. They bloom in the early Spring and then die down, to come up the next Spring.

No. on Map.	No. of Flowers to Plant.	How Deep to Plant.	Color.	Average Price.
(D.)	6 Emperor Daffodils.	4 inches.	Yellow.	25c for ½ doz.
(12)	6 Cottage Garden Tulips, called also May-flowering Tulips.	4 inches.	All colors.	15c for ½ doz.
D. T.	6 Darwin Tulips. Bloom later than "Cottage Garden" Tulips; grow taller.	4 inches.	All colors.	15c for ½ doz.
(G. 1)	6 German Iris roots, called also "Blue Flags."	4 inches.	Blue, purple, and yellow.	50c for ½ doz.

Hardy Perennials

The plants whose roots live on from season to season, or "winter over," and come up every Spring, are called Hardy Perennials.

The plants whose roots die **in the Fall, and do not** "winter over," are called Annuals.

When a boy or a girl undertakes **to** start a flower garden, how much more desirable it seems to plant, for the most part, Hardy Perennials, which will "come up" the next Summer and the next, and so on for years; instead of Annuals, the seeds of which must be sowed every Spring.

Of course, the seeds of Hardy Perennials may be sowed in the Spring, but *Hardy Perennial plants raised from seeds, seldom bloom until the next year after the seeds are planted.*

☞Therefore, it is best for the beginner, in **most cases,** to buy *plants* of Hardy Perennials.

If you wish to start seeds, however, see Chapter **LI on** "Perennials."

Gardens for Little Folks

Following is the list of—

Twelve Hardy Perennials for Little Folks Garden

No. on Map.	Name and Number of Plants.	Remarks.	Average Price.
(3)	2 Bleeding Hearts.	Pink heart-shaped flowers on graceful stems. Buy the plants in clumps in the Fall.	15c a plant.
(4)	Hardy Py-re-thrums.	Red, pink, white daisy-like flowers. When ordering, use the name: "Pyrethrum Hybridum." It is best to plant seeds in early Spring or August, to get plants which will "winter over" and bloom the next Summer. Plants may be purchased if you wish blooms the first year.	20c a plant. 10c a package.
(5)	Sweet-Williams (London Tufts).	"Biennials," which means the plants "come up" the second year, but do not do well after that. Plant every other year; preferably in August. Order mixed seed. Sweet-Williams often sow their own seed.	10c a package.
(6)	3 Hardy Phlox.	1 Salmon Pink: order "Elizabeth Campbell," or "Rheinlander." 1 White: order "Mrs. Jenkins." 1 Lavender: order "La Vague," or "La Mahdi."	20c a plant.

40 THE MARY FRANCES GARDEN BOOK

No. on Map.	Name and Number of Plants.	Remarks.	Average Price.
	Hardy Phlox—*Continued*.	Buy the *plants* of Hardy Phlox. The seeds are not generally satisfactory, because they should be sowed within a short time after ripening.	
(7)	Blue Thoroughwort ("Eu-pa-to-ri-um").	Order "Eupatorium Celestium." Blue misty flowers, sometimes called "Blue Mist," pretty in mixed bouquet. Bloom late in season. Buy the plant.	15c a plant.
(8)	1 Co-re-op-sis.	Order "Coreopsis Lanceolata Grandiflora." Yellow daisy-like flowers. A large, bushy plant. Keep the flowers well picked, to get continuous bloom. Easily raised from seed if planted early.	15c a plant.
(9)	1 Blanket Flower (Hardy "Gail-lard-i-a").	Large reddish-brown flowers with yellow edges, etc. It loves to bloom. If sowed very early, it often blooms the first season. Order *mixed* seed.	10c a package.
(10)	3 Chrys-an-the-mums.	Order "Hardy Pompon" (1 yellow, 1 red, 1 bronze). Bloom very late in the Fall. Buy the plants.	3 for 45 cts.

MARY FRANCES GARDEN CUT-OUT
No. 1—Continued

Hyacinths,
Rock-cress,
English Daisies,
Bleeding Hearts,
Moss Pinks,
Violets,

Yellow Alyssum,
Wall Flower.

SUNDIAL

MARY FRANCES GARDEN CUT-OUT
No. 1

For description of the flowers shown here see Chapter VII.

List of flowers shown in the Early Spring Hardy Garden

Snowdrops,
Narcissus or
Daffodils,

Cottage Garden Tulips,
Darwin Tulips,

Gardens for Little Folks 41

No. on Map.	Name and Number of Plants.	Remarks.	Average Price.
(11)	Roses (See Chapter XXXV).	Dwarf "Baby Ramblers": (a) 1 Fairy Rose—"Cecile Brunner." Little double flowers of soft rosy pink on a creamy white ground. (b) 1 Baby Tausendchon—"Louise Walter." Larger flowers of a tender shade of pink. Chinese Rose: "Hermosa"—pink.	50c a plant.
(12)	3 Hardy Asters ("Michaelmas Daisies").	Lavender, pink, white and purple little daisy-like flowers, growing in clusters on large tall bushes. Buy the plants.	15c a plant.
(13)	Iceland Poppies.	All colors. Sow mixed seed in August to grow plants which will bloom the next Summer. Cover with leaves in the Fall. Order mixed seeds of "Papaver Nudicaule."	10c a package.

Annuals

Sow the seeds of Annuals early in the Spring. The roots of Annuals do not live over Winter, and seeds must be sowed every Spring.

Annuals for Little Folks Garden

No. on Map.	Name.	Remarks.	Average Price.
(14)	Cos'-mos.	Easily grown in poor soil. Grow over 4 feet tall. Flowers: pink, white, garnet, with yellow centers. Buy mixed seed, "Summer or Early Flowering" Cosmos which will bloom early and continue until frost.	10c a package.
(15)	Sweet A-lys'-sum.	A charming edging plant. Order "Little Gem," which grows 4 inches tall, and blooms like a snow carpet.	5c a package.

Vegetables for Little Folks Garden

Name.	Remarks.	Average Price per Package Seed.
Nasturtiums. Buy "Tom Thumb" or Dwarf.	In the early Spring, sow seeds of *dwarf* nasturtiums for narrow border along the walk of the vegetable garden.	5c.
Lettuce. Buy "Early All-heart;" Early Cos; Late Lettuce.	Plant a small quantity of Early Lettuce seeds in the early Spring; when plants are two inches high, plant more seeds; thin plants out, that the ones left standing may grow large. Plant a few seeds every week until weather grows very warm.	5c.

GARDENS FOR LITTLE FOLKS 43

Name.	Remarks.	Average Price per Package Seed.
Lettuce—Continued.	Lettuce does not grow well in very warm weather. Plant late variety in early Fall. *Cos or Romaine lettuce* is easily grown, and stands the heat better than the other varieties. It has a very crisp fleshy rib in the leaf, but the leaf part is not so delicate as of the other varieties. *All lettuce needs very rich soil.*	
Parsley. Buy "Dwarf Curly."	Plant in early Spring. Soak seed overnight in warm water, mix sand in the water, and fling sand and seed over the prepared ground. Sometimes it takes six weeks for parsley seed to "come up." Except far north, it lives over winter if well covered with leaves. Plant some parsley every year, as what has "wintered over" goes to seed very easily.	5c.
Onions. Buy yellow "Onion sets."	"Onion sets" are tiny little onions which are set out in early Spring, about 2 inches apart in rows. Usually when they are partially grown, they are pulled, and green tops and bulbs are used for salads and in soup.	10c a pint.

Name.	Remarks.	Average Price per Package Seed.
Thyme.	A very pretty low-growing herb, used to flavor soup, and "stuffing" for meat. Grows easily from seed if sowed early. Lives over winter —except far north—if covered with leaves. Is, therefore, a "perennial." Plant in the Spring in the northern states. Plant in the Fall in the southern states.	5c.
Radishes. Buy Little Red Globe-shaped.	Sow a few radish seeds every week for four weeks, to have new young tender radishes ready for pulling each week. Radishes do not do well in very hot weather. The late or "winter" radish is planted in the early Fall.	5c.
Tomatoes. Buy 2 *plants* of early and 2 of late varieties.	Tomato seeds may be sowed in a box placed in a sunny window or under glass in the hot bed in very early Spring, but unless a large number of plants is needed, it is better to buy the young plants. A very interesting variety is "cherry tomatoes," which grow in little clusters of red fruit resembling cherries in appearance. Buy 1 plant.	2 for 5c.

The approximate cost of this garden for little folks is three dollars.

Seeds of all these vegetables may be started in the house. See Chapter XIV, page 81, "To Plant Seeds in Boxes." The young plants may be put out in the garden when they are of some size, about which you will read later.

CHAPTER VI

Gardens for Big Boys and Girls

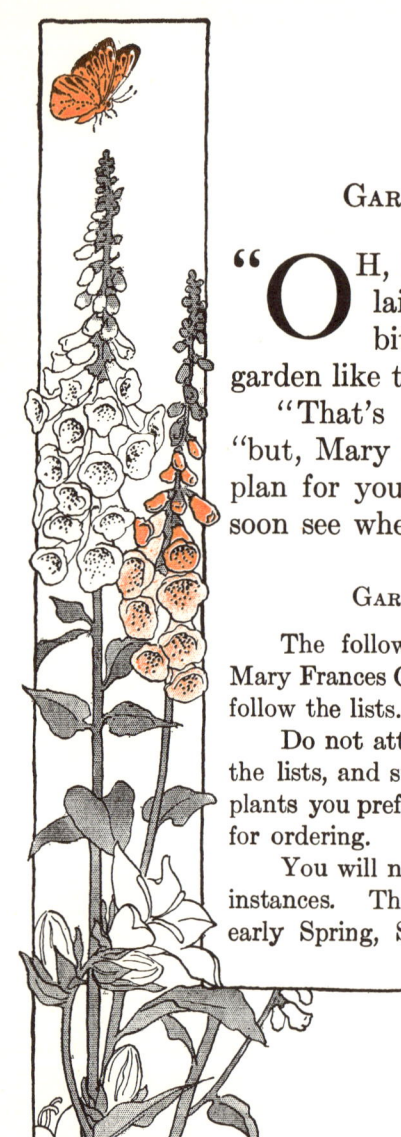

"OH, Billy," cried Mary Frances, as her brother laid down the paper, "that doesn't sound a bit babyish to me! If I could just have a garden like that——"

"That's an all-right garden," interrupted Billy, "but, Mary Frances, it isn't much compared with my plan for your wonderful play house garden, as you'll soon see when I give you the—

Garden Lists for Big Boys and Girls

The following-named flowers, which are pictured in the Mary Frances Garden Cut-Outs, are described in the outlines that follow the lists.

Do not attempt to plant all the flowers named, but read the lists, and study the descriptions carefully. Then select the plants you prefer for your garden, and make your own list ready for ordering.

You will notice that certain names are repeated in several instances. This is only to show the period of bloom, whether early Spring, Summer, or Autumn, or throughout the season.

Thirty-seven Hardy Perennials

Aster (Wild)	English Daisy	Phlox (Hardy)
Alkanet (Anchusa)	Forget-me-not	Pyrethrum
Baby's Breath	Foxglove	Poker Plant
Bellflower	Hollyhock	Rock Cress
Bergamot	Larkspur	Roses
Blanket Flower	Lupine	Sneezewort
Bleeding Heart	Marguerite	Speedwell
Campanula	Monkshood	Sweet Alyssum (yellow)
Candytuft	Pæony	Sweet-William
Centaurea	Pinks { Moss	Thoroughwort
Chrysanthemum	{ Hardy	Violet and Viola
Columbine	Poppy { Iceland	Wall Flower
Coreopsis	{ Oriental	Windflower

Twenty Annuals

Ageratum	Garden Geranium	Scarlet Sage
Cockscomb	Lemon Verbena	Snapdragon
Cornflower	Nasturtium	Sweet Alyssum (white)
Cosmos	Petunia	Verbena
Cigar Plant	Princess Feather	Wild Cucumber Vine
Everlasting	Periwinkle	Zinnia
Four-o'Clock	Phlox	

Eight Bulbous Plants

Daffodil	Lily of the Valley	Tulip
Hyacinth	Madonna Lily	Yellow Day Lily
Iris	Snowdrop	

A Letter About the Garden Cut-Outs

Dear Boy or Girl:

No doubt you will wish, just as Mary Frances did, to be able to cut flowers every few days from your garden, for your mother to use as a "center piece" on the dining table, or for your father's desk, or for your grandmother's dresser, or as a gift for a friend.

Now, anyone can have a few plants which will bloom at some time or other, but the garden you and Mary Frances have in mind is one which will have flowers in bloom from March, through April, May, June, July, August, September, October, and into November until ruined by frost.

Flowers over eight months of the year! Yes, that is possible in nearly every part of our country—if you study carefully the outlines following this page.

The first outline gives a list of plants which bloom in the Early Spring.

The second names the plants which bloom in Early Summer.

The third, the plants which bloom in Mid-Summer.

The fourth, those blooming in Autumn.

These lists are nearly like the ones given Billy by his teacher, which he and Mary Frances used in planting a garden in front of the Play House. As you read these lists, turn to the pictures of the Mary Frances Garden Cut-Outs, and try to recognize the flower named.

All that Mary Frances wished, she and Billy made "come true," and every day through the flowering season she gathered flowers

MARY FRANCES GARDEN CUT-OUT
No. 2

For description of the flowers shown here see Chapter VII.

List of flowers shown in the Early Summer Hardy Garden

Yellow Alyssum,
Columbine,
German Iris,
Lily-of-the-Valley,

MARY FRANCES GARDEN CUT-OUT
No. 2—*Continued*

Anchusa,
Lupines,
Tufted Pansies,
Bleeding Hearts,
Hardy Candytuft,
Forget-me-not,
Perennial Cornflower.

Gardens for Big Boys and Girls 49

from her garden—but that is part of the story, so now begin to read

A Few Hints on Growing the Flowers Shown in the Garden Cut-Outs

In using the following lists, if the garden space is small, select only the names marked with a star.

The height of each plant is given because it is always desirable to plant low-growing flowers in the foreground; and tall ones in the background.

The following-named Perennials (the roots of which live from year to year) may be grown from seeds, but *cannot be depended upon to bloom the first year.*

Instead of beginners starting *seeds* of *Perennials*, it is well to buy the young *plants* from a reliable dealer to start the permanent garden, and to experiment with seeds after acquaintance with those plants already established.

Do not buy many plants of any kind, as a few, well cared for, will increase in number the next year.

Annuals (the roots of which die in the Fall) will bloom the same season as planted. Start seeds early, either in a box in a sunny window, or in a warm sunny corner out of doors early in May.

The first step in garden-making is the planning of the garden.

(See Chapter LXII on "The Mary Frances Garden Cut-Outs.")

50   THE MARY FRANCES GARDEN BOOK

The second step is selection of the seed, and the ordering of the same from one of the *best* seed firms.

Never try inferior or untested seeds.   It is no economy.

In regard to "color scheme," see Chapter LX.

For artistic effect, it is usually best to plant the same kind of flowers close together to obtain "masses" of bloom.

CHAPTER VII

EARLY SPRING GARDEN

LIST No. 1

FIVE BULBS* FOR EARLY SPRING HARDY GARDEN

See Mary Frances Garden Cut-Out No. 1.

Plant the following named bulbs in the Fall.   See Chapter LVI.

Name.	Remarks.
Snowdrops.	Pure white small bells, blooming late in February or early in March, whenever the snow leaves the ground. Leave bulbs in the ground over Winter, covered with leaves. Plant 4 inches deep.
Nar-cis-sus or Daff-o-dils.*	Daffodil bulbs are very hardy, and increase in number from year to year. They should be covered with leaves over Winter. The best varieties are "Emperor"* and "Empress." Plant 4 inches deep. Barii Conspicuus, a Star Narcissus, is beautiful for cutting. Poet's Narcissus have beautiful white petals, with golden and red center.

* If garden space is small, select only the names marked with a star.

The Mary Frances Garden Book

Name.	Remarks.
Cottage Garden* (May-flowering) Tulips.	Beautiful large flowers of all colors, making the Spring garden bright and gay. Plant bulbs 4 inches deep. Plants grow 18 to 24 inches high.
Darwin Tulips.	These beautiful, stately tulips grow two feet high and more. Large globe-shaped brilliant blooms. They come in all colors except yellow. Plant 4 inches deep.
Hy-a-cinths.	Plant only a few hyacinth bulbs, because they do not "winter over" well; new bulbs should be added every year, as the old ones deteriorate. Colors: pink, purple, white.

Seven Hardy Perennial Plants which Bloom in the Early Spring

As pictured in the Mary Frances Garden Cut-Out No. 1.

Common Name.	Botanical Name.	Remarks.	Height.
Rock-cress.	Ar-a-bis Al-pi-na.	Little white flowers blooming in early Spring.	6–8 inches.
English Daisies.	Bel-lis Per-en-nis.	Little white and pink flowers, blooming in April and May. Pretty among Poet's Narcissus, or mixed in an edging.	3–6 inches.

* If garden space is small, select only the names marked with a star.

Early Spring Garden

Common Name.	Botanical Name.	Remarks.	Height.
Bleeding Hearts.*	Di-el-y-tra.	Pink heart-shaped drops on graceful stem. Raised from plants only. Buy clumps in the Fall.	24 inches.
Moss Pinks.	Phlox Sub-u-la-ta.	White, rose, lilac, little flowers blooming in April and May. Blooms make a carpet of flowers. Buy only a few plants as they soon spread.	4–6 inches.
Violets.		There are native and double Russian varieties. Buy plants of sweet-scented double Russian variety.	4 inches.
Yellow Alyssum "Basket of Gold."	A-lys-sum Sax-a-tile.	Little yellow clustered heads of flowers. Pretty for edging flower beds. Sow seed in August.	12 inches.
Wallflower.		Not perfectly hardy in all places. Fragrant brown and yellow flowers. Plant seeds in August, in a protected southern corner, where they may "winter over" if the weather is not very severe. Plant needs sun.	15 inches.

In order to obtain good Spring blooms, plant these flowers in August of the Summer before, or earlier.

* If garden space is small, select only the names marked with a star.

CHAPTER VIII

EARLY SUMMER GARDEN

LIST No. 2

ELEVEN HARDY PERENNIAL PLANTS WHICH BLOOM IN THE EARLY SUMMER

As pictured in the Mary Frances Garden Cut-Out No. 2.

Common Name.	Botanical Name.	Remarks.	Height.
Yellow Alyssum.*	A-lys-sum Sax-a-tile.	See List No. 1 for description.	12 inches.
Columbine.	A-qui-le-gi-a.	Airy, graceful plants, with spurred flowers, in red, blue, violet, white, yellow. Buy the seed of "Long Spurred Hybrids."	18–24 inches.
German Iris ("Blue Flags").	I-ris Ger-man-i-ca.	Lavender, purple, yellow, white. "Corm" roots which "winter over" and take care of themselves, "coming" up every Spring in increased numbers.	24–30 inches.
Lily of the Valley.	Con-val-la-ria.	Sweet-scented tiny white bells. Buy clumps and roots in Spring or Fall.	6 inches.

* If garden space is small, select only the names marked with a star.

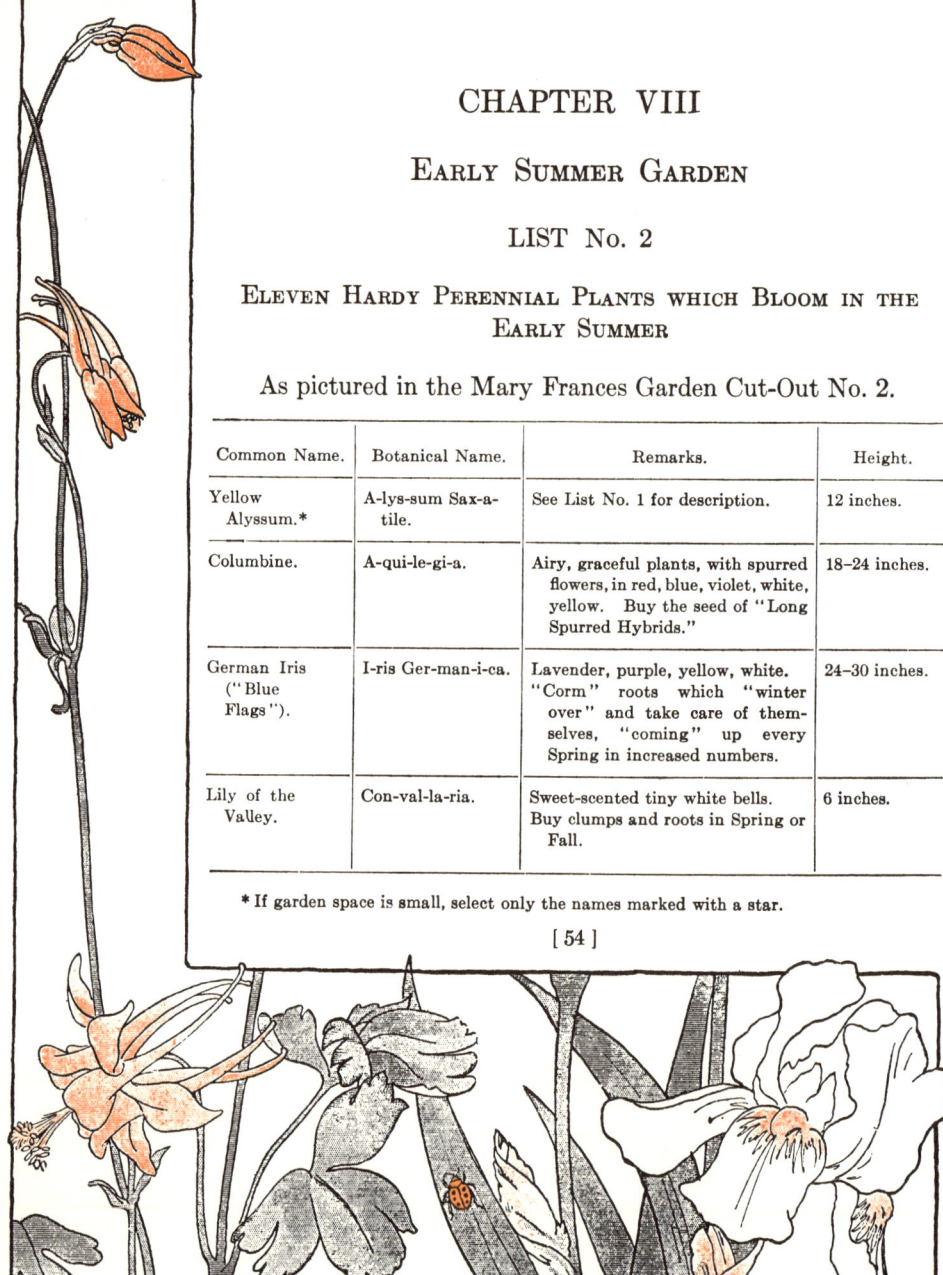

Early Summer Garden

Common Name.	Botanical Name.	Remarks.	Height.
Alkanet or Bugloss.	An-chu-sa I-tal-i-ca.	Buy "Dropmore" variety. Blue flowers. Buy the plants.	36 inches.
Lupines.	Lu-pi-nus.	Varieties in blue, white, pink	24–28 inches.
Tufted Pansies.*	Vi-o-la Cor-nu-ti.	Sow seed early. Resemble pansies, not so large; but bloom all Summer.	5–8 inches.
Bleeding Hearts.	Di-el-y-tra.	See List No. 1 for description.	
Hardy Candy-tuft.*	I-be-ris.	Buy "Iberis Sempervirens": white. Pretty for edging.	8–10 inches.
Forget-me-Not.	My-o-tis.	Buy "Myotis Palustris Semper-florens." Sky-blue little flower.	8–10 inches.
Hardheads or Knap Weeds. Perennial Corn-flower.	Cen-tau-re-a.	"Centaurea Montana" is known as the Perennial Cornflower. Bears large violet-blue flowers from July to September.	2 feet.

Rambler roses also bloom in early Summer.

* If garden space is small, select only the names marked with a star.

CHAPTER IX

Mid-Summer Garden

LIST No. 3

Twenty-four Hardy Perennial Plants which Bloom in Mid-Summer

As pictured in the Mary Frances Garden Cut-Out No. 3.

Common Name.	Botanical Name.	Remarks.	Height.
Hardy Larkspur.*	Del-phin-i-um.	Order plants of varieties named, "Belladonna" and "Formosum," which are turquoise blue and dark blue. Buy the plants, or seeds.	24 inches.
Pæony.		Bloom but once in the season. Beautiful showy large rose-like flowers. Foliage of plant dies down in Winter, coming up in young new "shoots" in the Spring. Colors: red, pink and white. There is also a "tree" variety. Most pæonies bloom in early Summer.	3 feet.
Alkanet or Bugloss.	An-chu-sa.	See List No. 2 for description.	

* If garden space is small, select only the names marked with a star.

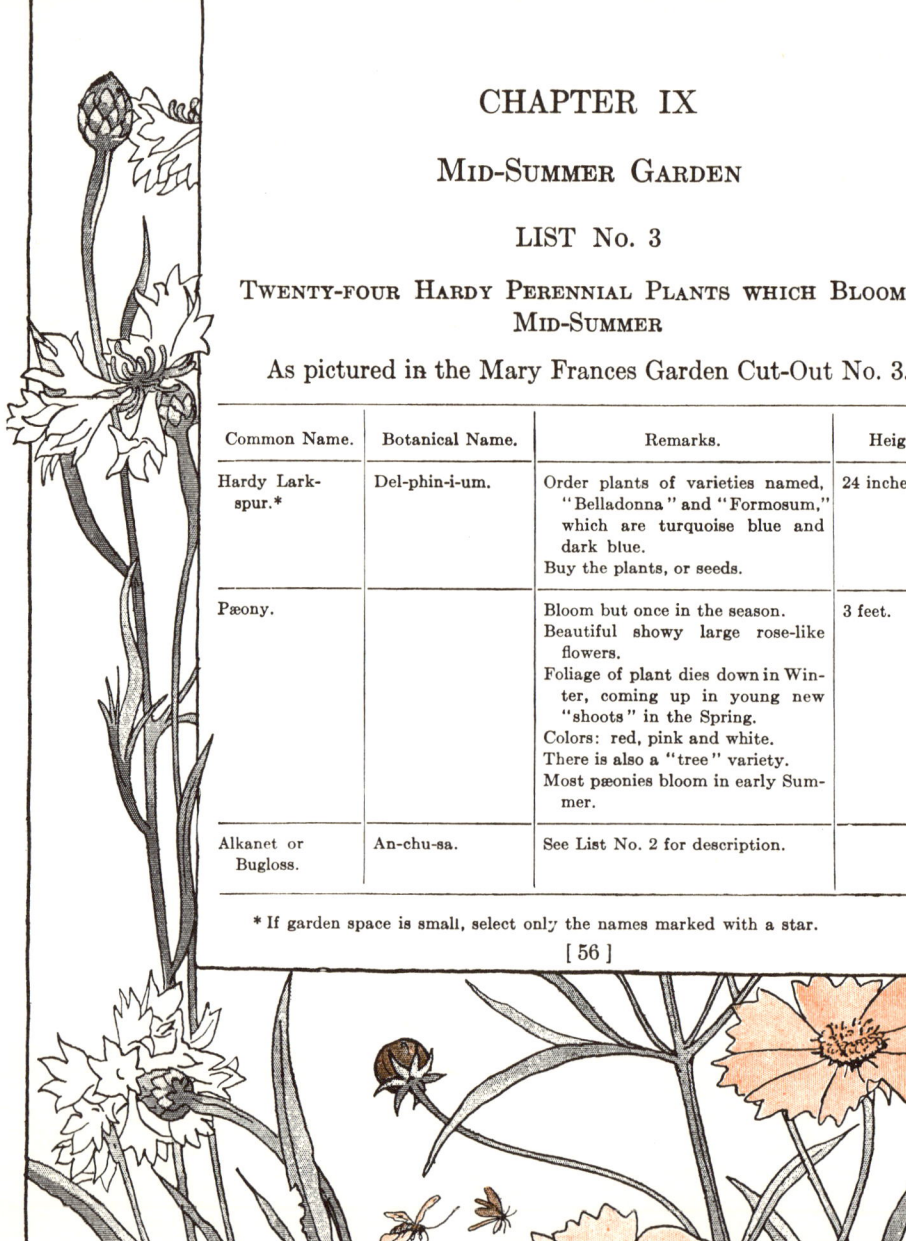

MARY FRANCES GARDEN CUT-OUT
No. 3

For description of the flowers shown here see Chapter IX.

List of flowers shown in the Mid-Summer Hardy Garden

Hardy Larkspur,
Pæony,
Anchusa,
Bellflower,
Madonna Lily,
Poppies,
Foxglove,
Sweet William,
Hardy Garden Pinks,

MARY FRANCES GARDEN CUT-OUT
No. 3—*Continued*

Marguerites,
Coreopsis,
Gaillardia,
Hardy Phlox,
Hardy Pyrethrums,
Tufted Pansies,
Baby's Breath,
Hardy Candytuft,
Hollyhocks,
Veronica,
Japanese Bellflower,
Summer Violet.

Mid-Summer Garden

Common Name.	Botanical Name.	Remarks.	Height.
Bellflower.*	Cam-pa-nu-la.	*Perennial Varieties:* (a) Campanula Carpatica (Carpathian Hare-Bell). Bloom from June to October. Blue. (b) Campanula Persicafolia (Peach Bells). One of the best. Large blue, and white varieties. (c) Campanula Pyramidalis (The Chimney Bellflower). Stately pyramid form plant, with many blue flowers. There is also a white variety. It is best to buy plants of the above. NOTE.—There are also biennial varieties of Campanula; namely, Campanula Medium or Canterbury Bells, and Campanula Calycanthema (Cup and Saucer). *Biennial* means of two season's duration.	8 inches. 2–3 feet. 4–5 feet.
Madonna Lily.*	Li-li-um Can-di-dum.	Pure white lilies, resembling Easter Lilies, growing on strong stems. Plant in the Fall (or possibly in the early Spring), 6 inches deep, preferably in the shade of some other perennial. Lay bulbs on the side when planting.	2–3 feet.
Oriental Poppy.	Pa-pa-ver O-ri-en-tal-is.	Very large showy poppies in various colors. Buy plants in clumps in August.	36 inches.

* If garden space is small, select only the names marked with a star.

Common Name.	Botanical Name.	Remarks.	Height.
Foxglove.	Dig-i-tal-is.	See tall flowers pictured on cover of this book. Various colors.	36 inches.
Sweet William.*	Di-an-thus Bar-ba-tus	Red, white and various colors. See Garden for Little Folks.	18 inches.
Hardy Garden Pinks.*	Di-an-thus Sem-per-flo-rens.	Buy plants. Various colors. Old-fashioned favorites, with spicy odor. Excellent for cutting. Also: "Dianthus Latifolius Atcroccineus." Hybrid Sweet-William, with brilliant crimson double flowers, blooming all Summer.	6–12 inches.
Iceland Poppy.*	Pa-pa-ver	Buy "Papaver Nudicaule" mixed seed. See description in Garden for Little Folks.	9–15 inches.
Marguerite.*	An-the-mis Tinc-to-ri-a.	Buy "Anthemis Tinctoria." Color: yellow. Buy plant.	15 inches.
Coreopsis.*	Co-re-op-sis Lan-ce-o-la-ta.	See Garden for Little Folks for description. Buy plant.	24 inches.
Blanket Flower.	Gail-lard-i-a.	Buy Gaillardia Grandiflora. Crimson and yellow. See Garden for Little Folks. Sow seed early.	24 inches.

* If garden space is small, select only the names marked with a star.

Mid-Summer Garden

Common Name.	Botanical Name.	Remarks.	Height.
Hardy Phlox.*		*Phlox Suffruticosa* are the Early-flowering Hardy Phlox. *Phlox Decussata* are the later Hardy Phlox, and are the variety most used. All colors: Crimson, white, salmon pink, etc. See List of Hardy Perennials for Little Folks Garden.	
Hardy Pyrethrums.*	Py-re-thrum Hy-brid-um.	Red, rose, white flowers. See Garden for Little Folks.	18–24 inches.
Tufted Pansies.*	Vi-o-la Cor-nu-ti.	See List No. 2 for description.	3–6 inches.
Baby's Breath.	Gyp-so-phi-la Pa-nic-u-la-ta.	Tiny white misty flowers, beautiful to use in bouquets, making a "cobwebby" filmy spray over the flowers.	20–30 inches.
Hardy Candytuft.	I-be-ris Sem-per-vi-rens.	White low-growing flowers.	8–10 inches.
Hollyhocks.*		A grandmother's favorite—picturesque in a garden background. Red, white, yellow, rose, pink. Cut down the stalks when the seeds are dry. Plant seeds; they will bloom the next season.	5–8 feet.
Speedwell.	Ve-ron-i-ca.	Blue, rose, white. Plant seeds in August.	12–24 inches.

* If garden space is small, select only the names marked with a star.

60 THE MARY FRANCES GARDEN BOOK

Common Name.	Botanical Name.	Remarks.	Height.
Hybrid Tea Roses.		See Chapter XXXV on Roses.	
Japanese Bellflower. Balloon Flower.	Plat-y-co-don.	Blue, and white flowers; deep-cupped and star shaped. Buds resemble tiny balloons. Easily grown. Buy plants.	
Yellow Day Lily.	Hem-e-ro-cal-lis.	Yellow and orange tall lilies. These are not pictured in the Cut-outs, but are very similar to the madonna lily in form. They will grow in the shade.	18–36 inches.
Summer Violet.	Vi-o-la Cor-nu-ti Pur-pu-re-a.	Resembles single violets, and very desirable, for flowers appear when blooming season of violets is passed.	4 inches.

Turn to Chapter LX on "Garden Color-Pictures," to read about combinations of color for the garden.

CHAPTER X

Autumn Garden

LIST No. 4

Thirteen Hardy Perennial Plants which Bloom in the Early and Late Fall

As pictured in the Mary Frances Garden Cut-Out No. 4.

Common Name.	Botanical Name.	Remarks.	Height.
Hardy Larkspur.	Del-phin-i-um.	See List No. 3 for description.	
Monks Hood.	Ac-o-ni-tum.	Curiously shaped blue and white flowers. Will grow in shade. Buy the plants.	3–5 feet.
Hardy Phlox.*		See List of Hardy Perennials for Little Folks Garden.	
Sneezewort.	He-len-i-um.	Yellow, old-gold, changing to terra-cotta, daisy-like flowers. Buy "Riverton Gem," "Riverton Beauty." Plant seed in August, or buy the plants.	36 inches.
Hardy Asters* ("Starwort").	Mich-ael-mas Dai-sies.	See Garden for Little Folks for description.	36 inches.

* If garden space is small, select only the names marked with a star.

[61]

Common Name.	Botanical Name.	Remarks.	Height.
Hardy Chrysan-themums.*		All colors except blue and purple.	15–24 inches.
Wind Flower.	A-nem-o-ne Ja-pon-i-ca.	Rose, pink, white flowers. If grown from seed, protect with shade-cover until started. Cover well in the Fall with straw or leaves. Will not grow in all soils.	2–4 feet.
Blanket Flower.	Gail-lard-i-a.	See Garden for Little Folks for description.	
Coreopsis.*		See Garden for Little Folks for description.	
Red Hot Poker. Flame Flower. Torch Lily.	Tri-to-ma.	Yellow-orange-scarlet showy flowers hanging downward in long clusters on "spike" heads. Buy plants. Not shown in the Cut-Out.	36 inches.
Tufted Pansies.	Vi-o-la Cor-nu-ta.	See List No. 3 for description.	
Hybrid Tea Roses.		See Chapter XXXV on Roses.	
Thoroughwort.*	Eu-pa-to-ri-um.	See Garden for Little Folks for description.	

NOTE.—Most seed houses furnish collections of seeds of Wild Flowers. They may be had in tall-growing and dwarf varieties for a very reasonable price.

* If garden space is small, select only the names marked with a star.

CHAPTER XI

SOME FAVORITE ANNUALS

A few Annuals may well be added to these lists. Even though Annuals must be planted every Spring, there are many worth the trouble; in fact, a garden would look lonesome without some of the old favorites.

A very convenient arrangement is to give one bed in the vegetable garden to the starting of Annuals.

The plants may be moved, when some size, to the hardy garden, near the place of some of the Perennials which die down; for instance, hyacinths, tulips, and other bulbs. Indeed, those having short roots may be placed directly over the bulbs after their leaves have withered and dried.

A border of low-growing Annuals along the vegetable beds makes the vegetable garden a place of beauty.

If you live where there is snow in Winter, in order to have early Summer blooms, the seeds must be started early, under glass protection, in a sunny window, or in a hotbed. A box with a glass cover is a good substitute for a hotbed. If the seeds of Annuals are planted out of doors, they rarely bloom before Mid-Summer, while many Perennials, which have been out all Winter, bloom in early Spring. Select from the following lists the flowers which from the description are most pleasing to you.

64 The Mary Frances Garden Book

List of Fifteen Annuals
(All may be raised from seeds. They do not "winter over.")

Common Name.	Botanical Name.	Remarks.	Height.
Cockscomb.*	Cin-e-ra-ri-a.	Crimson, showy flowers easily grown. Resemble the comb of a rooster. Bloom in the Fall.	24 inches.
Princess Feather. Feathered Cockscomb.	Ce-lo-si-a Plu-mo-sa.	Yellow and crimson, feathering spikes of bloom.	About 2½ feet.
Youth-and-Old-Age.*	Zin-ni-as.	All brilliant colors. Bloom late in Fall. Easily raised. Large-flowering Dwarf are the best seeds to plant.	2 feet.
Mad Wort.*	Sweet A-lys-sum.	Charming edging plant. Tiny white thick flower heads. Buy "Little Gem."	4 inches.
Wild Cucumber Vine.		A rapid Annual Climber.	
Floss Flower.	A-ger-a-tum.	Blooms from early Summer to late Fall. Buy "Blue Perfection;" small blue flossy flowers which grow in thick clusters. Excellent for blue among cut flowers.	12–15 inches.

* If garden space is small, select only the names marked with a star.

MARY FRANCES GARDEN CUT-OUT
No. 4

For description of the flowers shown here see Chapter X.

List of flowers shown in the Early and Late Fall Hardy Garden

Hardy Larkspur,
Monk's Hood,
Hardy Phlox,
Helenium,
Hardy Asters,

MARY FRANCES GARDEN CUT-OUT
No. 4—*Continued*

Hardy Chrysanthemums,
Anemone,
Japanese Wind Flower,
Gaillardia,
Coreopsis,
Tufted Pansies,
Eupatorium.

Some Favorite Annuals

Common Name.	Botanical Name.	Remarks.	Height.
Snapdragon* ("Biennial" plants).	An-tir-rhi-num.	Resemble sweet peas, but are easily cared for; need no trellis or support. Excellent for cutting, having stout stems. Sow in February or March in seed-boxes. Bloom from July to November. Best variety; large Flowering Half Dwarf. Colors: garnet, red, rose, pink, copper, orange, yellow, white. Plants sometimes sow their own seed for next season.	18 inches.
Scarlet Sage.	Sal-vi-a Splen-dens.	Brilliant red bloom from Summer through Fall. Too harsh a shade for a border plant. Use only in a mass in the garden.	24 in.
Cornflowers.*	Cen-tau-re-a Cy-an-us.	Sometimes called: "Bachelor's Buttons," "Blue Bottle," "Ragged Robin." Buy "Double Blue" variety.	15 inches.
Nasturtiums.		Orange, yellow, salmon color. Buy "Dwarf" variety. Excellent for edging. There is a tall growing variety which clings to a support, or "climbs."	10 inches.
Cosmos.		See Garden for Little Folks for description.	

* If garden space is small, select only the names marked with a star.

NOTE: For description of Sweet Peas, see page 356.

Common Name.	Botanical Name.	Remarks.	Height.
Verbenas.		Buy sweet-scented verbenas which come in red, rose, pink, purple, lavender, white.	18–24 inches.
Four-o'Clocks.	Mi-rab-i-lis Jal-ap-a.	Do well everywhere. Mixed colors. Give each plant twelve inches of room. Interesting because often visited by humming birds.	2 feet.
Mourning Bride. Pincushion Flower.	Sca-bi-o-sa.		

Our grandmothers loved also lady slippers, heliotrope, mignonette; but the perennial flowers have taken the place of many old-fashioned Annuals because they require less care.

Among the most interesting Annuals are—

Everlasting Flowers

which may be dried and will keep their color for years. They make charming winter decorations for the table. There are several varieties.

Do not try all of the varieties named, but select from the descriptions the one or two which would be most pleasing to you.

Some Favorite Annuals

Common Name.	Different Varieties.	Height.
Everlasting Flowers or "Immortelles" (pronounced im-mor-tél).	A-cro-lin-i-um. Pretty white and rosy-pink flowers, which should be cut and dried while in the bud state.	15 inches.
	Hel-i-chry-sum (Strawflower). One of the best "Everlasting" flowers. Plant 12 inches apart. Mixed colors.	30 inches.
	Xer-an-the-um. One of the prettiest of "Everlastings." Purple, white, rose.	
	Globe Am-a-ranth (Bachelor's Buttons). Resemble clover heads in white and purple.	12 inches.

In drying "Everlasting" Flowers, make a paper flower holder in the following manner:

Paper Flower Holder

1. Cut a large square from a heavy piece of paper. Eight inches is a good size.

2. Fold the paper across four times, as shown by the dotted lines in figures 1, 2, 3, 4.

3. Cut along dotted line A-B, figure 5.

4. Open to form figure 6. Clip a tiny piece off the point, and clip along the edges as shown.

5. Spread the paper open. Set it over the mouth of deep vase or jar, and let the stems of the "Everlastings" hang full length through the little openings cut in the holder until dried. This method of dried Everlasting flowers gives long straight stems.

"Some list, that," said Billy at length, "and we haven't yet thought of what we will plant in the

Vegetable Garden

See Chapter LVIII, "Some Hints on Growing Vegetables."

Peas	*Radishes
*Onions	Carrots
*Parsley (Dwarf Curly)	Beets
*Tomatoes	Beans—Stringless
*Lettuce	Beans—Bush Limas
*Thyme	Corn
Peppers	Leeks
Potatoes	Cucumbers
Sweet Basil—a soup herb	

* If garden space is small, select only the names marked with a star.

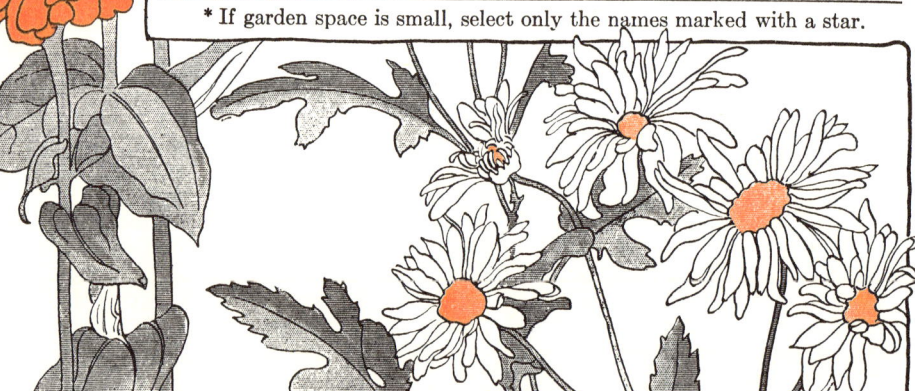

CHAPTER XII

Window Boxes

"WHY, Billy, the very thought of a garden like this almost frightens me," cried Mary Frances. "I don't believe I ever, ever can remember one-quarter of the names!"

"Pshaw!" exclaimed Billy, "that's just like a girl! I wouldn't let a few names scare me! Besides, there aren't so many names; some are *repeated* in each list. That's not a very difficult garden, if managed just as Miss Gardiner explained."

"Oh, I'm not scared—exactly," said Mary Frances, "not when I have such a wonderful teacher, ahem! Professor Billy, when does my next lesson come?"

"Can't promise," said Billy not knowing whether to be pleased or vexed, "next lesson begins work. Hello! I see by my note book, I've left out a part of this lesson. I suppose it is because we've never had window boxes that I overlooked this list."

"Window gardens are almost like a doll's garden, it seems to me," said Mary Frances, as Billy started to read:

THE MARY FRANCES GARDEN BOOK

SUGGESTIONS FOR PLANTING OF WINDOW BOXES

1. Have the boxes made with small holes, or outlets, so that there may be good drainage; for although plants love to drink water, they do not enjoy having "soaking wet feet" all the time.

2. In the bottom of the box place some pebbles or broken stone; this, also, to make the drainage good.

3. Fill box with sifted sand and humus (or manure) very much as for seed boxes. See Chapter XIV.

Following is a list of—

NINE EXCELLENT FREE-BLOOMING PLANTS FOR WINDOW BOXES

(Most are annuals, easily started from seeds)

Petunias.	Many beautiful colors. Sow the seeds indoors; the plants may be placed out as soon as danger of frost is passed. If seeds are saved, they should be taken from the weakest plants, as they will give better results than from stronger plants. Bloom until killed by frost. Buy double large flowering.
Zinnias ("Youth-and-Old-Age").	All colors except blue and purple. Buy "Dwarf Double" varieties. Bloom late into the Fall.
Phlox Drummondi (Annual Phlox).	Very many beautiful mixed colors. Easily grown.
Sweet Alyssum.	Buy the tall variety, of trailing habit: "Alyssum Maritimum." Plant near edges of box.
Cuphéa (Cigar Plant).	Interesting little plant, growing one foot high. Little scarlet flowers, shape of hollow cigars, with black and white tip, resembling ashes.

Window Boxes

Ageratum (Floss Flower).	Buy Dwarf Variety. See List of Annuals for description.
Verbenas.	Sweet-scented Verbenas. Colors: Rose, pink, white, purple, lavender, etc.
Vinca Major Varigata ("Variegated Periwinkle").	Excellent for trailing over the edges of window boxes. Leaves glossy green with light green edges. Flowers, blue.
Geraniums.	Too well known to need description. Easily grown from "cuttings." See Chapter XXXV. Do not expect geraniums to bloom the year round. Give them rest in Winter or Summer by pinching off the buds.

One of the prettiest shallow windows boxes is planted with Violas in mixed colors, with "Tom Thumb" Alyssum for edging.

"Oh, Billy, will you build me a window box soon for my play house?" asked Mary Frances with enthusiasm.

"Will I? Indeed, Mary Frances, what do you think! I don't believe you'll find another fellow——"

"Oh, Billy, I didn't think! I didn't! You're so good to give me these lessons! I'll wait until later for the window box."

"You'd better," said Billy; "you interrupted my notes. There is just one more flower mentioned in these lists. It is—

Lemon Verbena (not hardy).	An old-fashioned favorite, because of the sweet-scented foliage. It is better grown in the garden than in window boxes. The flowers are insignificant, but the lemon-scented leaves are a delight.

"Some 'lemon verbena' I shall have!" exclaimed Mary Frances. "I remember it well in Grandma's garden, don't you?"

"I remember it, but I remember another sweet-scented leaf better:

Ber-ga-mot.	Hardy, easily grown. Flowers: Brilliant red; pretty, but not beautiful. Leaves very fragrant. Humming birds often gather nectar from the flowers.

"Oh, Billy, I remember that, too. Wasn't it lovely! I know Grandma will give me some roots. Now, let's begin the next lesson. I am so anxious to get to the place where I really begin to do something!"

"Well, you could do something right away," said Billy. "You could start in this box which I filled with earth yesterday, and hung outside your play house window——"

Window Boxes

"Oh, Billy!" breathed Mary Frances, "I didn't see it! My, how pleased I am!"

"Humm!" Billy acknowledged her gratitude and continued: "You could start—

An Herb-Garden Window Box
A Soup-and-Sauce Garden

Parsley.	See List of Vegetables for Little Folks' Garden.
Sage.	A savory herb. Buy the plant. It grows about 15 inches tall.
Mint.	Used for "mint sauce." Easily grown. Buy the plant.
Chives.	Somewhat like small delicate green onion tops. Bear a pretty blue flower. Buy clump of roots.
Thyme.	Edge the box with thyme. See List of Vegetables for Little Folks' Garden.

"I'll start it immediately," declared Mary Frances, who was very fond of cooking, "I'll get my purse and go to the florist's right now to buy the plants."

"Good-bye, then!" called Billy, "I've done my part. My next help is in eating the soup—or sauce!"

CHAPTER XIII

Billy Tests the Soil

"Do you suppose, Professor—I mean Billy—do you imagine we can keep the garden a secret?"

The early Spring day was so lovely that the children were sitting in the summer house.

"I guess the folks will suspect something," answered Billy, "when they see us digging and spading, but they won't for a moment think of all we're planning to do."

"They can't help seeing things grow," Billy went on, "but how little they'll expect you to come in some day with radishes and lettuce from your own garden."

"You're just like Feather Flop!" exclaimed Mary Frances.

"Well, I like that!"

"I mean," Mary Frances caught her breath, "I mean you think only of the vegetables, and forget that I will bring in a beautiful bouquet of flowers for the table."

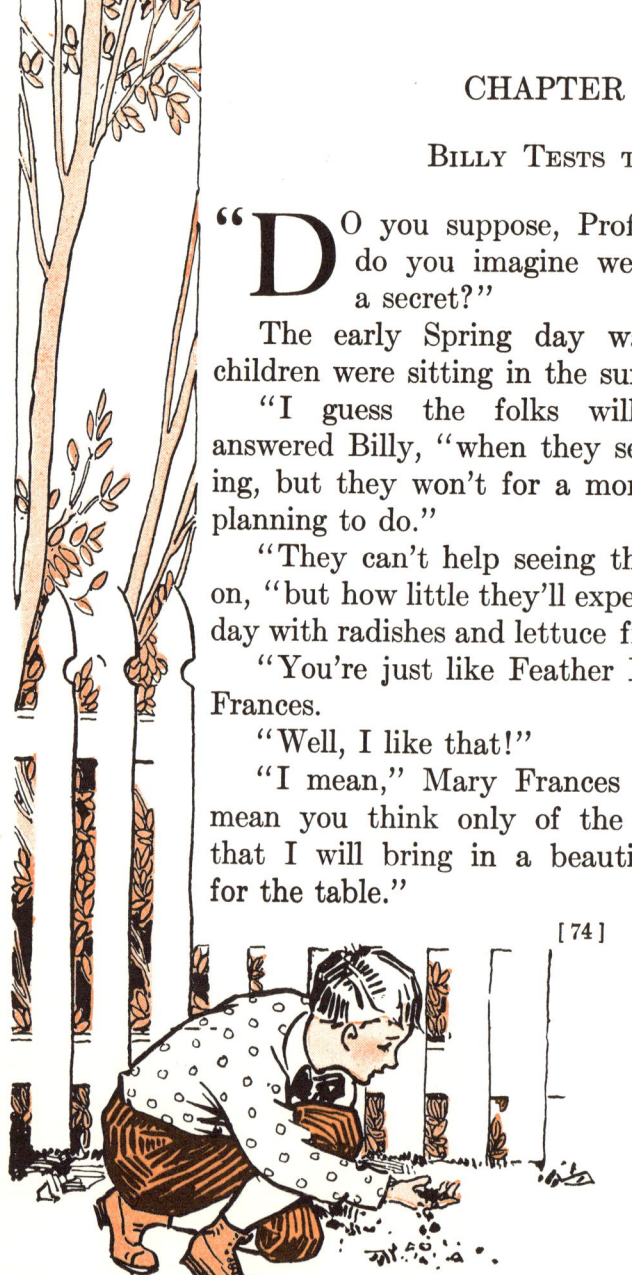

BILLY TESTS THE SOIL

"Oh, to be sure," nodded Billy, "but you won't have either unless we begin the next lesson. The first thing after making out the list, so our professor told us, is to understand about the soil. He said that after knowing what to plant, we must learn how to plant. So let us go have a look at the soil near the play house."

In front of the play house, Billy caught up a handful of earth.

"Listen, Mary Frances," he said, earnestly, "let us examine this closely. To test the soil is the most important point in gardening, as you will readily see after you have heard—

GARDEN LESSON No. 3
Testing the Soil

There are very few places where the soil is "just right" for plants.

In order to find out what kind of soil is in your garden, you may make a little test by squeezing some tight in your hand.

Almost any soil, if very damp, will "hold together;" that is, if a handful is squeezed, it will stay in the shape of the hand, so do not make the test until two or three days after a rain, when it will be quite dry.

Clayey Soil

If, in a couple of days after a rain, the soil is sticky, something like putty, and a squeezed handful holds together, and shows the marks of your fingers, it is clayey soil.

Now, if the soil in your garden is clayey, it will never, never do for plant babies. No indeed!

You see, it holds so close together that the little roots cannot push it apart, and cannot grow. So to clayey soil you must add something which will lighten it up; like sand, or even coal ashes, or stable manure which contains a large quantity of straw.

Deep digging and forking help a lot, too, in breaking up the tight hold which clay grains have upon each other. Sometimes that in itself will make the clay sufficiently light.

Sandy Soil

Little plant babies are so delicate that a very sandy bed would not do for them either, for a rain might wash away the soil from their roots.

All plants are very particular, and grow best if their bed is "just right."

So, if in a couple of days after a rain, a squeezed handful of your garden soil will not hold together at all, and sifts through your fingers, heavier material must be added.

A little clay worked into the sand and run over with a roller helps; but there is something even better—it is stable manure.

Billy Tests the Soil

Humus

Stable manure* not only helps hold sandy soil together and lightens clayey soils, but it contains a very great deal of plant food in the form of humus, and without humus all the other plant food in the soil is of very little value to the plant.

What Humus Is

I know you are going to ask me what humus is; but first I want to ask you to think what the soil is. Yes, dirt, that is right; but dirt came from where?

For the most part from broken and crumbled-up rock, for this earth was once nearly all of rock.

But dirt or soil is not only rotten and broken and crumbled-up rock, as you will see in one minute.

Do you remember how the leaves fell off the tree last Autumn, and how the grass died down? What became of the leaves and grass?

They died, yes, and turned into leaf mold, which is one form of humus.

You have guessed right, Mary Frances. Humus is decayed vegetable matter.

---

* Manure should be well rotted, otherwise plants cannot make use of it, for they must have food that has been "broken down," so that the plant roots can take up what they need.

Manure that is rotted has been piled up and left out in the weather with a board or two for cover to shed water. The pile has been turned over once a month, and dampened when dry.

What Humus Does

Humus mixed with water makes humus soup, which is the very best kind of plant food, and the plant babies love it. They drink it through their roots, you know.

Not only does humus help with the matter of food, but it holds moisture in the soil, and in some almost magic way makes other plant food into a form which the plant can use.

Of course, you wish to give your plants the best kind of food, and of course you will want humus.

But suppose you cannot readily get stable manure, or leaf mold from the woods, why then, you can make humus. Every day the very things you need to make humus may be going to waste.

To Make a Compost Heap

Save all the vegetable tops, leaves, grass, etc. Pile them up and let them decay. When decayed, they are humus.

Another way to make a compost heap is to dig grass sods about eight inches square, and make them into a pile about two feet high, with layers of earth and manure between, and let stand in the weather to decay. Turn over when decayed. When wanted for use, cut some down, knock apart and spread.

You have heard of sowing rye or oats, and "ploughing the crop under" to enrich the soil; this makes humus out of the green rye or oats and their roots.

The plant baby and big plants, too, need many different kinds of food, but the most important is humus.

CHAPTER XIV

How to Plant

"OH, yes," continued Billy "I'm going to tell you how the plants eat, and why they are so fond of plant-food soup, and why they like bones (of course, for soup! that is right); but I think you would prefer that story later on, and would rather talk now about—

Garden Tools

The best small garden tools are a "Ladies' Set," for they are strong and yet small and pleasant to handle.

A fork for digging; a rake and a hoe and a "cultivator" are necessary.

To Dig up the Garden

1. Drive the fork down into the ground, with your left foot on top of the prongs, and lift the clod of earth high enough to turn over.

2. After dropping it, "spank" it apart into little lumps and dust.

Commence this work at the back of the garden, and step

backward over the untouched earth, until you have covered the entire plot. Begin at the left-hand corner "A" and across to the right.

In this way, you will not step on the loosened soil, nor pack it down.

Of course, in large fields, this work is done with a plow.

To Prepare the Soil

1. Spread humus or manure, or both, all over the surface and dig it in, in the same manner in which you first dug up the garden, if you wish to be entirely certain of having success.

But even then, the soil is not fine enough. No. I see you shake your head. But, Mary Frances, if you want a lovely garden, you must get the garden table ready for the plant roots in the most enticing way.

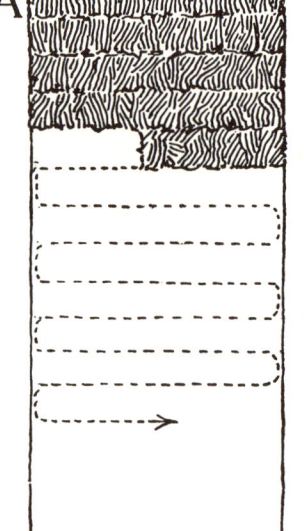

Spading the Garden

2. Next, take your rake and "comb" the earth to and fro until it is all light and feathery.

Of course, in large fields, this work of raking is done with a harrow.

3. After planting the seeds, pat the soil down firmly so that

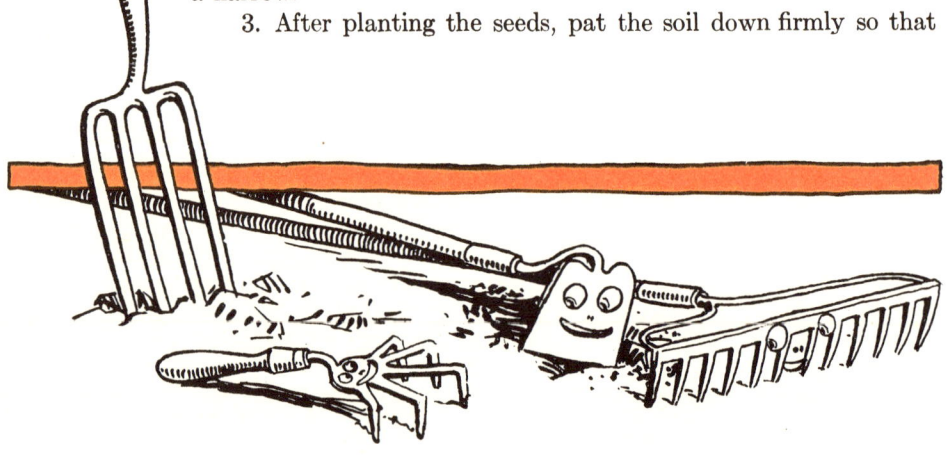

How to Plant

it will be firm enough for the little rootlets to "get a hold," yet will be movable so that they may grow.

To Plant Seeds in Boxes

Little seeds are not always started, or planted, out of doors.

Instead, early in the Spring, seeds are often started in boxes in a sunny window, or in hotbeds. (See Chapter LVII.)

We'll make a hotbed of our own one of these days, Mary Frances, but at present we'll have to be satisfied with seed boxes.

Preparing the Soil

1. For starting seeds indoors, use shallow boxes, placed in a sunny window.

Cigar boxes are of a convenient size for children to use. The soil should be fine and rich in humus.

2. Sift some soil from the compost heap, or some leaf loam (soil from the woods), or some well rotted stable manure,* through a large mesh sieve (ash sifter) and mix with the same amount of fine sand.

3. Fill the boxes with this mixture; water it well with a fine sprinkler.

---

* Manure is sold by the pound in powdered form by all leading seed houses.

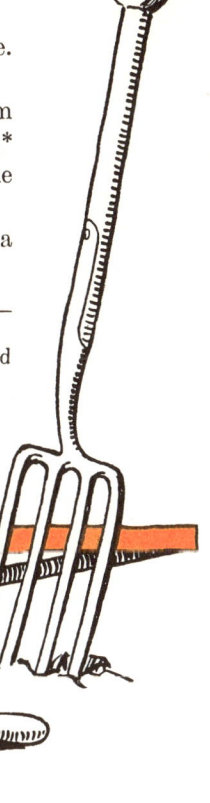

Sowing the Seed Boxes

1. Sow the seeds thinly, sprinkle them like pepper from a shaker on the surface, and over them spread a very, very little sand.

2. If possible, cover the box with glass to prevent the soil from drying, but let the *air into the box by tilting the glass* on one side, using a cork on the edge.

Watering the Seed Boxes

1. Do not water often, but when necessary to do so, use the finest sprinkler possible.

2. Water seed boxes in the morning. For if watered at night, the tiny plants may "damp off," or mildew.

"Oh," exclaimed Mary Frances, "how careful a gardener has to be! What lovely beds must be made for little seeds!"

"Exactly so," agreed Billy. "I see you get the point of the lesson. It is really about how to make the beds for the seed babies."

"The dear little things," said Mary Frances. "Billy, I had no idea how easily I would learn to love the thought of them."

"Well, then you'll enjoy the next lesson," said

Billy, turning over the leaves of his note book. "Our professor told us next a good deal about the seed babies."

"Can't we go right on now with that lesson?" asked Mary Frances, in delight at the willingness of Billy to teach her.

"I guess so," replied Billy, looking at his watch. "The ball team doesn't meet until two-thirty."

CHAPTER XV

THE OUTDOOR SEED-BED

"LET me see," said Billy. "What lesson is this?"

"It's the fourth lesson," Mary Frances counted on her fingers. "I remember perfectly."

"Right you are," replied Billy, rising and bowing; "and I shall begin this lecture by reciting a little piece of poetry, called—

TWO LITTLE ACORNS

Two little acorns
    Sitting on a stem—
One little acorn
    Says, "Ahem!"
Other little acorn
    Says, "Oh-ho!
I wonder, now,
    What makes us grow?"

The Outdoor Seed-Bed

"I don't know,
    But this I see;
It must be someone
    Wiser than we."
Other little acorn
    Says, "Oh-ho!
Indeed, indeed,
    That must be so!"

Billy made a deep bow, and Mary Frances clapped her hands; then Billy opened his note book, cleared his throat, and began:

GARDEN LESSON No. 4
THE OUTDOORS SEED-BED

Having found how to get the outdoors seed-bed ready, we will next learn how to plant the seed.

Of course, you have made your list of the seeds needed, and have received them from the dealer.

If possible, it is best to run the planting of the rows or drills north and south so that *the sun will shine* upon the rows of plants all day, from the east in the mornings; from the west in the afternoons.

You will need a garden line to make a straight first row.

To Make a Garden Line

1. Cut two sticks about as large around as a broom handle, each eighteen inches long.
2. Point the ends so that they may be easily stuck into the ground.
3. Tie one end of a strong twenty-five foot cord to each stick. Roll the cord on the stick.

To Use the Garden Line

1. Decide where you wish the first row of plants to grow.
2. Push the stick, not having the roll of cord, down into the ground at the end of this imaginary row.
3. With the other stick in hand walk back, unrolling the cord until you reach the other end of the imaginary row of little plants. Try to make this row very straight, as all the other rows will be measured from it.

By the way, this row should be quite near the edge of the bed, so that you will not have to step on the loose "feathery" soil.

4. Drive the other stick down into the earth, drawing the cord tight.

Planting in Drills

1. Prepare the rake to mark the little rows, or drills, for the seed. Have ready three good-sized corks. Stick the middle tooth of the rake half way through one cork.
2. Do the same to the two end teeth.

The Outdoor Seed-Bed

3. Run one end tooth of the rake along the stretched garden line keeping all the teeth parallel with the line. Continue to use the rake across the entire bed. This is a convenient method of getting straight rows. Make the drills (hollows) about a half inch deep.

Broadcasting

Seed are often not sowed in "drills," but are "broadcast;" where plants are to be thinned out when they come up, and not to be transplanted, the *drills* are better.

Broadcasting is throwing the seeds lightly over the surface of the ground, so that each will fall a little way apart from the other, like sprinkling with pepper from a pepper shaker.

Covering the Seeds

After the seeds are sown, draw the earth lightly over them either with your hands or with the back of the rake. It is best to sow seeds just before a rain, except when the seeds are very small; then, just after a rain. If there is no rain, sprinkle lightly, but thoroughly dampen the earth.

Pat the earth down gently with the palms of your hands or with a board.

A board is much the better if seed has been broadcast.

The reason? Oh, yes, the reason is that the soil will be too light and airy unless firmed.

The little seed rootlets need close-packed light earth, with

no lumps. Just imagine how tiny they are, and how near to them must be the tiny grains of sand for them to take hold on.

To Mark the Beds

After the seeds are planted, drive down at the ends of the first and last rows little stakes, marked with the names of the kind of seed planted in the section.

"Perhaps you think you will remember what kinds of seed you've planted; but one is never certain. Once I thought I had planted carrots and when the plants grew, I had beets. It is not safe to try to remember.

So much, then, for how to put seed babies into their beds.

By and by, they are going to wake up, and we must understand how to take care of them. The best way to learn how to take care of them is to find out what they are, and what they need."

CHAPTER XVI

Seed Babies and Their Nurses

"FIRST of all, we must understand that the seed has a coat which holds the living, sleeping baby. You see, the baby itself is so tiny and delicate that it would not be safe for it to be out without its seed coat. The wind and the sun would soon dry it up and kill it; then, too, it would die of hunger, for it is too little to find its own food. So its mother wraps the baby up in its strong seed coat, and puts its food in beside it, in the same coat. And there the seed baby lies sound asleep until—until everything is just right for it to wake up. The time it likes best to awaken is in Spring, when the weather is getting warm.

Seed Babies in Their Coats

You will put your seed babies, coats and all, into the warm ground early in the Spring, when they will feel like growing. Then you will dampen them, for without moisture and food, the seed baby will not wake up. The moisture swells the seed coat, and wakens the baby, and gets the food ready for the baby to eat.

The baby begins to eat the food its mother put inside the seed coat; it stretches itself, and pretty soon sends down into the earth a "teeny-weeny" rootlet. This rootlet takes a little food from the earth up to the baby. Oh, yes, plant soup, that is the kind of food it takes. Plant soup is mixed earth and water.

How good it is for the plant child, depends on how sweet the soil is, and how much humus or compost or manure food is in the soup. Humus soup tastes wonderfully good to the baby plant.

Cotyledons

Well, not only does the baby plant send down this tiny rootlet, but its tiny stem grows upward, and bursts through the seed coats and show two tiny leaves.

The two tiny leaves which appear on top of this stem, while down in the soil grew larger, threw open the seed coat, and came up to the surface for the air and sunshine.

These leaves are called the seed-leaves, or cŏt-ў-lē'-dŏns. They are not the true leaves of the plant baby, but are nurse-leaves which go ahead of the leaves of the baby plant, and really hold the true leaf of the baby between them.

These nurse-leaves take care of and feed the tiny plant baby until it can send out its own tiny leaves to gather air and digest food for itself.

If you pull up a Lima Bean Seed Baby after it has started to grow you will see the nurse-leaves.

Seed Babies and Their Nurses

No plant should be moved or transplanted until at least two true leaves, or leaves of its own, not nurse-leaves (cotyledons), have appeared.

Of course, when the little plants first come up there will be so many that each will choke the other, and so we must learn about—

Thinning Out the Plants

When the little plants are about two inches high, pull up all the weak plants, leaving the stronger ones from one to six inches apart, according to the kind of plants.

The little plants will need moisture, too—not just "watering," but the moisture which lies far beneath the surface, and which can only be had by keeping the surface soil in good condition, so as when the plants grow one of the most important things we have to learn to do is—

To Cultivate

"Cultivating" means breaking up the soil where it hardens about the plant. *It is the most important part of gardening* after planting, except "thinning out."

Cultivating is done by use of the hoe and "cultivator," the rake-like tool which has but few prongs. Draw the cultivator between the rows of plants every day or two. Use the hoe in smaller spaces. Use the hoe to chop down weeds below the surface of the ground, being careful not to cut into the roots of the garden plants.

In breaking up the hard soil, or "cultivating," the weeds are destroyed, but hard soil is a worse enemy of plant babies than weeds even, although every child knows how dreadful it is for a garden to let weeds steal all the food from the baby plants.

Baby plants need $\begin{cases} \text{air,} \\ \text{food,} \\ \text{moisture.} \end{cases}$

Now if there is a hard crust of soil around the roots, they cannot get the *air;* so we *cultivate* or break up the hard soil to give them air.

Baby plants cannot get *food* if big strong weeds steal it from them; so we *cultivate* to kill the weeds.

Baby plants need *moisture*, perhaps more than anything else, so we cultivate; for cultivating keeps in the moisture that is down in the soil. I will explain this in a very little while.

So you see *Cultivating* is the most important garden work.

WATERING

Perhaps you think watering the garden most important. If so, you are mistaken. Yes, the garden must be watered from time to time; but when it is watered it should be drenched soaking wet, never sprinkled a little every day or two. One soaking in a week is better than a light sprinkling every day. Light sprinkling brings the roots to the surface, where the sun dries them up in a short time. On the other hand, the rain or a thor-

Seed Babies and Their Nurses

ough drenching soaks down, down, down, into the earth, where it is stored up for future use.

The Importance of Cultivating

Now, I am going to tell you why cultivating is so important in regard to moisture.

If the soil is all soft and fine and loose, the rain can easily run down through it to the roots.

If it were hard, the water would run off to lower ground. That's easily understood.

But immediately after the rain, when the sun comes out and the wind blows, the surface of the soil begins to dry.

Then the sun "coaxes" and "pulls" the water up, up, up, to the surface it has dried, something like the way you pull the juice of an orange up through a stick of lemon candy. Now let me ask you—could you pull much orange juice through the stick of candy if the stick of candy were crumbled or broken apart at the top? No, you could not.

Neither can the sun pull the moisture up through the tiny little tubes in the soil if we break those little tubes and crumble the tops into dust. No, you need not look for these tubes, Mary Frances; they are too tiny for you to see, but they act very much like blotting paper to bring the under moisture up to the surface, and unless they are broken and crumbled, the deep earth moisture goes sailing off into the air to meet the sun, as fast as if it ran out of a little spigot running it off, and the poor plant baby dries up for want of deep moisture near its roots.

How shall we break these tubes (the sun's lemon candy stick)?

Yes, that's right, Mary Frances!

By CULTIVATION.

"Jiminy! what a long lesson!" exclaimed Billy, wiping his forehead, "What're you going to do for me, Mary Frances, for all this wonderful instruction?"

"I'll give a dinner in your honor, Professor, and let you invite whom you please."

"On one condition," said Billy, "that every thing we have will come out of your garden!"

"Agreed!"

"To-morrow we begin real work and put into practice some of these remarkable lectures," added Billy earnestly.

"Oh, how glad I am!" exclaimed Mary Frances. "Billy, it seems too wonderful! My, I'm glad Mother and Father sent you away to school, though I did miss you terribly, but you learned such a lot that it makes up for it."

"Augh! Mary Frances, you make a fellow feel queer, I wasn't such a perfect little *angel* in *school*."

Seed Babies and Their Nurses

"Oh, certainly not, certainly not, Billy," laughed Mary Frances, "that's the wonder of it—to think a bad boy like you could learn so much, that's the puzzle to me."

"Humm!" said Billy to himself as he looked after Mary Frances' fleeting figure, "It's lucky for that girl that I'm a scout."

CHAPTER XVII

NAMES OF PARTS OF FLOWERS

THE children worked in the garden early and late for days, and if the grown-ups in the big house suspected they were gardening, they did not hint that they thought of such a thing.

Billy spaded, and Mary Frances planted, and Feather Flop looked on from a distance whenever Billy was anywhere to be seen.

One day, Mary Frances met him as she came to the compost heap, where she was going to throw some weeds and grass cuttings.

"Why, Feather Flop," she exclaimed, "I haven't seen you for ever-so-long! Where have you been?"

"I've been—I've been—watching," said Feather Flop, "and when I've thought I dared, I've weeded your garden; yes, I have. Haven't you noticed how few weeds there were?" he asked anxiously.

"I have, Feather Flop, indeed I have; only the other day I said to Billy, 'I almost could imagine

someone had been "cultivating" the garden this morning.'"

"That was the morning I got up before daylight, and went out there and scratched, and scratched, where I felt *sure* I would not disturb anything which ought not to be disturbed," said Feather Flop, delighted.

"My," said Mary Frances, "how perfectly dear of you, Feather Flop; I can't begin to tell you the wonderful fairy-story-feeling I have, to know that all the time that Billy and I are studying and working, you are so interested and kind, so anxious to help me!"

"Oh, yes, dear Miss," sighed the happy rooster; "but I certainly do wish I could do more and be with you oftener."

"Never mind, Feather Flop," said the little girl. "Some day when Billy goes to town, we'll spend the whole day together."

"Good!" cried Feather Flop, delighted. "Good! and now, please let me show you where I found so many cut-worms."

Mary Frances and he walked over to the garden.

"Right there," explained Feather Flop, going toward the tomato plants and pointing with his wing: "right down there. About twenty, I guess there were, and I had some difficulty——"

"Get out of that garden, will you, Feather Flop!" roared Billy, coming with a stick. "Say, Mary Frances, why don't you chase that old good-for-nothing rooster off? If he doesn't look out——"

"Oh, Billy," cried Mary Frances. "Oh, Billy, you ought—he was—he has eaten a lot of cut-worms. I know he has! You don't understand!"

"I don't understand! Well, I guess I don't! Get out of here, you old busybody of a rooster!" said Billy.

Mary Frances felt so sorry about the rooster she couldn't have helped crying, and out came her handkerchief.

"Oh, Billy," she sobbed, "he's so interested—in the—garden."

"I should say he is!" said Billy. "I should say so! But whatever can be the matter with *you*, gets me! For pity's sake, dry up those tears. I was going to give you the next lesson."

At that Mary Frances dried her eyes.

"Oh, were you, Billy—will you?" She was delighted.

"Yes," said Billy, "if you'll stop weeping. The next lesson is a real one in Botany, or the study of flowers and plants; and since I've found these few buttercups, which I pressed in my collection of dried flowers, if you wish, I shall begin—

GARDEN LESSON · No. 5
NAMES OF PARTS OF FLOWERS

Not all flowers have every part. The buttercup (or better, the single geranium) is an excellent flower to study to show the various parts.

To learn the name of each part, our teacher told us—

THE STORY OF LITTLE BUTTERCUP

Little Buttercup has on a yellow collar.

Her collar is called a cô-rŏl-lá.

Her corolla collar is made of five scallops; each scallop is called a pĕt′-al.

The petal scallops of Little Buttercup's collar corolla are held in place about her neck in a little green cup-shaped holder.

This holder is called a cā′-lўx, or cup.

The calyx cup has five pointed scallops.

Each scallop is called a sĕp'-ăl.

Little Buttercup wears not only a beautiful yellow collar corolla made of shiny yellow petals, held in place by the green sepals of the calyx cup, but she has a lovely necklace of fringe close about her neck.

Each thread of fringe is a stā'-men.

Each stamen is made of a thread called a fĭl'-ă-mĕnt, and on the end of each filament dangles a little bead, called an ăn'-thĕr.

Proud little Buttercup not only wears all of these beautiful things, but she uses powder!

On each anther bead Little Buttercup carries some yellow powder.

This powder is called pŏl'-len.

She must be very proud when she gets all dressed up in the lovely Spring days in her best finery—a shiny corolla collar, made of yellow petals, held in a calyx cup, made of green sepals, and a stamen fringe necklace, powdered with pollen!

Oh, yes, she wears a lovely dress of green lacey leaves. The leaf is made strong, just as children are, by a bone, a leaf-bone or a mid-rib.

All other flowers dress in a similar way, but not every flower has as many beautiful things to wear as has little Buttercup.

When you see flowers after this, look for the lovely corolla, calyx, stamens, and other parts of the flower, which you have learned to know through Little Buttercup.

Names of Parts of Flowers

There is another part to a buttercup, called the pis-til, but I shall tell you about that part of flowers in the next lesson, in just the way our teacher told us.

"Oh," cried Mary Frances, as Billy finished, "What a delightful lesson! Never again will buttercups seem the same. Although I always loved them, they will be so much more interesting after this."

CHAPTER XVIII

Good Mrs. Bee

"GETTING tired?" asked Billy as Mary Frances finished planting the last of her radish seeds.

"Not so very," answered Mary Frances, "but I would like to take a little rest," sitting down on the garden bench. "Doesn't everything look lovely—the beds all laid out, and neat as biscuits in a baking pan!"

"It is some garden, believe me!" agreed Billy, wiping his brow. "I guess I'll stop for a few minutes, too," throwing himself down at the foot of the tree.

"Oh, Billy, you oughtn't to lie there on the ground," chided Mary Frances; "you'll take your death of cold."

"Ha! Ha!" roared Billy, getting up. "Yes, Grandmother, certainly, your darling grandchild understands your kind admonition and obeys," taking a seat beside Mary Frances, who made room for him.

Good Mrs. Bee

"Oh, Billy, don't tease," she begged. "Please don't! I've enjoyed my Garden Lessons so much, and you've been so kind——"

"Say, Mary Frances, if you want me to go away, just keep on praising me, will you," interrupted Billy.

"All right," said Mary Frances, "I'll stop, but I've gone over and over in my mind the lesson about the seed babies. It all seems so wonderful to me. Do you know, Billy, I've often wondered how the little seed babies are made. Where does their mother get them?"

"Well," began Billy, "I guess I can explain."

"Oh," shrieked Mary Frances suddenly. "Oh, Billy, excuse me, please, but that bee nearly dashed in my face."

"It's not after you, Mary Frances," laughed Billy. "That's good Mrs. Bee looking for honey. And she'll have hard work to find it to-day, I'm thinking. Still, I saw a few very early blossoms out on the shrubs at the end of the garden."

"I saw them, too, Billy. Isn't it lovely that we have such beautiful things to enjoy."

"That's what Mrs. Bee thinks, too," said Billy;

"and in fact, the flowers are made beautiful, not for us especially, but to attract the bees and moths and butterflies."

"But I can't imagine why," said Mary Frances; "the bees only steal honey from them."

"Only steal honey!" exclaimed Billy. "But then, I used to think so myself, Mary Frances, until about a year ago, when I learned better. You see, the bees do every bit as much for the flowers as the flowers do for the bees."

"Oh, do they? That's wonderful, Billy. Please tell me about it?"

"If you'll move over far enough on this bench to let me be comfortable," growled Billy.

"Oh, certainly, certainly; excuse me." Mary Frances almost fell off the end. "Oh, say, Billy, let's go over under the trees and I'll swing in the hammock, and you can take the bench."

"All right," said Billy, following Mary Frances.

"Now," suggested Mary Frances, settling herself in the hammock, "I know you feel just like telling me the whole story."

"All right," agreed Billy, "and I have a surprise

Good Mrs. Bee

for you—I just caught that honey bee you saw. Here, in my cap."

"Oh, let's see it, Billy," Mary Frances put out her hand.

"Take care!" warned Billy. "I guess you forget how a bee stings. Go get a large-mouth bottle and I'll slip it in."

Billy gently slipped the bee into the large bottle Mary Frances brought.

"Notice, Mary Frances, how furry its little body is."

"Why, it's covered with yellow!" exclaimed Mary Frances. "I thought bees were rather dark in color."

"Yes," said Billy, "yes, this bee is quite dark in color; the yellow you see is pollen powder."

"Oh, off the anther bead!" exclaimed Mary Frances. "It's off the anther bead of some flower!"

"Guessed right that time," said Billy. "That's what it is, all right. I wish I could tell you the whole story of the bee and of fertilization the way Miss Gardener told us in class."

"Won't you try to remember, Billy; won't you try?" begged Mary Frances.

CHAPTER XIX

The Story of Fertilization

"WELL, as nearly as I can remember," began Billy, "Miss Gardener said she had been studying very hard on the formation of parts of flowers, and the story of fertilization. It was pretty dry stuff, too, as it was taught when she was young; but the way she told it was so interesting that I took notes which will help me in telling you about

The Birth of Seed Babies. Formation of the Pistil

The pistil is the tall green center stalk generally found in the midst of the stamens.

The pistil is very interesting, for it has to do with the way in which the seed baby is born.

The pistil has three parts { the stigma (the top), the style (the stem), the ovary (seed holder).

"The stigma is the real mother of the seed babies.

The Story of Fertilization

"Here, Mary Frances, I am going to cut a flower off that geranium in the window, down the center to show you. Mother will not object."

When Billy had cut the flower down lengthwise he explained further

The Need of Pollen

Now, the pistil needs pollen off the anthers of some other flower in order to bring seed-babies to life. Oh, yes, Mary Frances, I'm coming to the part about the bees. The pistil needs pollen, as I said; sometimes a pistil needs the kind of pollen which is on the anthers of the same plant, sometimes a pistil needs pollen from the anthers of some other plant, but it must have pollen to give seed babies life.

How Can the Flowers Get Pollen

Now, flowers cannot walk, nor can the pistils or stamens of flowers walk. How can they get the pollen powder to their pistils? How can the pollen powder get to their pistils?

The Flowers Spread a Feast for Insects

In some cases the breeze blows some pollen upon the pistils of a few flowers, but it is a very *uncertain* way, to depend on a breeze; so the wonderful flowers *spread a feast* of just the most delightful food for *bees*, and sometimes for butterflies, and

sometimes for moths; and not only do they get the most enticing food ready for such insects, but they put out the most beautiful signs telling them the feast is ready.

They make the sign just as attractive as they possibly can for the particular kind of insect they wish to come to them to eat.

They use the loveliest colors and the most delightful odors, which please the bees, the butterflies, the moths, more than they please even you and me, by their wonderful beauty and fragrance.

Nectar

The food they give the bee is—no, Mary Frances, it is not honey, it is *nectar*, out of which the bees make honey.

Honey Bee's Honey-Churns

Yes, I know you want to learn how they make it. No, they do not churn it in a churn; they really churn it, though. That is a good guess. They churn it in their honey-sac stomachs. The honey bees love pollen, too. It is their flour—pollen flour—and they carry it to their hives in little basket-like places on their legs.

The Insects Carry Pollen

Now, the bees in coming to get this feast of good things to eat—the nectar for honey, and the pollen for bee-flour, both of which are very necessary for bees—do just exactly what the

The Story of Fertilization

flowers want them to do above everything—*to carry pollen* from some anthers to the pistil. This they do without knowing what a great kindness they are bestowing upon the flowers.

They think they are just doing their duty in gathering nectar to make honey and pollen for bee-flour, but in dipping their heads down into the deep calyx where the nectar is stored, they get their furry bodies covered with pollen, and when they come out of that flower, or go to visit another, they spread pollen all over the stigma of the pistil! And when the pollen is spread on the stigma of the pistil, somehow, in some wonderful way it sinks down through the style into the ovary where the dear little seed baby is born.

If you cut open an old bloom going to seed you will see a number of seed babies in the ovary from which they will fall when they are ripe.

Bumble Bees Help

Sometimes flowers are very particular as to just what insect shall do this work for them. For instance, the clover hides its nectar too deep for the honey bee's tongue to reach; so the bumble bee and butterfly do most of the work of pollination for the clovers.

The little butter-and-eggs flower depends upon bumble bees, too, to bring pollen to the pistil, for she closes the nectar holder with so tight a lip that the weight of the honey bee is not heavy enough to open it.

Animals Would Starve Without This Work of Insects

By the way, it is a dreadful thing to kill bumble bees. They do the work of pollenizing for many a deep-cupped flower, and *without their aid and the aid of some such insects, everybody would starve*, for there would be no seed and no new plants to take the place of the old ones as they died, and animals and birds and mankind would perish of starvation.

Moths and Butterflies Help, Too

This work of pollenizing depends for the most part on bees, but many butterflies and moths feed on nectar in the same way. Most moths' tongues are very long, and many long-necked flowers depend upon them to bring pollen on their soft, furry bodies to the pistils. The moths fly at night, so many long-necked flowers, like the moonflowers, do not open their blooms nor shed their sweet odors in the day time, but wait to show their sweetness until their favorite insect is flying.

Now you see that Beauty Butterfly and night moths are not just a gorgeous bit of living color. Such moths and Beauty Butterfly accomplish much good.

"Well, Miss Gardener said she lay out in the hammock, just as you are lying, Mary Frances, studying just what I have told you, only in a much more difficult way, and she kept saying over and over to

The Story of Fertilization

herself, 'Corolla, calyx, sepals, stamens, pistil,' in order that she might know her lesson, when all at once her book began to slip out of her hand and she could not seem to cling to it at all. She heard the dull thud as it hit the ground."

"Are you ready?" asked a strange buzzy voice. "I'm always in a hurry, you see. Are you quite ready?"

"I'm ready," answered Miss Gardener; "ready for anything; but please, where are you, who are you, and what am I to be ready for?"

And again the buzzy voice spoke: "Ready to go with me?"

Miss Gardener looked around toward where the buzzy voice seemed to come from. There, sitting on a rose nearby, was a honey bee.

"Oh," gasped Miss Gardener, "I'm—that is—I——"

"You're afraid!" buzzed the bee, coming near her. "You're afraid I'll sting you!" She laughed. "We never sting unless we think we need to take care of ourselves or our lovely children."

"Oh," apologized Miss Gardener, "I—that is, I—I'm ready, Mrs. Bee."

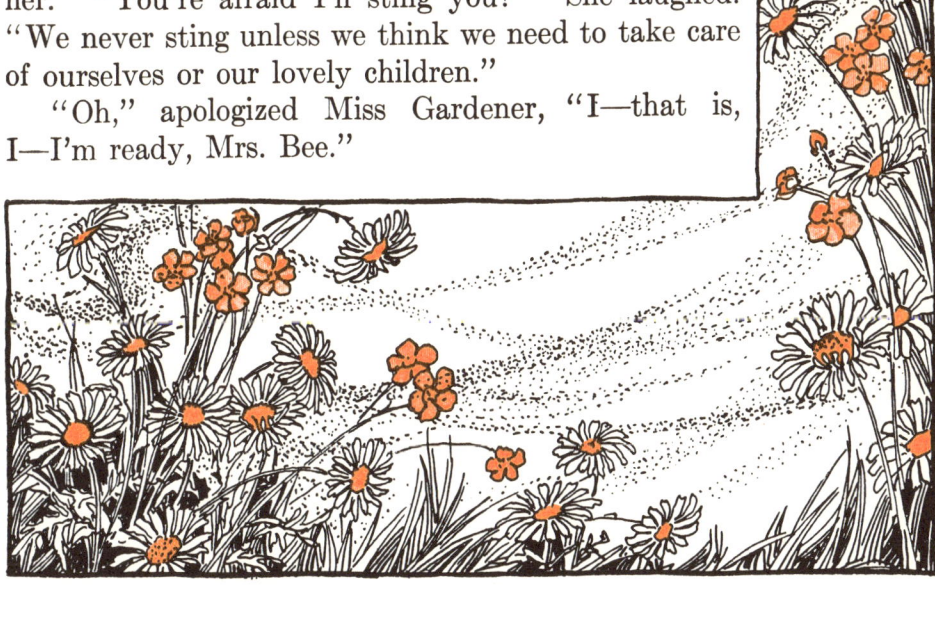

"All right, then," buzzed the bee, flying nearer. "Are you certain you're not afraid?"

"I'm not," declared Miss Gardener; but she said a little shiver went down her spine.

"Very well," buzzed the bee, coming straight at her and hitting her between the eyes.

Miss Gardener tried to scream; before she could do so she had the queerest sensation. Before she could think whether the bee had stung or not, she began to sink down, down, down, down, down, down, until she was just the size of the bee.

"You've wondered so long," said the bee, "about what a beehive was like inside, I am going to take you on a visit to ours. But we must hurry, or I shall not get my duty to the hive people done. Besides, you cannot enter without some pollen or nectar; so here, stop and get a bit."

"How can I?" began Miss Gardener.

"Fly over to that rose I was on," said the bee. Miss Gardener flew and gathered some pollen, and, together, Mrs. Honey Bee and she winged their way over to the hive.

CHAPTER XX

THE STORY OF THE HONEY BEE

"NOW," began her strange little friend, "I shall tell you about the honey bees.

There are two thousand different kinds of bees known at the present time, but the most useful and best understood are the honey bees. The homes (usually wooden boxes) furnished by man for bees are called hives, but the wild bees live ordinarily in hollow trees or caves. The prettiest and gentlest family of the honey bees are the Italian Bees.

Perhaps you think you lead a busy life. If you worked from earliest morning to dark you could not be busier than good Mrs. Honey Bee, for she never trifles nor wastes a minute.

Perhaps you think she goes leisurely from flower to flower, sipping the sweet nectar, and has a very delightful time simply enjoying herself.

You are mistaken, then, for the worker honey bee is not thinking of herself at all, except to eat just enough to keep her well.

She is working for the good of the whole Bee family, and especially for the little Baby Bees.

You begin to see in all your studying, that almost all living

things seem to live with the purpose of helping baby things like themselves to live.

So good Mrs. Bee is not gathering honey and pollen bee-flour to "gobble" them up, but is going to pack much of them away for the use of the bees who will live over winter, and for the baby bees, and for the male bees who have no way of gathering food from the flowers for themselves.

The Bee City

A Beehive city is a wonderfully busy place.

From twenty thousand to forty thousand, or more, inhabitants live in the Bee City, so no wonder it is a busy place. You would think that everything would be in confusion, but on the contrary everything is in marvelous law and order. Every inhabitant knows just what part it is expected to do, and each kind of inhabitant is particularly fitted to do its own particular part.

In every Beehive City there are
{
A Queen Bee,
Many Worker Bees,
Quite a number of Drone Bees.
}

The Queen Bee

The Queen Bee is the mother bee, and it is her duty to lay eggs, out of which Baby Bees are hatched.

The Story of the Honey Bee

Worker Bees

The Worker Bees do the work of the Beehive City. They gather food, and feed and care for the inhabitants, and keep the city clean.

Drone Bees

The Drone or male Bees do not work. Their bodies help keep the hive warm, but they cannot do any real work. One of them is the husband of the Queen Bee, but after she first marries him she doesn't pay any attention to him. She is too busy laying eggs in the cradle cells the Worker Bees have made.

Why the Workers Kill the Drones

Yes, it is expensive to feed the Drone Bees, and when the weather begins to turn cool, perhaps in September or October, the Worker Bees who up to that time have cared for the Drones, begin to rid the Hive City of them. They bite off their wings, and bite them in half sometimes—anything to kill them or send them away. No, it is not as cruel as it sounds, for you see, if Drone Bees kept on living they would eat up the honey which is so much needed in the Winter by the Worker Bees and the Queen who live over to care for the new Baby Bees in the Spring.

The Wonderful Bodies of the Bees

Now, each different kind of honey bee has a body which is particularly fitted to the work it has to perform.

The Body of the Worker Bee

The Worker Bee, the one you see so often on flowers, has a body made especially for the kind it is to do. It has many excellent eyes which look to you like but two eyes, unless you see them under the magnifying glass, and wonderful an-ten-næ, and a tongue in its head. The antennæ are its horn-like feelers, and they resemble your arms in the way they reach out, and examine objects by "handling" them.

The Antennæ

The antennæ are so delicate that the bee can tell the shape and size of any object by just passing them over it. On the antennæ are smell-hollows with which the bee "scents out" the honey.

Legs, Wings, and Claws

On the bee's body, as you know, are the legs and wings. At the end of each leg is a pair of claws.

Pollen Baskets

On each hind leg of the Worker Bee is a hollow in which she packs the pollen flour which she gathers. These are the pollen baskets.

The Wings

The front pair of wings is larger than the hind pair, and often in older bees who have done much work, the edges are frayed and torn.

The Story of the Honey Bee

The Industry of the Worker

A Worker Bee does not live often over five weeks. She actually works herself to death!

Just think. A bee has to visit nearly one hundred flowers to fill her honey-sack with nectar, and when it is full, it does not contain a full drop!

Wax Pockets

Under the body of the Worker Bee are the little wax pockets. The wax is very important, as it is used to make the cells in which the honey is stored, and the cells in which the eggs are laid.

The Honey-Sac

The honey, you remember, is carried to the hive in the honey-sac of the Worker Bees.

The Body of the Queen Bee

The Queen Bee, or Mother Bee, is longer than the Worker Bee and has a tapering, graceful body. She has no pollen basket, because it is not part of her work to gather pollen or honey, her work being to lay eggs—sometimes as many as three thousand in twenty-four hours, equal to about twice her own weight!

The Sting

Both the Worker Bees and the Queen Bee have a sting to use as a weapon of defense.

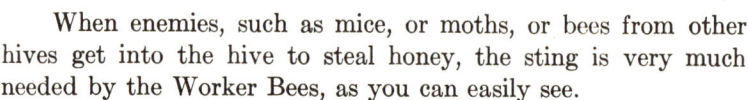

When enemies, such as mice, or moths, or bees from other hives get into the hive to steal honey, the sting is very much needed by the Worker Bees, as you can easily see.

The Queen uses her sting in a different way, as I shall tell you later on.

The Body of the Drone

The Drone Bee differs much in appearance from the Worker and Queen, his body being broad and blunt. His eyes are very large and wings strong. He has no wax pockets nor pollen pockets. His tongue is not long enough to get honey from the flowers. He cannot even find food for himself, and when driven out of the hive, as sometimes in the Autumn, he starves to death in a short time.

CHAPTER XXI

How the Bees Work

As I said, the work in the Beehive City is divided up.

The Worker Bees are divided into various groups: who forage for nectar; who gather pollen; who guard the entrance to the hive from enemies; who clean the city; who build the comb; the nurse-bees, who feed the babies; the undertakers, who carry away the dead; and a group whose duty it is to fan the air to keep the hive cool.

The Ventilating Workers—The Fanners

They keep their tiny wings vibrating so rapidly that sometimes the draught they make will put out a lighted candle flame held at the entrance of the hive at night.

The Comb Builders

When a colony or swarm of bees first enter their new home or hive, the comb builders set about making the comb. The comb is formed of food-cells, in which to store honey and pollen; and cradle cells, in which the queen may lay her eggs.

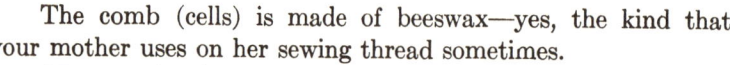

The comb (cells) is made of beeswax—yes, the kind that your mother uses on her sewing thread sometimes.

After getting in the right position on the ceiling of the hive (for bees build downward), the bees take from their wax pockets some little scales of wax, and begin kneading and chewing them into the correct degree of softness, and they or their helpers fix it in position. They make the cells six-sided, and there is no wasted space.

The Queen's Work

All the time the comb builders have been working, the queen has wandered about in an excited way. When she sees that there are cells ready for her, she begins to lay eggs. She is attended by a number of bees who feed her, and massage her, and wait upon her, and feed her "royal jelly."

Worker Baby Bees

In three or four days each egg (which looks like a tiny grain of rice) hatches into a little white grub, and later the nurse bees begin to feed it—no, not honey, but a kind of milk—honey bee milk—which the nurses make. The little grub feeds on this for three days, then is given richer bee-milk, and grows very rapidly, turning into a chrysalis on the fifth or sixth day. It spins around itself a silken cocoon, and is sealed into its cell by another set of worker bees.

How the Bees Work

In about two weeks it turns into a full-fledged worker bee; but there she is all sealed up in the cell. How can she get out?

It doesn't take long for her to discover she has a sharp pair of jaws, and she bites her way out. She is very pale and weak, so the nurse bees begin to clean and feed her.

As soon as she gains strength, she gets right to work on some task like feeding grub-babies; and perhaps after two weeks of such work, she flies away to gather nectar.

The Drone Baby Bee

The Drone Bee is hatched in the same way, only it takes longer for him to become perfect.

The Queen Baby or Princess

But the Queen Bee is different.

When the worker bees decide they need a queen, the comb builders make three or four queen cells, or "royal cradles," which are ordinary cells made large by cutting away parts of the next-door cells and building a hanging cell.

In these larger cells are placed the eggs. When the first egg is hatched, it is a princess bee.

Why Bees "Swarm"

The old queen, knowing the princess will be the new queen, "swarms" with the bees who wish to follow her to a new hive.

The new queen, as soon as hatched, goes to the other royal cells and stings the other little princesses (who might try to be queen if they hatched) to death, and commences to be mother-queen of the Bee City.

How Bees Spend the Winter

The bees spend the winter in a kind of sleep. They cluster together to keep warm.

When the early Spring days come, and some of the bees begin to bring in pollen and nectar, the queen begins to lay eggs.

These eggs will be hatched out into worker bees to carry on the work of the hive, and the bees that lived over winter will live only long enough to care for them until they can carry on the work of the hive.

At length the Bee sighted her hive. "We are home," she said to Miss Gardener, "and I will explain to the guard bees that it is all right for you to enter, as you are one of us."

Miss Gardener thanked her. They flew to the Bee City entrance gate, and her new friend disappeared within.

Miss Gardener just poked her head inside to see how it seemed, when all the guard bees started toward her, and the foremost one stung her and stung her

until—she woke up shrieking, to find that there was a hive of bees swarming on the tree just over her head.

"Oh," cried Mary Frances, "did they sting her?"

"No, not really," said Billy; "it was only a dream, but somehow the fact that the bees were swarming there must have made her dream of the stinging."

"Well, I just believe Miss Gardener never had to study the lesson about the bees," said Mary Frances. "I imagine her wonderful dream taught her."

"But she was always sorry, she said, that she did not get inside the hive in her dream," replied Billy.

"What wonderful little creatures bees are!" exclaimed Mary Frances. "When people sell honey, do they steal it from the bees?"

"Yes, practically that," said Billy; "yet it is not a serious theft, for the bees generally store up much more honey than is needed, and the bee keeper always leaves enough for them to use."

"Billy, wouldn't it be lovely to have a hive?"* said Mary Frances.

* For information as to Bee Keeping write for Farmers' Bulletins on Bee Culture, U. S. Dept. of Agriculture, Washington, D. C.

"I've thought of it myself," acknowledged Billy. "One hive would make from four dollars upward in a year, but I don't think we'd better experiment along any other line than gardening this year at least."

"Well, I guess you're right, Billy," laughed Mary Frances, "although you're a pretty good manager, we don't want too many 'bees in our bonnets' at one time, do we? Oh, Billy, do you remember the verses we used to say when we were little—

"The great round sun is sleepy,
    And wants to go to bed;
So he hides his face so shiny
    Behind a kerchief red.

"Then all the little clovers
    That dot the velvet lawn,
Begin to nod their tiny heads
    And put their night-caps on.

"Good-night, you winsome clovers,
    All snug in grassy beds;
You'll dream of busy bumble bees
    A-buzzing round your heads."

How the Bees Work

"That would please 'most any youngster," remarked Billy, as Mary Frances finished, "but I think it is about time for us to let this honey bee fly away. She is anxious, no doubt, to get to work," as he opened the bottle.

"Good-bye, good Mrs. Bee!" called Mary Frances as it flew away.

CHAPTER XXII

The Children's Money-making Plans

THE children were in the garden, pulling weeds and "cultivating."

The little plants had come up quite a way through the soil.

With her hoe Mary Frances was drawing little mounds of earth quite high around the stems of the plants.

"Now, Mary Frances," exclaimed Billy, "you're doing just wrong! That is one of the garden 'don'ts.' Don't pile the earth high over the stems."

"Why, if you please, Mr. Billy?" asked Mary Frances.

"Because—" started Billy; then: "Oh, you must know, Mary Frances."

"I suppose because the little rootlets need rain, and little hills would make the water run off," guessed Mary Frances, "and I'll do it right after this; but, really, Billy, I'm afraid I'll never learn all my lessons as well as you know yours. It is a marvel to

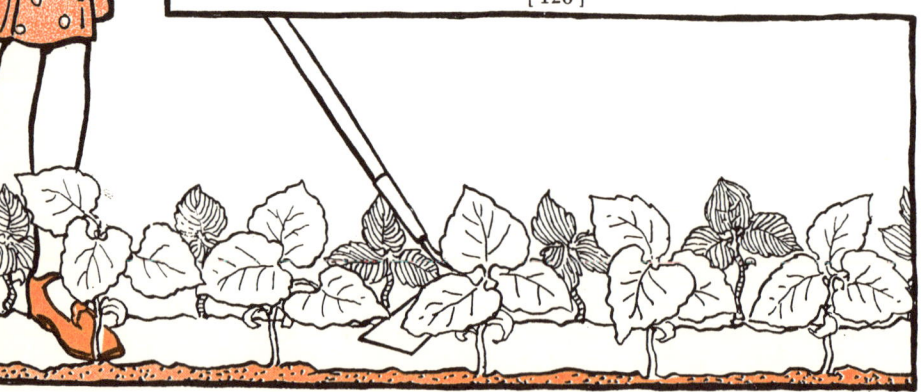

me how much you know. How you must have studied!"

"Humm!" said Billy, hoeing away. "I did study; but, somehow, I like gardening so much, it didn't seem hard work."

"You must have worked hard, though, or you wouldn't have won that garden prize of five dollars at school. Billy, you must feel rich! What are you going to buy with it?"

"I don't think I'll buy anything with what I have left; it seems fine to me to just keep it in my bank account."

"Oh, dear," sighed Mary Frances, "I wish I could make some money—not just save some of what is given to me."

"Why don't you?" asked Billy.

"Why don't I what?" Mary Frances looked up from her work.

"Make some money," said Billy.

"How could I?" asked Mary Frances in bewilderment.

"Why, sell some of the vegetables you raise in the garden."

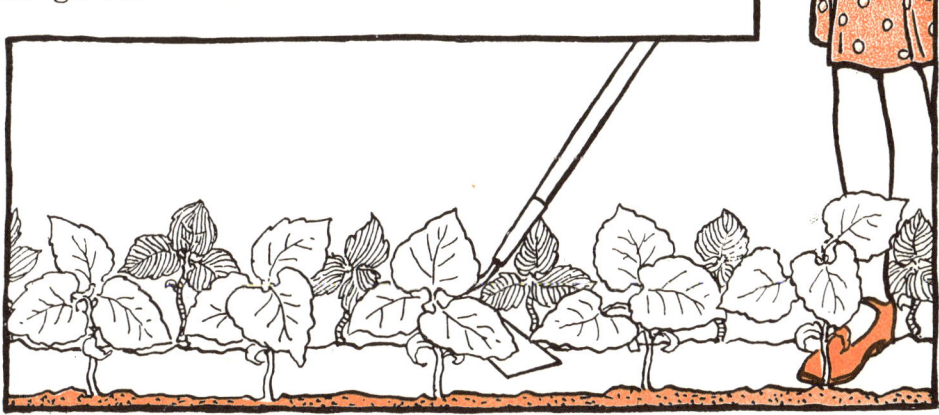

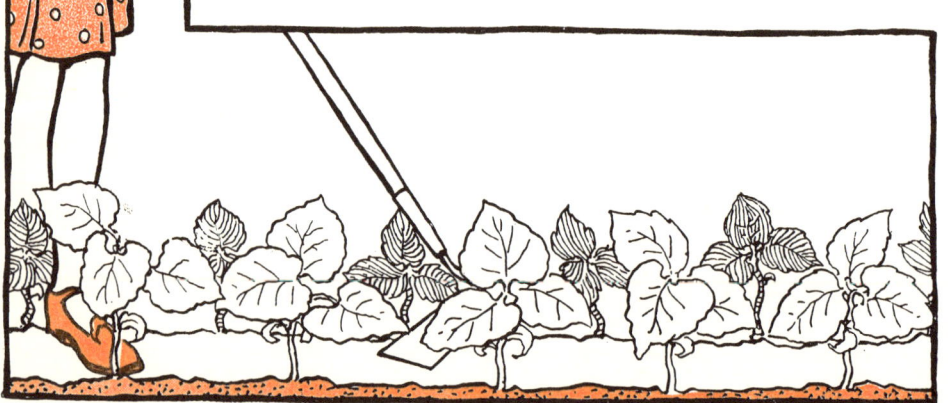

128   THE MARY FRANCES GARDEN BOOK

"Oh, Billy! Billy!" cried Mary Frances. "Do you suppose for a minute I could?"

"Course you could," answered Billy, "if I helped you, especially. I would like some spending money myself. Suppose we go into partnership?"

"Oh, let's!" cried Mary Frances. "How much better than trying to do such a thing alone! And I wouldn't want you to help me unless we divided the profits."

"And I wouldn't want to help you on any other basis," agreed Billy.

"But," exclaimed Mary Frances suddenly, "what about your own garden? You'll not need any partnership with me. You yourself will raise all you can sell."

"Have you noticed what I have growing there, Mary Frances?"

"Billy," said the little girl shamefacedly, "I haven't. I haven't noticed at all. How selfish I am!"

"Well," laughed Billy, "I don't mind at all, so you needn't feel bad, but I'll tell you. Chiefly rhubarb and asparagus; and they are both plants which

The Children's Money-making Plans 129

need two years, or three, before they may be disturbed, so you see why I'm so generous with my offer."

"I understand now, Billy," smiled Mary Frances. "My, won't you be rich when the rhubarb and asparagus are ready to sell!"

"I do expect to make some money," said Billy. "Father said he would pay me something for what is used by the family. It cost quite a sum to buy the little plants I set out—all I spent of the prize money was for them."

"Well, I certainly am glad you will help me, Billy," said Mary Frances, falling to work.

"All right; then it is settled," Billy said. "It won't be long before that lettuce and those radishes will be some size."

"But the parsley bed has shown only the tiniest little green leaves here and there! I wonder if it's never going to come up!" exclaimed Mary Frances.

"It often takes six weeks for parsley to germinate," explained Billy.

"Germinate?" inquired Mary Frances.

"Yes," answered Billy, "for the seeds to grow—start up, you know—wake up from their sleep."

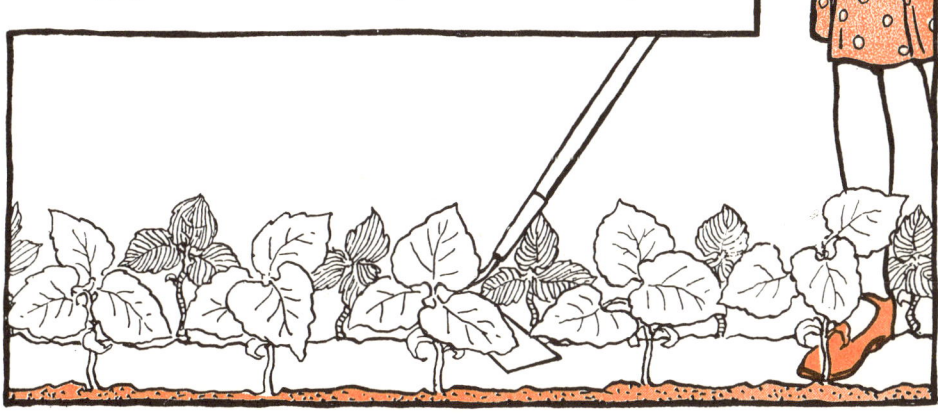

"Oh," said Mary Frances, "I understand." Then suddenly, "Oh, Billy, I can scarcely wait until we can begin to sell things! I believe, I really believe I can cut some flowers to sell!"

"Certainly you can if they are beautiful enough!" said Billy. "Well, I must make a start or else I'll never get over to the camp, and the fellows are down on me now for being away so much. So long—get all that hoeing done."

"Good-bye, Billy; it will all be done when you reach home," called Mary Frances.

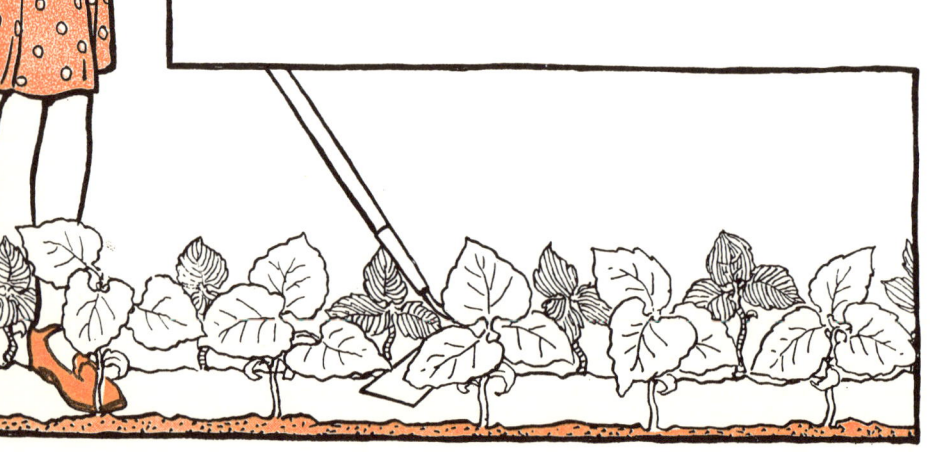

CHAPTER XXIII

Mr. Hop Toad Hops In

SHE worked away very hard for half an hour.

"My," she thought, "this is such warm work I guess I'll take a little rest," and she sat down under the tree nearby.

She was just going to sleep when she thought she heard someone speak. Yes, it was Feather Flop, and he seemed to be arguing with someone.

"He wouldn't talk to a stranger," thought Mary Frances, "I wonder who it is. I don't dare peep, for fear they'll stop talking if they see me."

Pretty soon the voices came nearer.

"I tell you," Feather Flop was saying in a boastful tone, "I tell you I am of the greatest benefit to the garden."

"If so, why so?" The question was asked in a funny, croaking voice.

"If so, why so?" mimicked Feather Flop. "Because it is so. So there!"

"Yes, certainly, if saying so makes it so," replied

the voice. "But it is not so in my opinion. For instance—pardon me till I catch that fly—how many snails do you imagine I have eaten today?"

"Oh, I don't know," said Feather Flop; "but I do know this. I know I am the biggest benefit to the garden."

"I beg pardon, sir," answered the other; "I think I can easily prove I am the biggest benefit to the garden."

"Cluck! Caw!" exclaimed Feather Flop. "You mean you are the biggest toad in the puddle, Hoppy, you poor old toad!"

"Ho! Ho!" thought Mary Frances. "So it's a hop toad! I just believe it's that big fellow that lives under the stepping stone. I think I'd know him. I believe I'll peep!"

She looked cautiously around the tree. "It is! It is that same fellow I really believe! My, I wish I could ask him some questions!"

"Indeed, I do not mean anything of the kind, Mr. Feather Flop," retorted the hop toad, and Mary Frances could see his throat swell with indignation. "I mean that I am actually and truly one of the most helpful living things to have in a garden."

Mr. Hop Toad Hops In

"Now, now, don't get angry," begged Feather Flop, "I want to hear about that! I want to find out, Hoppy, how you are more beneficial to the garden than I am."

"Well," answered the hop toad, blinking his eyes with a satisfied smile, "it's this way: suppose I begin with the baby toads——"

"A crow told me they taste very good," interrupted Feather Flop.

"For shame!" whispered Mary Frances. "Isn't that awful of Feather Flop!"

The rooster must have heard her, for he suddenly bowed his head, saying, "Oh, I beg your pardon, Hoppy—really I do! Please excuse me!"

"I suppose you don't know any better manners," answered the hop toad, "so I'll have to excuse you, and I'll tell you—if you don't interrupt—

The Story of the Hop Toad

My mother told me that one lovely day early in May she awoke from her winter's nap. Oh, yes, that's what we do in winter—sleep in the ground.

Well, my mother awoke, and went happily hopping down

to the meadow pond to lay some eggs. Perhaps you don't know them when you see them—toads' eggs. They look like tiny black pills in strings of transparent jelly. This jelly either drops to the bottom of the pond or fastens to water weeds.

Tadpoles

The eggs grow larger and larger and pretty soon become baby toads, or tadpoles.

Well, I was one of the tadpoles that spring, and my brothers and sisters and I soon ate some of the jelly, and then some of the delicious slime in the pond.

Yes, we lived in the water and breathed somewhat the way fishes do.

When we were about ten days old, our mouths grew much stronger and our jaws grew horny so that we could bite off pieces of plants.

How lovely it was! I can remember now how cool and pleasant it felt to swim about in the pond. We had long flat tails which we used for swimming.

Now, Feather Flop, if you interrupt again I shall not finish my story! No, we didn't eat our tails; of course not. Our tails were absorbed into our bodies to help with their growth.

When we were about an inch long we had but stump tails, and found we had to come to the surface of the water for more air every day, we decided we were no longer tadpoles, but real hop toads. We swam to the shore of the pond and hopped away.

MR. HOP TOAD HOPS IN 135

TOADS' ENEMIES

Many of my little brothers and sisters, alas! were eaten by snakes, and—yes, Feather Flop—gobbled up by crows.

No, Feather Flop, dogs wouldn't bite us, because—do you see the warts on my back? They are very useful to me. When I want to disgust an enemy, I can send out of those warts a disagreeable, biting secretion, and I am dropped pretty quickly.

No, of course, we cannot make warts on people's hands. No toad ever did anything of the kind! It's a horrible untruth. Certainly we seem cold to people's touch. That's because our blood is of the same temperature as the air. Their blood is warmer.

Well, as I said, almost any enemy drops one of us grown-up toads quickly but snakes! They don't seem to mind us at all. Ugh! when I see one I either hop away with all my might, or I bury myself in the earth. No, Feather Flop, I can't teach you how! I do it with my hind legs. See how I can kick!

There are two more ways in which we escape our enemies.

In the first place, if you notice carefully, you will observe that I am almost the color of the leaves on which I am sitting. If I should hop out there on the path, my coat would change in a short time to nearly the color of the path. Oh, I do not care to try it now. The sun is shining there, and I certainly do not like sunlight and heat! The fact of our color being nearly the shade of our surroundings prevents enemies from seeing us. Yes, you are right, we shed our skins several times a year, and we

swallow them. We generally do this when no one is looking. The other way we escape notice is the fact that we feed mostly at night, while our enemies are asleep.

How Toads Help the Garden

Speaking of food, Feather Flop—have you eaten any of those delicious tent caterpillars? No? Well, you should try some. Don't you like them? They stick to your throat? Oh, I didn't know that, but I've noticed that you didn't seem to eat them, nor "thousand-leggers." That's the reason I said I was of more benefit than you to the garden.

Just listen until I tell you what I had this early morning for supper. No, not breakfast! I told you I feed at night. Early morning brings my supper time! Well, these are what I had:

*6 cutworms
5 thousand leg worms
6 sow bugs
9 ants
1 weevil
1 ground beetle

We eat also snails, injurious beetles, grasshoppers, worms, potato bugs, and lots more of harmful creatures. Well, ants and spiders may be useful, but ants are a question, and we eat

---

* This list is taken from U. S. Farmers' Bulletin No. 196, Usefulness of the American Toad.

few spiders. Spiders are lots of fun to catch, though. See, there is one! See how my tongue shot out at him? My tongue is fastened to the lower jaw at the front of my mouth. You didn't see it? Well, I suppose we toads do use our tongues pretty quickly. They have a sticky substance spread over them, so we're pretty certain to make our "catch."

"Now, Feather Flop, I think I've told you almost everything. Is there anything else you'd like to know?"

Mary Frances had been listening with all her ears.

"My, there are things I'd like to know," she thought. "How I wish he'd talk to me!"

"No," said Feather Flop in a crestfallen voice, "I don't think of any. I certainly must acknowledge that you are usefuller than I thought!"

"Thanks! All right!" replied the toad, taking a hop.

"Hold on, please, Hoppy!" Mary Frances ventured to call.

The toad turned.

"Please, Mr. Hop Toad," she begged, "please will you tell me something? I've overheard your

wonderful story. If it is not too inquisitive, may I ask why your throat puffs all the time?"

"Certainly, certainly," croaked the toad, "my voice is hoarse, Miss, but I'll do my best to answer. You see, we toads have no ribs to use when we breathe, so we have to swallow every bit of air we use."

"Oh," said Mary Frances, "that is it. I am so much obliged to you for telling me. Here is a fish-worm—or do you call them angle-worms, or earth-worms?—for you!"

"A fish-worm!" exclaimed the toad. "That is fine. Throw it down, please. No, that is the wrong end toward me. Fish-worms wear rough rings along their bodies which hurt the throat if swallowed the wrong way foremost. They're pretty large to get down, so I may have to rub it down my throat with my hands."

This the funny little toad did, and after getting it down, patted its little stomach. "My, it was so good. I shut my eyes while I swallowed!" he said.

Mary Frances laughed outright. "I'm glad I

MR. HOP TOAD HOPS IN

gave you a treat," she said. "I wish I knew something else I could do to make you happy."

"Then just take a stick and scratch my back, please."

Mary Frances did as requested.

Feather Flop looked on all the while without a word. At length he blurted out, "You told me, little Miss, I think, that fish-worms were good for the garden—that they stir the soil and make it light and porous. I've never eaten one since you told me that!"

He looked scornfully at the toad.

Mary Frances smiled. "Oh, Feather Flop, indeed I thank you, but you see, we don't need so many of them. You could take one once in a while."

"I must be going," said the toad, "and I thank you, Miss. You're much more polite and kind than some people I've known!" glancing at the rooster.

"He means the boy that stoned him," said Feather Flop.

"Excuse me, I did not refer to him," said the toad; "but really, boys are terribly hard on us!

And think of all we do to help them. We eat the dreadfully destructive insects."

"I wonder if my brother Billy ever—" began Mary Frances.

"No, not any more," said the toad. "I've lived here in this garden five years and it's over a year since he's troubled any of us."

"He never will again," promised Mary Frances. "I shall certainly tell him your story."

"Good-bye, and thank you very much!" suddenly exclaimed the toad, hopping away very rapidly.

"Oh," called Mary Frances, "I want to ask you something else. Won't you talk to us again?"

This time the toad did not turn around nor answer a word, but hopped more rapidly than ever.

"I can catch him!" exclaimed Feather Flop, "and I'll peck him as hard as ever I can, too, for treating you that way!"

"Don't you dare, Feather Flop," called Mary Frances, running after him. "I'm ashamed of you!" catching him up.

"Oh, dear," sighed Feather Flop, "and I wanted

Mr. Hop Toad Hops In

to help you so much! I am always doing something wrong!"

"Listen, Feather Flop," explained Mary Frances, "that probably frightened him so he'll never speak again."

"I'll be to blame for that, too," mourned Feather Flop. "Oh, I'm sorry, so sorry."

"Never mind, my friend," said Mary Frances; "I appreciate the kindness you meant to show even if you made a mistake."

"Are you sure you forgive me, little Miss?" asked the rooster.

"Quite sure," answered Mary Frances. "But I can't promise about the hop toad!"

"I don't care a hop about Hoppy," said the rooster, "just so you forgive me."

"I guess a rooster, even if as clever as Feather Flop, can't understand such things," mused Mary Frances to herself.

"Please be polite to him for my sake, then," she said.

"I will! indeed I will!" promised Feather Flop.

CHAPTER XXIV

MR. CUTWORM, THE VILLAIN

"IF he mentioned cutworms," said Billy, as Mary Frances finished telling him the story of the hop toad, "If he mentioned cutworms among the insects he eats, I certainly am glad to make his acquaintance. Will you introduce me to him?"

"Certainly I will, Billy; come right down into the garden."

The children looked all over the place for the hop toad, but were unable to find a trace of him.

"I remember," said Mary Frances, "that he told me he slept in the day time."

"Oh, of course," replied Billy, "that's the reason we don't see him. I might have thought of that!"

"Hello, he's been lazing on the job though," he exclaimed. "Look at those three young tomato plants, all cut off near the roots. Neat work, that. Mr. Cutworm the Villain's, I'll bet!"

"Oh, dear! Billy, won't they grow up again?"

Mr. Cutworm, the Villain 143

"Not much!" exclaimed Billy. "No, indeed; we'll have to put in new ones in their place. "We've had so little trouble with cutworms that I forgot to take precaution."

"What's that?" asked Mary Frances.

"Precaution—why, means to keep him from the plants. We could have used—

Paper Collars to Protect Plants from Cutworms

Cut strong paper into rectangles about 2½ x 5 inches. Wrap a paper loosely around the stem of growing tomato plants and other tender stems before packing the earth around them. Let the paper extend about an inch above the ground, but make it narrower if it covers the roots.

"Oh, how funny," laughed Mary Frances, "for plants to wear paper collars."

"They would cheat Mr. Cutworm out of several good meals," said Billy. "It's provoking to find plants cut off that way. You see, the worms do their villainous work at night!"

"Oh, do they live under ground all the time?"

"No, we learned in school that they are the larvæ, or young, of a certain night-flying moth. They live

in the ground until they change into cocoons (or worms-in-cases), which they weave about themselves. Finally the cocoon comes out of the case as a moth. Here is a picture of the villain."

"Ugh!" shuddered Mary Frances.

"Hello, here is the real thing," exclaimed Billy as he kicked aside some earth.

"Oh, isn't he ugly!" exclaimed Mary Frances.

"We'd never preserve him for his beauty," agreed Billy. "Some farmers make poison bait for cut-worms by mixing a little poison and molasses with bran or clover, and throw it on the ground at night when birds and chickens have gone to bed. They are careful to take it up early in the morning so that no other creature will get it by mistake."

CHAPTER XXV

BIRDS AS PLANTS' FRIENDS

"NOW, Feather Flop said—" began Mary Frances; "I mean, if Feather Flop had been in the garden there wouldn't have been so many cutworms."

"Mary Frances!" exclaimed Billy. "How ridiculous! You don't seem to understand that that old rooster would have eaten up all the young plants himself!"

Mary Frances bit her lip to keep from laughing as she saw Feather Flop peeping around the tree in back of Billy.

"If that rooster were a robin or a wren it would be different," went on Billy. "Just listen, Mary Frances!" pulling a paper out of his pocket.

"'One robin has been known to feed his family five yards of worms a day.

"'A chicka-dee will dispose of 5500 eggs of the canker-worm moth in one day.

"'A flicker eats no less than 9000 ants a day.

" 'A pair of wrens have been seen to carry 100 insects to their young in an hour. They are especially fond of plant lice and cutworms.

" 'Little humming birds lick plant lice off foliage with lightning rapidity.

" 'The yellow-billed cuckoo eats hundreds of tent caterpillars in a day.

" 'Seed-eating birds destroy myriads of seeds of destructive weeds—actually eating hundreds of tons of seed.

" 'The Department of Agriculture of the United States estimates that the tree sparrow alone saves the American farmer $90,000,000 in a year by eating seeds of weeds.' "

"That isn't the English sparrow," laughingly interrupted Mary Frances.

"No," replied Billy, "not so much can be said in its favor."

"How do people know what the different birds eat?" asked Mary Frances. "Did someone watch to see what each different bird took for a meal?"

"No." Billy referred to his clipping. "Scientists have examined the contents of the stomachs of the

Birds as Plants' Friends

birds, and have learned what food each kind of bird uses. There was a time when people imagined that robins stole so many cherries and berries that it was a good deed to kill them. Now they have found that they destroy so many injurious insects that they do not begrudge them a few cherries. Besides, if mulberry trees are planted nearby, they will prefer their fruit to the cherries."

"Oh, Billy," cried Mary Frances, "isn't it wonderful! Not only do birds help us by destroying harmful insects and seeds, but they help us by their beauty. I believe they are the most beautiful of living things! They could have helped us just as much, and have been as ugly as—cutworms."

"Yes," laughed Billy, "I believe that is so, but it takes a girl to think such things out. The most remarkable fact to me, however, is that without birds we would die of starvation. It has been estimated that if they were absent for one season alone, the United States would lose over $300,000,000, and if they disappeared entirely, agriculture and farming would be impossible within a few years."

"Bees and birds," commented Mary Frances softly, "keep us from starving. How wonderful it all seems. Why, Billy, it must have all been planned out when God made the world!"

"I have thought of that myself, Mary Frances," said Billy; "it's one of those thoughts a fellow doesn't often speak out loud. I don't know why."

"Everybody ought to take care of birds," went on Mary Frances. "Surely the reason they don't, is because they do not understand how wonderfully they help us. Do you recall Miss Carey's poem—'An Order for a Picture'? I learned a part of it in my literature course last winter:

* * * * * * *

" 'Afraid to go home, sir; for one of us bore
A nest full of speckled and thin-shelled eggs,
The other, a bird, held fast by the legs,
Not so big as a straw of wheat:
The berries we gave her she wouldn't eat,
But cried and cried, till we held her bill,
So slim and shining, to keep her still.

Birds as Plants' Friends

"'At last we stood at our mother's knee.

* * * * * * *

You, sir, know
That you on the canvas are to repeat
Things that are fairest, things most sweet,
Woods and corn fields and mulberry-tree,
But, oh, that look of reproachful woe!
High as the heavens your name I'll shout,
If you paint me the picture, and leave that out.'"

"I know just what that means," said Billy, "for one day—only I've never told it, for I knew how it would grieve mother—I killed a little wren. I was quite a little chap and had no real intention of doing such a thing. I aimed a stone at the little thing, and down it came—dead."

"Well, Billy, there's this comfort," said Mary Frances; "it didn't suffer. That's very different from injuring it and letting it live on in agony."

"Yes," said Billy, "you see I didn't understand; boys don't, I guess."

"Birds and bees," Mary Frances repeated, "keep

150 THE MARY FRANCES GARDEN BOOK

us from starving. I suppose you know of many other beneficial animals or insects."

"Oh, Billy, let's have lots of birds in our garden!" she went on.

"Why, how?" asked Billy. "Perhaps we could put food out for them."

"Yes, but I wasn't thinking of that. I thought maybe we could put houses where they would build."

"Of course," replied Billy; "and we could keep a small bath tub full of water for them."

"What fun!" exclaimed Mary Frances. "Billy, do you know how to build the right kind of houses for each different kind of bird?"

"No, I do not," answered Billy; "I know of only a few. They are the ones our manual training teacher showed us. I have some pictures right here in my book. It's queer I didn't think of them!"

"Let me see," cried Mary Frances. "Oh, Billy, will you make some later on?"

"I'm to make them in school next term," explained Billy. "Mr. Carpenter, our teacher, told me about these houses one day when we were out walking. We

Birds as Plants' Friends 151

happened to talk of what Professor Weed had told us in a lecture on birds, you see."

"Do let me read about these houses," begged Mary Frances, looking over his shoulder at the picture of—

A Robins' Sleeping Porch

Robin Redbreast will not live in an enclosed house, but desires merely a shelter where the family can have plenty of fresh air.

"I believe in living out-of-doors," says Mrs. Robin Redbreast, "and I shall not send the children to school in a schoolhouse, no matter how sanitary. They shall be educated in the open air. There is a lot more to be learned outdoors than indoors."

Robins' Sleeping Porch

A Bungalow for Wrens

Wrens' Bungalow

Jenny Wren and her husband like a little perch to rest upon before entering their home. In order to keep the English sparrow from being inquisitive and troublesome, make the entrance only 1 inch in diameter where Mr. and Mrs. Sparrow cannot enter.

"They are not a bit nice neighbors," fusses gentle Jenny Wren. "They pick a quarrel over nothing, then peck our family to pieces if they can."

The Martens' Hotel

Do not charge Mr. and Mrs. Marten for lodgings. Instead be thankful that they bring their friends and relations with them, for Martens come in companies and love to linger where invited. They destroy myriads of insects.

MARTENS' HOTEL

The Blue Birds' Cottage

These heavenly blue birds, with pinkish plumage on their breasts, add great beauty to our home gardens, and fortunate is the owner of the bird house which they select "rent free." They are desperately afraid of English sparrows, or more of them would tenant the houses round about the home garden. Blue birds eat up whole families of garden pests at a meal.

BLUE BIRDS' COTTAGE

"My, aren't those bird houses dear!" said the little girl. "I hope we'll have one of each kind some day. Then we'll feel that our garden is well protected from injurious insects. Are there any other creatures which destroy them beside toads and birds?"

CHAPTER XXVI

Little Ladybird

"CAN'T say with certainty," replied Billy, "until I look in my note book."

"Well, it's just inside the play house, isn't it?" asked Mary Frances.

"I'm getting rather tired, Mary Frances," said Billy.

"Oh, go get it, Billy," Mary Frances begged, "please do, bring it out to the garden bench—that's a good fellow."

"Well, if it were any other subject than gardening, you couldn't persuade me, young lady; but I guess I'll go."

"There are lots of beneficial insects named," he said, coming out of the play house, "but the one you know best is a different kind of a bird from the feathered——"

"I know! I know!" eagerly interrupted Mary Frances, repeating the old rhyme—

" 'Ladybird, Ladybird, fly away home!
Your house is on fire, and your children will burn.' "

"Good!" exclaimed Billy. "Ladybird or ladybug; but why they are given so charming a name, I can't imagine."

"I can imagine, Billy. Have you ever noticed, besides being so very pretty, how neat they are; how ladylike they look when they fold their wing covers and tuck in their inside wings; and did you ever see them wash themselves? They do it so carefully! I don't wonder at their being named Ladybirds."

"Humph, Mary Frances, you certainly have an enviable imagination. I should say they were more fittingly named Possumbugs. Have you ever noticed how they 'play possum' when you try to pick them up?"

"Indeed I have," Mary Frances laughed at the remembrance. "Maybe they do that to save their lives just as opossums do; but they are so very pretty that I'd call them Ladybirds for that reason alone."

"Not all are pretty alike," commented Billy.

"Why, don't they all wear shiny red dresses with black polka dots?" asked Mary Frances.

"No," smiled Billy, "some wear shiny black

dresses with red or yellow polka dots; sometimes the dress is yellow with black spots."

"Oh, isn't that interesting!" cried Mary Frances. "I never tried the rhyme on any but the red ones with black dots."

"I never 'tried' the rhyme. How do they act?" asked Billy.

"Well," laughed Mary Frances, "usually, if you blow your breath upon them, they fly away; if you just watch them, they generally turn around and run as fast as they can in the opposite direction from which they were going."

"Probably looking for food," said Billy.

"Probably running to save their children's lives." Mary Frances was quite indignant.

"Perhaps my notes will tell," said Billy, opening his note book again and beginning to read:

Ladybirds or Ladybugs

The Ladybird is a little beetle about a third of an inch long. There are many species of ladybirds; they all are of the same general shape, somewhat like a split pea, but much smaller. They are usually of brilliant shiny colors with spots of contrasting colors: sometimes red with black spots; sometimes black with

red or yellow spots, sometimes yellow with black spots. The young or larvæ of the ladybird are not in the least like their mothers. They are little black, rough, worm-like creatures with six legs, having reddish-yellow or rusty spots on their backs. Both the young and the parents are very helpful to the garden because they eat harmful insects—scale insects and aphids or green plant lice.

One species of ladybird which the California fruit growers brought from Australia has been the means of exterminating a scale insect very injurious to the orange and lemon trees of the Western coast. The larva of the ladybird turns into a hard encased pupa, and later into a full-grown ladybird insect.

"My," exclaimed Mary Frances, "another garden friend! Why, Billy, one is never alone in the garden. There are always lots of friends about."

"And enemies too," said Billy. "Some time I'll tell you about one of the silliest of enemies, which Professor Weed called an 'animated honey drop' or aphis."

"Tell me now, Billy? Oh, do tell me now!"

"Not much! Not much! Some other time, Mary Frances. Do you think I'm an animated encyclopedia—always ready to deal out information, or do you think—? Oh, so long!"

Before Mary Frances could answer, Billy had disappeared.

CHAPTER XXVII

Curly Dock

"JUST in the nick of time," said Billy as Mary Frances came racing with Eleanor around the front of the house. "Why, hello! who's here? Excuse me, Eleanor, I didn't know you were to arrive until this afternoon," shaking hands with Mary Frances' "best girl friend."

"She wasn't expected until afternoon," explained Mary Frances, "but some friends of her father's were coming this way in their car, so she's here quite early. Oh, I'm so glad!" as she kissed Eleanor again.

"I wish we'd never moved away, Mary Frances," said Eleanor, returning her embrace.

"You said I was just in the nick of time, Billy," Mary Frances suddenly exclaimed. "Why, so is Eleanor. We can share the secret with her!"

"Another of Mary Frances' secrets!" cried Eleanor. "Please tell me about it!"

"Oh, Mary Frances makes so much out of

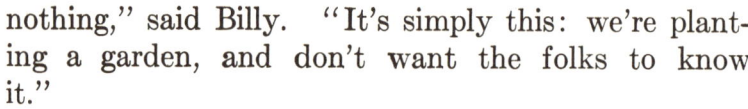

nothing," said Billy. "It's simply this: we're planting a garden, and don't want the folks to know it."

"That isn't all, Eleanor," said Mary Frances, "Billy is teaching me how to garden. He took a course in gardening last year, and he explains to me everything his professors taught him."

"Jiminy!" exclaimed Billy. "Everything! Well, not much! I'm trying to tell her just a little bit of what they tried to teach us fellows. By the way, doesn't Bob garden?"

Eleanor began to giggle. The children looked at her in surprise. Finally she answered: "Such gardening! Believe me—no garden can raise a crop of weeds equal to his. I must tell you what I was laughing at. Early in the Spring Bob planted in a box some seed one of the boys had given him, and Father allowed him to put it in the sunniest window. He watered and tended it, and finally set the little plants out. The fellows told him that he'd be surprised at the wonderful plants he'd get; that he could have them served as 'greens' for our dinner."

"What were they?" interrupted Mary Frances.

Curly Dock

"Hush!" exclaimed Billy, who was much interested. "Eleanor will come to that soon."

"Well, the plants certainly did grow! They grew large, broad leaves, quite curly, but no one seemed to know what they were. One day Bob asked the farmer who sold us potatoes to look at his garden, and I'll never, never forget how that man laughed. He roared; he shook; he doubled up with laughter. He struck his knee with his hand, and tried to speak, but no words would come. Bob looked on at first with amazement, and then with anger, finally with disgust.

"'If you wouldn't mind telling the joke,' he said, 'we might share in the fun.'

"In a few moments the farmer spoke: 'Well, sir,' he said, 'that's the finest crop of curly dock weed I ever seen!' and he began to laugh again."

"My, I bet Bob was 'sore'!" laughed Billy.

"Yes, he was, but that wasn't the best of the joke," Eleanor went on.

"'I'll serve a mess of it to those fellows!' he cried. 'And Dick Willoughby's got to eat the most—even if I'm compelled to have the doctor there to keep him from being poisoned.'

"'That would be a treat,' the farmer said. 'Curly dock makes one of the best "greens" in the Spring. Just boil the leaves until tender, and serve like spinach. Only, young feller, next time you want a mess, just come over and weed out my meadow. Don't you take up your time and your pa's land a-cultivating what grows wild and can be had without the asking.'"

CHAPTER XXVIII

The Stupid Honey Drops—Aphids

BILLY and Mary Frances enjoyed Eleanor's story very much, and laughed heartily over Bob's discomfort.

"Well, Eleanor," said Mary Frances, "you'll be able to teach Bob a lot about gardening if Billy will let you share the lessons he's been giving me. By the way, Billy, what did you mean by 'just in the nick of time'?"

"Nothing much," replied Billy, "only I wanted to show you some of the 'animated drops of honey' about which I spoke."

"Oh, where are they?" cried Mary Frances.

"What in the world do you mean, Billy?" Eleanor exclaimed.

"Follow me if you want to know," commanded Billy, leading the way to one of his mother's rose bushes.

He lifted a long new branch.

"How funny the tip looks!" exclaimed the girls. "All bristling, like a burr."

"Look more closely," said Billy.

"Oh, Billy," laughed Mary Frances. "Billy, it's not a green burr at all! It looks that way because of thousands of those little tiny green plant lice!"

"Yes," acknowledged Billy, "nothing but aphids. I'll now try to repeat a little of our lesson on—

Aphids or Plant Lice

There are several species of aphids, but those most commonly seen are little green ones.

Nearly all delight in feeding upon the sap of young tender* shoots. They thrust their tiny sharp beaks into the stem, and, with their hind legs or claws in the air, suck the juices into their soft little bodies. The sap is turned into honey-dew in their stomachs, and ants use them for their cows! But they give them honey, and not milk. Perhaps ants like honey-milk better than we like cow's milk. Aphids seem very insignificant. They are helpless little creatures, and are very easily killed. Indeed, they are so stupid they don't seem to know when they are being killed. Even though they are stupid, they do a great amount of harm in the garden, stealing the vital fluids of the plants.

They multiply so rapidly that their many enemies do not do away with all of them, so almost all gardeners use a "spray" to kill them.

---

* There are a few aphids which feed upon roots.

The Stupid Honey Drops—Aphids

One of the most interesting of their enemies is the—

Aphis-lion

This little worm-like creature is hatched from the egg of the mother lace-wing, an airy green fly with light lacey wings. She places eggs on a leaf nearby a group of aphids. The little creature that is hatched is very hungry and immediately begins to look for food.

It seizes the first aphis it can find in its strong pincers, and lifting it high in the air, drinks the honey juice in its body with great enjoyment.

"Greater than Mary Frances shows when drinking chocolate soda?" queried Eleanor.

"That's a question," laughed Billy. "I've never seen many aphis-lions eat, but I have seen Mary Frances drink chocolate sodas 'galore.'"

"But, Billy," reminded Mary Frances, after they had finished laughing, "you haven't told us what other enemies the aphids have, nor what you mean by using a spray."

"Oh, if you stop to think, you'll realize that spiders and several different kinds of birds will eat them. They are such stupid little creatures that it's not difficult to find or catch them."

"But what about spraying—is that difficult?" asked Eleanor. "You see, I want to surprise Bob with my superior knowledge."

"Oh, Billy, do give us just as many lessons as you can possibly squeeze into the time Eleanor visits us, won't you?" cried Mary Frances. "Do tell us about spraying or any other thing we ought to learn about gardening."

"Why, Mary Frances, you talk as though I knew a lot on the subject!" said Billy, "when, as a matter of fact, I don't begin to know anything. It seems to me that the more I study, the more there is to learn.

"I'm willing," he went on, "to tell you girls what I can remember of what Professor Weed told about insect pests and insecticides—but I do wish you were both boys!"

"We don't, though. Do we, Eleanor?" said Mary Frances. "I shouldn't think you'd mind. You're always with boys during the school term, and—I don't believe they'd listen anything like as well as Eleanor and I will."

CHAPTER XXIX

Some Sprays for Garden Pests

"REALLY, there is some truth in that," said Billy. "I'm not certain that I can remember much about the subject; but, since you are so anxious to learn, my children, I'll refer to my trusty note book, and read to you about—

Garden Pests

If we examine the various insects which injure plants, we find they do the harm in two different ways, according to their method of feeding. The different methods of feeding are by—

(*a*) biting; or,
(*b*) sucking.

Biting insects have *mandibles*, or jaws.

The biting insects most familiar to you are beetles, grasshoppers, and many "worms," or larvæ.

If you catch a grasshopper, and hold a blade of grass in an upright position close to its mouth, you will observe that the jaws do not move up and down, but sidewise. This is true of all insects.

It is quite easy to see the holes in leaves, bark, flowers or fruit where biting insects have been feasting.

166 THE MARY FRANCES GARDEN BOOK

Sucking insects, instead of jaws, have a *haustellum* or proboscis, which is a sucking tube, or beak, somewhat like a sharp hollow bristle.

This they use to thrust down through outer layers of bark or leaves into the inner tissues where they draw up the sap or lifeblood of the plant.

Among the sucking insects are aphids and scale insects.

Now, it is an easy matter to throw poison on the parts of the plants that biting insects devour, where they will eat and swallow it, and then die; but it is almost impossible to place poison in the inner portions of the plants where sucking insects feed.

Fortunately, most sucking insects have soft bodies which are easily destroyed; but it is a rather difficult task to do this work of destruction of sucking insects, because every insect must be touched by the destroying material to smother it, or destroy its breathing pores. Every farmer is familiar with some insecticides, or insect poisons.

The trouble with using poisons, however, is that most poisons which will kill insects will also kill people, so it is better for young gardeners to use remedies harmless to human beings, but deadly to insects, of which there are a few.*

---

* The small amount of arsenical poisons used by market gardeners and farmers is not dangerous unless the plant is used immediately after their application. The danger lies in having such poisons within reach of children.

Some Sprays for Garden Pests

Insecticides or insect poisons are applied to plants in two ways: by—

(a) dusting with powder; or,
(b) spraying with a liquid.

A "sulphur gun" is a great help in applying powder; although an old can with holes in the top may be used as a sprinkler.

Liquid sprays may be applied with a patent "sprayer," which may be purchased from any seed house; or with a whisk broom.

It is absolutely essential to reach the *under* sides of the leaves in applying insect destroyers.

Among the best insecticides which are non-poisonous to human beings is Hellebore.

Following is a list of remedies for insects oftenest found in gardens.

Hellebore

Remedies for Biting Insects

> For spraying: use two tablespoons Hellebore to a gallon (four quarts) of water.
>
> For dusting: mix two tablespoons Hellebore with fifteen tablespoons flour. Keep in a closely covered can. After a day or two this flour may be sprinkled on the upper and under sides of the leaves. This is best done while the dew is upon them. The use of the flour is simply for the sake of economy.
>
> Wood ashes and also insect powder discourage cabbage worms.

Various Remedies for Sucking Insects	For dusting: insect powder, snuff, sulphur, tobacco dust. Tobacco stems (laid on the ground) will discourage them. For spraying: Dissolve 1 lb. caustic Whale Oil Soap in ½ gallon (2 quarts) hot water. Mix one cup of this mixture with five cups of water for plant lice, etc. Hot Water for Aphids or Plant Lice. Hold the branch under water at a temperature of about 125°, or as hot as possible to hold the hand under.

Fungi of various kinds attack plants. Mildew is a form of fungi.

For Fungi— Mildew	Dust the plant well with Flowers of Sulphur. Bordeaux Arsenate of Lead is used as a spray in early Spring, to prevent fungi, but it is deadly poison and should not be used by children.
For Insects that Feed Under Ground	Severe poisons are generally used, the fumes of which kill the insects. Tobacco tea, made by boiling a pound of tobacco stems in a gallon of water, or Ivory soapsuds, if thrown on the ground, will discourage these insects.
For Cutworms, and Insects Feeding on the Surface of the Ground	Poison Baits are used: that is, bran or grass is sprinkled with sweetened poison. (NOTE: It is better for children to use the precaution of paper collars as already explained to Mary Frances in the talk on the Cutworm.)

There are also many excellent remedies sold by seed firms under commercial or "patent" names.

"Well, Billy," cried Eleanor, "if I remember one-tenth of the lesson, I'll be satisfied!"

Some Sprays for Garden Pests

"And I, too!" echoed Mary Frances.

"If I'd thought," continued Eleanor, "you were such a wiseacre, Mr. Professor Billy, I'd have brought a note book."

"Oh, you girls can see my notes any time," said Billy, pleased with their compliments.

"What I didn't like, Billy, was the constant reference to 'children,'" Mary Frances went on.

"Now, little girls," began Billy, "that is just for 'Safety First.' When you are a little older and more experienced in gardening——"

"Oh, Billy, if you tease, you'll spoil everything!" declared Mary Frances. "Do keep your old poison secrets. I don't like the idea of killing bugs even."

"Nor the fellow 'who needlessly puts his foot upon a worm,'" quoted Billy. "I bet Bob would rather like that lesson, even if you and Eleanor didn't."

"I'm going to write down what I can remember for Bob," declared Eleanor. "May I use your desk, Mary Frances?"

"Nothing could please me better," answered her friend, leading the way through the play house door.

CHAPTER XXX

Early Vegetables

"YOU will tell me, won't you, Mary Frances, how you started the garden, and how in the world you induced your brother to give you lessons?"

Eleanor looked up from the notes she had made.

"If it hadn't been for Feather Flop," began Mary Frances.

"Feather Flop!" exclaimed Eleanor. "Do you mean your pet rooster?"

"Yes," declared Mary Frances, "he really had a great deal to do with it, although Billy ridicules the idea."

"I can't quite understand it myself," Eleanor said. "I thought chickens were very injurious to a garden."

"Not Feather Flop! He has been so interested from the very first that I myself have been amazed. Eleanor, you should hear about the cutworms and other insects he has eaten, and the weeds he has taken out of the garden."

Early Vegetables

Mary Frances grew excited in being able to praise the rooster to someone.

"He made little piles of weeds at the end of each vegetable patch, and I had to pretend to Billy that I did the weeding, for he'd never, never have believed that Feather Flop did the work."

"Isn't it wonderful!" exclaimed Eleanor. "Do tell me more about him!"

"Hush!" exclaimed Mary Frances, "here comes Billy."

"Hello, girls, want to see something fine?" Billy looked in the play house window.

"Of course!" cried the girls at once.

"Come on out then—follow me."

Billy led them to the vegetable garden.

"What is it?" asked Mary Frances.

"Just brush a little of the earth away from that radish," replied Billy, pointing to one of the largest plants.

"Oh, look!" cried Mary Frances, as she pulled the little red ball root, and held it up for admiration.

"Oh, Eleanor, it is ready to eat! The very first thing from my garden. Let's give it to Eleanor, Billy!"

"Indeed, no!" declared Eleanor. "I think, Mary Frances, you should have the very first of the crop!"

"I know what!" exclaimed Mary Frances. "I'll cut it up into three pieces!"

"Augh, count me out!" exclaimed Billy. "I don't want any! Besides, I guess there are several others nearly that size."

"But no other first ones!" declared Mary Frances. "My, if the garden weren't to be a surprise, I'd want to divide this with Mother and Father, too."

"So would I!" exclaimed Eleanor.

"Well, if girls aren't silly!" Billy looked almost disgusted. "If you want the radish, eat it up. The garden can't be a secret much longer anyhow, for in a day or two you can pull a couple of bunches of radishes and several small heads of lettuce."

"Oh, it seems too good to be true!" exclaimed Mary Frances, dancing around in joy at the thought.

"But," said Eleanor, "surely your parents know you are gardening. Anybody with eyes could see that."

"Yes," exclaimed Mary Frances, "they know we are doing some work near the play house, but I asked

them not to try to find out anything about what we were doing, and they haven't come near! They want to be surprised! I know they do!"

"But how did you get the money to buy the seeds and plants?" asked Eleanor.

"Mother gave me permission to use some money from my bank, and Billy loaned me some from the money he won as a prize in school. I have to pay that back."

"When we sell some of the vegetables," said Billy.

"You don't wonder that I'm excited, do you, Eleanor?" cried Mary Frances.

"Indeed I don't," said Eleanor. "I wish Bob and I had just such a garden."

"You can have," said Billy; "I hope Bob will be able to make me a visit as soon as he has finished being 'coached' in his Latin!"

"That won't be for some time," replied Eleanor. "Meanwhile, I'll try to learn all I can about gardening, and we'll be ready to start in earnest next Spring."

"Oh, won't that be lovely!" cried Mary Frances. "I'm so glad you're here to see our experiment. How

soon did you say, Billy, we could take the radishes and lettuce to Mother?"

"About day after to-morrow," answered Billy, examining the vegetables closely again. "And a picking of peas in about ten days."

"Oh, goody! I love the vegetable garden almost as well as the flower garden," cried Mary Frances, "although the flowers are so interesting and are growing beautifully. Come, let us go look to see if any are ready to bloom," leading the way to the front garden.

"Excuse me," said Billy; "I'm going fishing."

"Good luck!" cried both the girls. "Wish you'd take us!"

But Billy pretended he didn't hear.

CHAPTER XXXI

Feather Flop's Temptation

"QUEER," said Feather Flop, as he stopped crowing for a moment early the next morning, "queer, that I can never get to see my little Miss alone any more. How I do hate to see company come, for then I can't get a word with her! Never mind, I'll go over to the vegetable garden in a few minutes to see how everything is getting along. I'll crow very loud now; she might possibly hear and come out."

He flapped his wings and swelled out his breast, and began to crow loud and long.

He looked at the windows of Mary Frances' room.

"No sign of her yet. Well, I'll go over to the garden now, and I'll work hard to help her."

He walked over to the play house garden, occasionally stopping to give an answer to a neighboring hen or rooster.

"You're earlier than usual this morning," crowed the rooster in the next neighbor's yard.

"Cock-a-doodle-doo," answered Feather Flop. "It doesn't take much to beat you! Good-morning, though!" and walked on.

When he arrived at the vegetable garden, he fell right to work pulling weeds from between the rows of onions and peas.

When he came to the lettuce, he stopped his work.

"My," he said. "My, doesn't that look good! Oh, how sweet and tender that looks! I don't believe anybody would miss a leaf or two of the little leaves inside those largest heads."

He picked at the inside of the largest and most beautiful head in the garden.

"Good!" he ejaculated. "Good! I should think so! I wish I had more!"

"I hope nobody saw me," he whispered as he looked around. No one was in sight. "Nobody would miss that little peck! I'll try another head."

"That's better than the other," he said, swallowing the dainty morsel and blinking hard. "I'll take a little from each of these large heads, and nobody will know anything about it."

Feather Flop's Temptation 177

"That's all I'll try now," he decided finally. "I don't wonder human beings like such stuff."

He fell to work again and stopped only when he saw Mary Frances and Eleanor come out of the house and go to the hammock. Then he ran near enough to hear what they were saying.

"To-morrow morning," Mary Frances began, "to-morrow morning I can take in the beautiful lettuce. Oh, Eleanor, such perfect heads. I can scarcely wait one more day."

"If we hadn't promised to go over to Cloverdale, we would work in the garden all day to-day, wouldn't we, Mary Frances?" said Eleanor.

"Eleanor, I believe you love a garden almost as much as I!" declared Mary Frances. "Well, we can't work in the garden to-day; we must get ready for our little journey."

"But, oh—lettuce for to-morrow!" cried Eleanor, throwing her arm around Mary Frances' waist as they skipped up the walk into the house.

Feather Flop watched them from behind the tree where he was hiding. "Maybe I oughtn't to have touched it after all," he said.

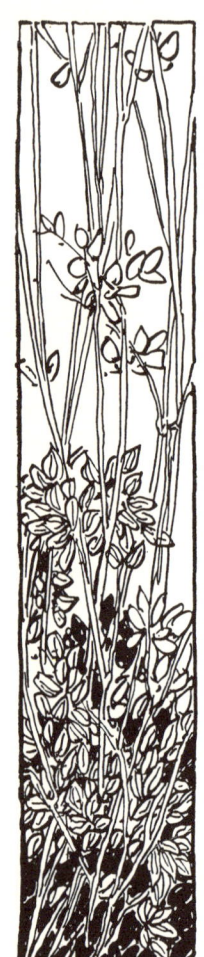

CHAPTER XXXII

Feather Flop Gets Angry

FEATHER FLOP was in the vegetable garden the next morning long before the children came for the radishes and lettuce.

When he saw them coming, he ran around a corner of the play house, where he could hear every word, but could not be seen.

"Oh, Billy," cried Mary Frances, happily, "isn't this just fine! Eleanor and I will pull the radishes and you can get the lettuce."

Eleanor began to help Mary Frances, and Billy went to the lettuce bed.

"Well, of all things!" He shouted so loud both the girls jumped.

"What in the world's the matter?" Mary Frances dropped the radishes she had in her hand.

"Matter!" roared Billy. "Matter! That old rooster of yours has eaten the hearts of the lettuce! That's all! Darn him!"

"Oh, Billy, don't use such language!" cried Mary

Feather Flop Gets Angry

Frances. "Maybe he didn't do it. Maybe it was a cutworm or a sparrow, or—or—"

"Look here!" demanded Billy. "Who took that bite?" pointing to a hole in the lettuce just the size of Feather Flop's beak.

"Oh, dear!" exclaimed Mary Frances, "I'm afraid it was Feather Flop! Oh, how could he have done such a thing!"

"That's not the only one!" went on Billy, examining further. "Every one of these big heads has just such a bite taken out!"

"What shall we do!" exclaimed Eleanor. "What a disappointment!"

"I'm ready to cry!" said Mary Frances. "I wonder if any of it is fit to use!"

"Yes," answered Billy, "of course, you can use some of the leaves, but the beauty of each head is spoiled! Here, you girls take these things to the house."

"Where are you going?" asked Mary Frances.

"I'm going hunting—hunting for a bird!" replied Billy grimly.

"Oh, don't hurt him!" called the girls.

"Not if I can help it," said Billy.

"What are you going to do with him?" again called Mary Frances.

"Come help me catch him, and you'll see. I'm going to make a prisoner of him!" Billy just then caught sight of Feather Flop as he half ran and half flew across the lawn.

The rooster gave them a long chase, but finally Billy caught him and tucked him under his arm.

Feather Flop meanwhile kept up an incessant chatter.

"We know you're not pleased, old fellow," said Billy as he put him into a coop and held it down, "but you're going to be put into a safe place. No pleading off for you! Now, I've got you fixed."

"Yes, you bad boy!" said Mary Frances.

At twilight, however, a little girl crept out with a plate of lettuce to the old hen-coop where Feather Flop was prisoner.

"Feather Flop," Mary Frances whispered softly, "Feather Flop!" but there was no answer.

She stooped down and looked into the coop. At

first she didn't see the rooster, then she espied him leaning up close to the farthest corner.

"Why, Feather Flop," she exclaimed, "are you ill? Why didn't you answer?"

"I'm not sick," muttered Feather Flop.

"Why, what is the matter then, old fellow?" said Mary Frances.

"Are you going to let me out?" asked the rooster sullenly.

"Not to-night, Feather Flop, I'm afraid. I think, myself, you need a little punishment. Tell me, why did you do it?"

"I'll not answer," said Feather Flop. "I'm mad!"

"Oh, Feather Flop!" exclaimed Mary Frances. "Oh, Feather Flop! You did wrong, and now you're angry! What is the matter with you? You used to be so nice!"

"Oh, let me alone," answered the rooster.

"All right, then," said Mary Frances. "All right! I'm going away now."

"I don't care! You could have saved me from being a jail bird!" said Feather Flop, turning tail.

"Excuse me, I don't care to answer another word!" he declared, putting his head under his wing.

Just then her mother called her, and Mary Frances had to leave him to go into the house.

"Poor old Feather Flop!" murmured the little girl. "Maybe I should have saved him from being locked up like a real thief! I don't believe he meant to be so bad!"

CHAPTER XXXIII

Father and Mother's Surprise

"Perhaps you suspected, Mother dear," said Mary Frances after showing the radishes and lettuce, and telling about the garden lessons Billy had taught her. "Perhaps you and Father suspected we were gardening."

"We had an idea that something was being done in that line," smiled her mother, "but we did just as you requested. We didn't try to find out."

"Wasn't that dear!" exclaimed Eleanor. "I think Mary Frances has such wonderful experiences!"

"She has had a happy life," said the mother, looking sympathetically at Mary Frances' little friend, for Eleanor's mother had died two years before.

Only for a few moments did the tears stand in Eleanor's eyes, then she said:

"Mary Frances has been so good about sharing her splendid times with me. Do you remember the cooking lessons, and the sewing lessons, and Mrs. Paper Doll's housekeeping lessons, girlie?"

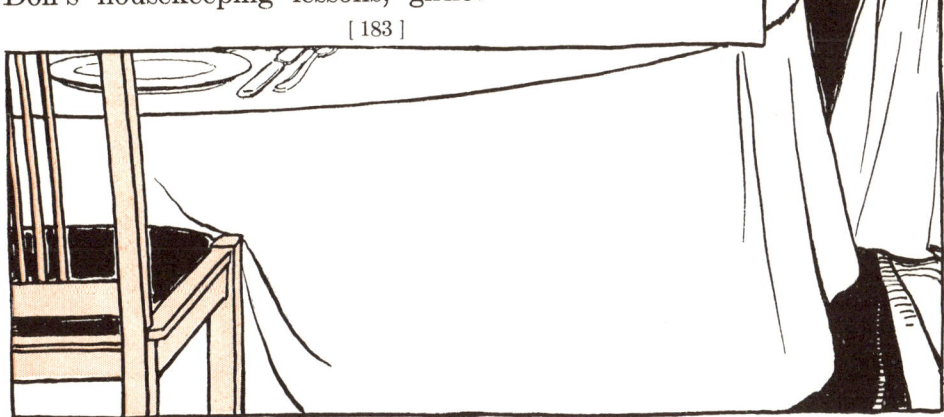

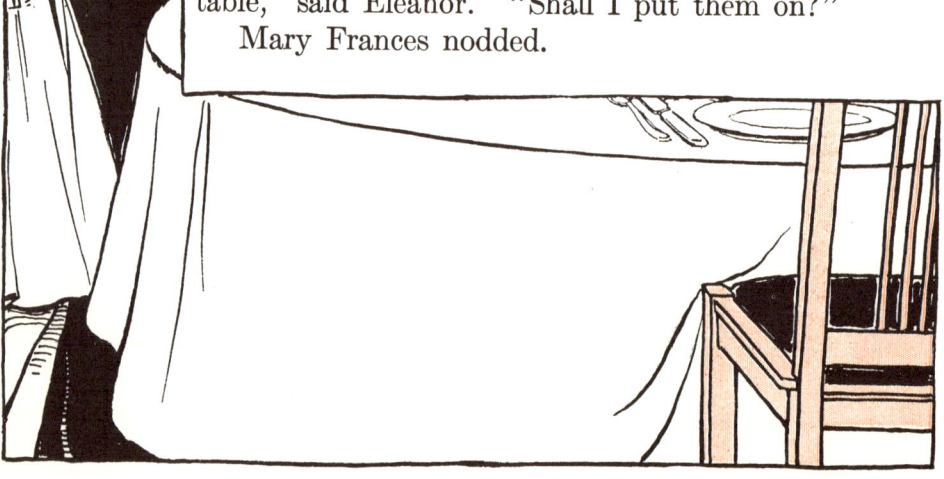

"They're not so far past that you can't remember," smiled Mary Frances' mother, "but you girls are growing up fast. I hope that, even when you are young ladies, you will delight in just such lessons as you have already had."

"I feel sure I shall," declared Mary Frances.

"I do, too," said Eleanor.

"Play lessons," went on the mother, "keep fun in your hearts and 'fun keeps one young,' you know."

"Well, these garden lessons were fun," said Mary Frances, "but they had a great deal of hard work attached. Oh, Mother dear, I'll ask you what I meant to! May we serve the lettuce and radishes for dinner, and not say a word to Father about them? Then, perhaps he'll say, 'What fine radishes! What tender lettuce! Where did you get them, Mother?' Oh, wouldn't I just love that to happen!"

"I don't doubt that he will say it, Mary Frances! I would, I know, for I've not seen any so fine this year," replied her mother.

"I have the radishes all washed and ready for the table," said Eleanor. "Shall I put them on?"

Mary Frances nodded.

"Just put them in the refrigerator until nearer the meal hour," said her mother, "then they'll get more crisp!"

"How about this lettuce?" asked Mary Frances, who had it well washed by this time. "Feather Flop didn't hurt it so much after all," she said to herself. "I don't think I'll say anything about what he did."

"Put it in this glass-covered dish and place it on the ice to make it crisp in the same way."

. . . .

"Here comes Father!" exclaimed Mary Frances, and she and Eleanor ran to meet him.

"Dinner's about ready, Father," said the mother, greeting him and nodding her head to the girls to put their "surprise" on the table.

"Billy will be here in a minute," he replied. "I saw him as I turned in the walk. There he is, now."

"Why," he exclaimed, as he looked at the table, "where did these beautiful little red radishes come from? We haven't seen such beauties this year! And that lettuce! Who's been sending in such a treat?"

Mary Frances was delighted.

"It's our surprise!" she explained. "They are from my own garden, Father!" and she told about the lessons.

At least she tried to tell, but Billy, and Eleanor, too, helped in telling the story.

"Such interesting lessons, Father!" said Mary Frances. "My, I had no idea gardening is so wonderful."

"Fine!" exclaimed her father. "Billy boy, I see it paid to send you to a practical school."

"I wish," said Eleanor, "that Bob was going to study gardening, too."

"Can't you persuade your father to send him away to Billy's school this Fall?"

"Wouldn't that be splendid!" exclaimed Eleanor. "I never thought of it. I'll try my best!"

"But, Father, you and Mother both had an idea of what we were about, hadn't you?" asked Billy.

"We knew 'something was up,' Billy," smiled his father, "but we didn't know radishes and lettuce were."

Everybody laughed.

"Now, that we're all in the secret," Mary Frances declared happily, "I like it better than ever."

Father and Mother's Surprise

"Father can give us a lot of information I don't know a bit about," said Billy.

"I believe Mother knows a lot she's not telling," said Mary Frances.

"Father, won't you give us some lessons on the wild flowers?" asked Billy.

"That would be delightful," his mother said. "We could all share in such lessons. For instance, some day soon we could all take a walk in the woods."

"Won't that be a picnic!" Billy was enthusiastic. "When shall we go? Can't you make a holiday of it, Father? Let us take our lunch."

"If it suits all parties, we'll go day after to-morrow," said his father.

"It just suits me!" declared Billy.

"It just suits me!" echoed Mary Frances.

"It just suits me!" said Eleanor.

"How about you, Mother?" asked the father.

"It will charm me to accept the invitation," smiled the mother.

"Don't you girls oversleep!" warned Billy.

"Oh, Billy, we're not the sleepy-heads!" laughed Mary Frances, shaking her finger at Billy.

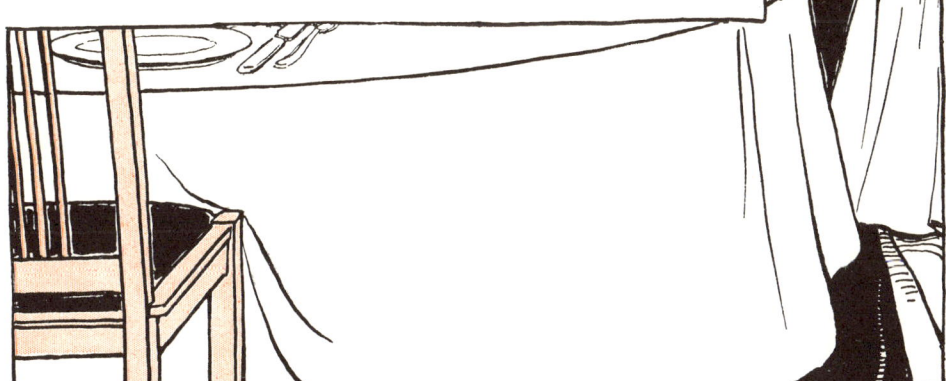

CHAPTER XXXIV

Feather Flop Makes Up

"UNLESS you speak to me, Feather Flop," said Mary Frances, when she took his breakfast to the coop next morning, "unless you speak to me, I am not coming out again! I'm going to get Billy to bring you your food," and she turned away.

Feather Flop stuck his head between the slats of the coop, and a tear rolled out of each eye.

"Oh, please don't go away," he begged. "I'm so awfully ashamed of myself I don't know what to say. That's the reason I didn't answer."

"You poor dear old Feather Flop," cried Mary Frances, opening the slats. "You poor old fellow!"

"I'm so awfully ashamed," went on the rooster, "that I'd gladly have you chop my head off and make a potpie of me."

"Oh, Feather Flop, don't feel quite so bad as that," exclaimed Mary Frances. "I forgive you, my friend."

For the first time, Feather Flop looked up.

Feather Flop Makes Up

"Do you?" he asked. "Please tell me again."

"I forgive you, Feather Flop," repeated Mary Frances, gathering him up in her arms. "The lettuce wasn't so badly hurt, after all."

"My, I'm so thankful," said Feather Flop, "though I don't see how you can forgive me. Are you certain that you do?"

"Very certain!" smiled Mary Frances. "As certain as I am that you'll never do such a thing again!"

"Never again!" solemnly declared Feather Flop, holding up one claw. "Never again!"

"Well, now, eat your breakfast," said Mary Frances, putting him down and gently stroking his beautiful feathers.

"I—haven't—eaten—a—beakful," said Feather Flop between hungry pecks, "since—I—was—put—in prison,—so—you—can—imagine—how—awfully—hungry—I—am."

"Indeed I can," laughed Mary Frances, delighted to see him his own self again.

"Does being forgiven always make a person feel hungry?" asked Feather Flop.

"Well, being unforgiven makes a person feel very unhungry," said Mary Frances.

"A strange thing about me, I guess," said Feather Flop, "is, that after I've eaten a full meal, I'm not hungry."

"Of course not," laughed Mary Frances. "Nobody ever is."

"It's very sad, though," declared the rooster.

"Why," began Mary Frances, "I don't see anything sad about that."

"It's sad, because it's so much fun to be hungry and eat. I'd like to eat every minute myself—when I'm forgiven."

"You do pretty well, Feather Flop," said Mary Frances. "I wouldn't complain. It's far worse to be hungry and not to be able to get food."

"I hadn't thought of that," said Feather Flop.

"What's the next lesson?" he asked abruptly.

"Next lesson?" echoed Mary Frances. "Oh, about roses. Isn't that a nice one?"

"Call on me for anything I can do," said Feather Flop. "I'd starve a year and a half before I'd touch anything good in the garden again."

"Oh, thank you, my friend," said Mary Frances. "Thank you! I'll call upon you, never fear. I must go now, though."

"Shake hands?" asked Feather Flop, holding out his claw. "Just to show real forgiveness."

"Certainly," said Mary Frances, taking his claw in her hand and shaking it in a most serious fashion.

As much as she wanted to, she did not smile.

CHAPTER XXXV

Roses

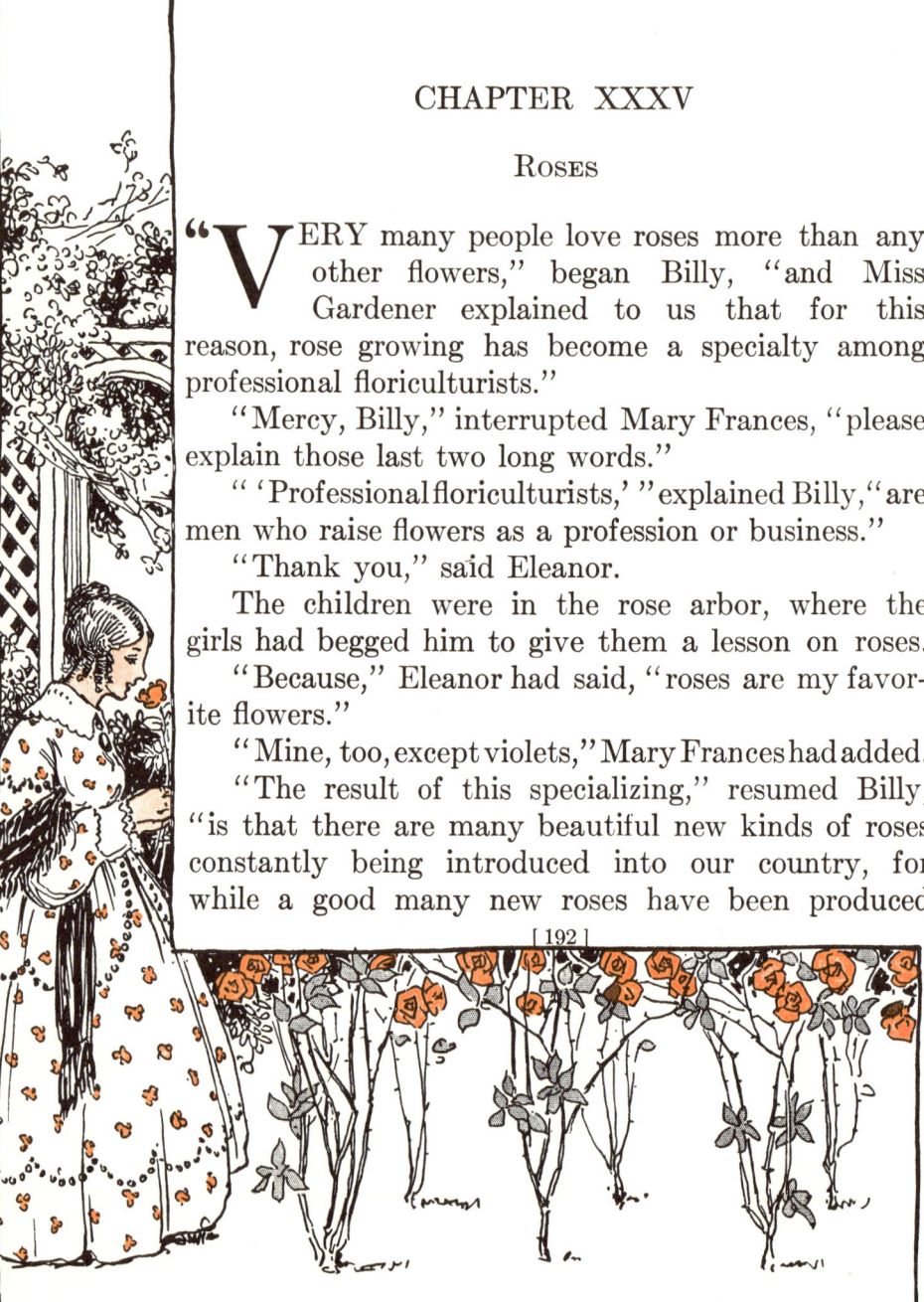

"VERY many people love roses more than any other flowers," began Billy, "and Miss Gardener explained to us that for this reason, rose growing has become a specialty among professional floriculturists."

"Mercy, Billy," interrupted Mary Frances, "please explain those last two long words."

" 'Professional floriculturists,' " explained Billy, "are men who raise flowers as a profession or business."

"Thank you," said Eleanor.

The children were in the rose arbor, where the girls had begged him to give them a lesson on roses.

"Because," Eleanor had said, "roses are my favorite flowers."

"Mine, too, except violets," Mary Frances had added.

"The result of this specializing," resumed Billy, "is that there are many beautiful new kinds of roses constantly being introduced into our country, for while a good many new roses have been produced

ROSES 193

here, the most have been produced by growers across the ocean, in Ireland and France."

"I never knew that," exclaimed Eleanor. "I thought that roses were—just roses."

"So did I!" declared Mary Frances. Then suddenly, "Oh, here comes mother! Don't stop talking, Billy! Mother will love to hear!"

"Oh, I don't think—" began Billy.

"Please let me listen, Son," interrupted his mother's pleasant voice. "You know how I love roses, I would certainly appreciate hearing what you learned from your teachers about them."

"Well, all right, Mother," said Billy, "but I'll stick more closely to my notes than I generally do, since we are honored by your presence."

The girls made room for her on the arbor seat, and Billy opened his note book.

"Here is the place," he said in a moment. "Here commences the lesson on Roses—

Old-Fashioned Roses

A flower garden would be lacking in interest and beauty, indeed, without the Queen of Flowers, the rose.

No matter how small the garden space, some roses may be grown, and their loveliness and perfume will well repay the work of caring for them.

There were no such beautiful roses in your grandmothers' gardens as you may grow to-day, for more beautiful and more perfect roses come into existence every year.

Perhaps you have heard of "Damask," and "Cabbage," and "China" roses; old-fashioned sounding names they are, very familiar to the ears of your grandparents.

They were the great-great-grandparents of the hardier and lovelier roses of to-day, the "Hybrid Perpetuals," and "Hybrid Teas."

How New Roses Came About

Some few of the new roses were accidents, so called because good Mrs. Bee carried some strange rose pollen to the pistil of one or more of the old-fashioned roses, and the new rose seed-babies took on a new nature. When the little plants from the new rose seed-baby bloomed, rose lovers were delighted with the more perfect loveliness of the new flower.

They carefully saved the new plant, and tenderly cared for it. When it was old enough and strong enough, they took "cuttings" from its shoots, and grew more plants like it.

Now, rose lovers after noticing what good Mrs. Bee had done by accident, thought, "I wonder if a person could not dust the pollen from a very different rose on the pistil of some particular rose." This was tried, and to-day we have such wonderful improvements on the old-fashioned roses that no other flower gives quite the pleasure to garden lovers as the rose.

How Roses are Propagated

No, the seeds of the new varieties would probably not bring plants like themselves. More likely they would resemble closely their parents or grandparents. Besides, it takes a long time to raise a plant from a rose seed.

So the safest and surest way to propagate, or grow more of, the new varieties is by:

      (*a*) Cuttings, or
      (*b*) Budding.

Cuttings

Cuttings are "slips" cut from the plant, which if kept in damp sand will take root.

New geranium plants are usually procured in this way. In fact, the old plant is often cut entirely up into sections and each section is planted in an earthen pot. They are kept damp, and soon throw out roots. The new plants of the geranium will bloom much better than the old one, especially in winter, in the house.

Many roses will readily grow out-of-doors from cuttings. Among these are the Rambler roses, the Dorothy Perkins being one of the easiest to raise. Among the Hybrid Tea roses, the La France grows readily from cuttings.

Cuttings, however, do best if raised under glass, in a greenhouse.

Each little cutting may have its own greenhouse. This is arranged by—

Growing Rose Cuttings Under Glass Jars

At any time in warm weather some cuttings will take root under an inverted jar. The best time to experiment, however, is in the Spring or in August.

The tip cut from a strong growing shoot, or cane, does best. It should have at least three joints, one of which is near the base. After all the leaves but one, and the tip are cut off, the "slip" is placed in damp sandy soil up to *one-third* of its length, and covered over with an inverted quart jar. The glass jar is the little cutting's own hot-house where it will have wonderfully good conditions for "taking root."

Do not lift the jar for many a day, but keep the soil well watered.

After a number of weeks, most likely you will notice new leaves putting forth, and will know that the cutting has become a little plant with its own roots. Let it grow under the jar until the tip reaches the glass; then uncover.

It is not necessary to make cuttings especially for the purpose, for rose* bushes have been raised from the stem of a blooming rose after the blossom has faded.

---

* Mary Frances has several rose bushes blooming, which she made from cuttings. She saved some especially beautiful cut roses which were given her. When the flowers had wilted she cut them off and followed the directions Billy had given.

Roses

Cuttings are inexpensive, and the method is an easy one for obtaining a large number of plants; but there is a better and quicker and more certain way for professional rose growers. This is by—

Budding

In order to find what is meant by budding, you must understand that the "bud" referred to means the little green "eye" on the stem of the plant where a branch will grow.

This "eye" is cut off with a sharp knife, and slipped under the bark of some wild rose plant, called the "stock."

The advantage of budding is that the growth is rapid and commences with the strong roots of the wild plant.

If you buy rose plants from the dealer, they will probably be budded plants. Now, watch for—

"Suckers"

You see, in budding, after the "bud" or "eye" has begun to put forth leaves, all the branches of the wild rose plant are cut away, and only the new bud allowed to grow. Sometimes the *wild rose stock* or root will send out a shoot after the new rose bush is planted. If this is allowed to grow, it will use all the food sent up by the roots, and the new budded growth will die out, unless the *wild rose shoot is cut off close.*

"Suckers" are very easily discerned. They are full of prickles, are light green in color, and usually have seven leaves. Cultivated rose bushes with few exceptions have five leaves.

You do not want to find any of your lovely rose bushes killed in this way—so watch out for "suckers!"

Billy looked up from his note book, "I haven't read exactly as I have taken these notes," he said; "I've made the lesson shorter. Do you wish me to go on?"

"Oh, please do!" cried the girls.

"Yes, Son," said his mother, "that is, if you are not too tired. I imagine we are coming to that interesting point where we will learn what roses were recommended to you for planting."

CHAPTER XXXVI

THE BEST ROSES TO PLANT

"YOU are quite right, Mother," replied Billy, "but before we were given the lists, we learned a little more about the history and—

CLASSES OF ROSES

If we should go back many years, and give the names of the old roses and follow their history until the present time, you could scarcely remember their names.

Already you have heard of "Damask," "China," and "Cabbage" roses, and have been told that they were among the grandparents of the roses of to-day.

THE HOMES OF CERTAIN ROSES

Perhaps it would interest you to know that Damask roses were found around Damascus, in Syria, and taken to Europe in about the year 1573; that the "Cabbage", or "Provence", rose is supposed to have been known to the Romans, and later was grown extensively in Provence, in the South of France; that the "China" rose was brought to Europe sometime in the eighteenth century from China, where it is a native or "wild"

[199]

rose; that the beautiful, fragrant and delicate Tea rose was brought from China to England about 1815.

About Hybrid Perpetual Roses

It is not necessary to tell what particular old roses became the great-grandparents of our present roses. Indeed, it would be a difficult matter, for commercial rose growers have guarded well the secret of just what roses they used to produce the new ones.

The term given to a new flower is *hybrid*, which means a *mixture*. When, about the year 1825, a new class of roses, called the Hybrid Perpetual, was brought into existence, everybody was glad, because these new hybrids bloomed longer than any of their parents; were of good strong growth; and were perfectly *hardy*.

Perfectly hardy *means that they would live out-of-doors over severe winter weather.*

Hybrid Perpetual roses are among our most prized roses of to-day for these same reasons; but we now have a still more valuable class of hybrids, with a longer season of bloom, which were derived from—

Tea Roses

Perhaps the loveliest of all roses are the Tea roses, because of their beauty and enchanting fragrance; but they are delicate. Very few Tea rose bushes can live out-of-doors over *cold* weather. Not only are Tea roses most beautiful and fragrant, but they *bloom almost continuously* during the entire season.

About Hybrid Tea Roses

So, as I have said, garden lovers who lived where the winters were severely cold and bring snow, could not have the lovely Tea roses in their gardens.

You can imagine their delight when another new class of roses appeared—roses which bloom freely like the Tea roses, and have much of their fragrance, yet are hardy and can live out-of-doors in winter weather, except in the "way north country."

The name of this wonderful new class of roses is Hybrid Tea; which means, as you already know, that the new roses are the result of a mixture of Tea roses with others.

Hybrid Tea roses are, in fact, a mixture of Tea roses with Hybrid Perpetuals.

What Roses to Plant

For blooms for cut flowers, you will plant many Hybrid Tea roses, and some few Hybrid Perpetuals; for, while Hybrid Perpetuals bloom plentifully only in June, and have a few blooms in the Autumn, they are so large and magnificent that no one wishes to do without the following:

Hybrid Perpetual Roses (Abbreviation: H. P.)

Hybrid Perpetual Roses bloom profusely in June, and a few times in Summer; quite well in the Fall. They are very hardy. Prune after June blooming to get Autumn blooms.

Paul Neyron:
   One of the largest roses in existence; a deep pink in color.

Frau Karl Druschki:
   Pure white, large and perfect in form. Buds sometimes 3 inches long. Blooms well.

Hybrid Perpetual
Roses—*Continued*
{
Mrs. John Laing:
  Soft pink, very fragrant and free flowering; one of the best.

Prince Camille de Rohan:
  Deep crimson maroon.
}

There are several other very desirable Hybrid Perpetual roses, but the name of one only of each color has been listed, because one has so much more pleasure in cutting a half dozen buds of the same color and form than a mixture of different kinds.

Even if one has space for many rose bushes, there is a great deal more satisfaction in having two or more bushes of the same variety than many different kinds, for a bouquet of the same kind of flowers is so much more beautiful than an assortment.

Perhaps you thought that the words Hybrid Perpetual meant continuous blooming. Many a grown person has made this mistake in looking over the seedsmen's catalogs. Probably the name Perpetual refers to the fact that the plant lives over from year to year and has such a long life. In England, however, Hybrid Perpetuals bloom for a much longer time than in our country, for the climate is better suited to roses.

Of the many, many beautiful Hybrid Tea roses, you will wish red, white, pink, and yellow; and you will be pleased if you grow some of the following:

The Best Roses to Plant

Hybrid Tea Roses
(Abbreviation: H. T.)

Hybrid Tea Roses are free-blooming, hardy, and combine to a large degree the beauty of color of the H. P. with the fragrance and continuance of bloom of the Tea roses.

Red:
  1. General McArthur.
      A satisfactory bloomer, crimson scarlet. Good for cutting.
  2. Gruss an Teplitz.
      Bright crimson. Pretty foliage. Flowers in clusters on a weak stem. A constant bloomer, and very desirable for that reason, and for the color and form of foliage.

White:
  1. Kaiserin Augusta Victoria.
      Pearly white, tinged with light yellow. A very satisfactory rose.
  2. Innocence.
      White. A good bloomer.

Pink:
  1. Caroline Testout.
      Very good for color and hardiness. Fragrant; blooms freely.
  2. Killarney.
      A general favorite, because of good color and form, and a continuous bloomer. Subject to mildew.
  3. La France.
      Excellent. Very fragrant. Charming in color.
  Other excellent pink roses:
      Lady Ashtown.
      Killarney Brilliant.

Yellow:
  1. Duchess of Wellington.
      Deep yellow and orange. Excellent bloomer.

Hybrid Tea Roses—
Continued

Yellow—*Continued*
2. Mrs. Aaron Ward.
   Indian yellow; free blooming.
3. Marquise de Sinety.
   A magnificent rose of sunset shades, but not so easily cared for, nor so free blooming, as Duchess of Wellington.

In looking over these lists, perhaps you are wondering why you do not find the name of the rose, American Beauty, so dear to American hearts. The American Beauty rose is not hardy, and is grown under glass, and as we are considering only out-of-door roses, it is not listed.

If you happen to live in the warm climate of the South or in California, you can have the luxury of growing the more tender roses, and I am giving you a list of some of the best Tea roses.

Do not attempt to raise them if you live where there is much snow in winter; a few of these might "winter over" if well protected, but with the many exquisite Hybrid Tea roses, it is only a waste of time for young gardeners to experiment.

List of Tea (Scented) Roses

Tender roses which require extraordinary winter protection in the vicinity of New York.
Do not prune severely.

Red:
   There are no dark red tea roses, the nearest perhaps being Souvenir de Catherine Guillet, coppery-carmine, shaded with yellow.
White:
1. Mrs. Herbert Stevens.
   Beautiful in form. Sometimes tinged with faint pink shadings.
2. White Mamam Cochet.
   White, sometimes tinged with pink.

The Best Roses to Plant

List of Tea (Scented) Roses—*Continued*
{
   Pink:
     Mamam Cochet.
       Hardiest of all Tea roses; excellent for cutting. Free blooming.
     Duchesse de Brabant.
       Most fragrant. Silvery pink.
   Yellow:
     1. Lady Hillingdon.
       Reddish yellow; a beautiful rose.
     2. Souvenir de Pierre Notting.
       Canary-yellow, deeper in center.

Below is a list of Climbing Roses. Climbing roses were brought into existence in a way similar to any of the other new roses.

Hardy Climbing Roses (For places where the winters bring snow)
{
   Red:
     Excelsa.
       A great improvement on the Crimson Rambler, the foliage being nearly free from mildew. Blooms in June.
     American Beauty Climbing Rose.
       Resembling the American Beauty in shade; blooms are of quite good size, on weak stems, but rather good for cutting. A desirable rose, but not for showy effect.

   Pink:
     Dorothy Perkins.
       A splendid rose; grows very rapidly, sometimes 20 feet in a season. Flowers in clusters. Foliage charming. Blooms in June.

206   THE MARY FRANCES GARDEN BOOK

Hardy Climbing Roses
—Continued

> Debutante.
>   Fragrant, very desirable because blooming sometimes in July, in September and October.
> Tausendschön.
>   Sometimes called "Rose of a Thousand Blooms." Flowers early in large clusters. Very hardy; beautiful foliage. Color, blush pink and white.
> American Pillar.
>   Grows very rapidly. A brilliant pink single rose, borne in clusters. Foliage excellent.
>
> White:
>   White Dorothy.
>   Flowers at the same time as the Pink Dorothy Perkins.
>
> Yellow:
>   Shower of Gold.

In warmer parts of the country there is a great variety of beautiful climbing roses, among which may be named:

Climbing Roses for the South and Pacific Coast

> Pink:
>   Climbing Bridesmaid.
>   Rose pink with crimson shadings, very fragrant.
>
> White:
>   Climbing Devoniensis. ("Magnolia Rose.")
>   Large creamy white roses with pink center.

The Best Roses to Plant

Climbing Roses—*Continued*
> Yellow:
>   Marechal Niel.
>   This well-known magnificent climbing rose bears masses of double fragrant blooms which are excellent for cutting.

There is another class of roses about which you should know:

Wichuraiana Roses (Evergreen or Memorial Roses)

These roses will live in our coldest climate.

The first were brought from Japan in 1892. The Wichuraiana roses are highly valued where the winters are severe or where the plant cannot receive special care, as in a cemetery. (For this reason they have been called "Memorial.") Once planted, they seem to care for themselves. They trail along the ground, or over rocks, and often climb over any support.

Do not plant them in the rose garden where you need space to grow bushes for blooms which are lovely for cutting.

Wichuraiana roses bloom in June and July and sometimes later. Insects do not trouble the beautiful shiny foliage, which stays green nearly all winter.

The single roses, if not cut, become red berries in the Autumn. "*Wichuraiana*" is the catalog name of the single variety.

Blooms of the Wichuraiana roses are small compared with the Hybrid Tea or Hybrid Perpetual, but some are beautiful.

The Best Wichuraiana Rose
> Gardenia.
>   Sometimes called "Hardy Marechal Niel," bears lovely yellow buds which open into double flowers of cream color, resembling a Cape Jessamine.

Suppose you live at the seashore or in the mountains; suppose you have very poor soil for roses; then you will be glad to plant—

Rugosa Roses

Sometimes Rugosa Roses have been called, "Ironclad," because of their thick leathery foliage, which is seldom, if ever, troubled with insects; and because of their wonderful hardiness and ability to live under trying conditions.

They bloom early, in large flowers, some of which resemble large single wild roses; others resemble large "double wild roses," if you can imagine such roses. Many make the Autumn gay with their brilliant red seed berries.

Do not make the mistake of planting Rugosa among the rose bushes you are growing for cut flowers.

They are used where heavy growth is needed; as among shrubbery or for a hedge. A single plant looks well on a lawn or at a corner of a house. The Rugosa roses grow from four to six feet tall.

In case you wish one or two of these, the following are—

The Best Rugosa Roses (Ramanas, Japanese)

Of very hardy heavy growth, with large single or semi-double flowers, many bearing red seed pods in Autumn.

White:
  Blanc Double de Coubert.
    Pure double white blooms.

Pink:
  Conrad F. Meyer.
    Silvery rose; double; one of the best.

The Best Roses to Plant

"There," said Billy, looking up from his book, "isn't that a long lesson? Well, the reason for it all is this: Miss Gardener and Professor Weed are rose enthusiasts—'rose crazy,' we boys called them."

"Their love of roses was an excellent thing for you boys," said his mother, "for I believe you know more on the subject than most grown-up people."

"Just listen!" exclaimed Mary Frances, "Billy, don't you feel repaid for giving us the lesson? What comes next?"

"Next comes—let me see," replied Billy. "Oh, yes, it's about planting and caring for roses, I remember."

"When will you give us that?" asked Eleanor.

"Does it tell about 'Tree Roses?'" asked Mary Frances eagerly before Billy could answer Eleanor.

"I'll tell you *now*," he said, "about—

Tree Roses

Tree Roses are Hybrid Perpetual or Hybrid Tea or other roses, budded or grafted high up on strong stock, or wild growth, and cut or pruned to the form of trees.

They are very attractive in a formal or "set out" garden, or for edging walks, but such great care must be taken to keep

them warm during cold weather that it is best not to try them except in places where there is little snow in winter.

For winter bed covers, place boards around the plant and fill with earth.

"Miss Gardener said," went on Billy, "that English and Irish rose growers are constantly sending new varieties of roses over to Americans, but the new roses have to be tested in our climate before we can be certain if they will do well here. That's all the lesson for to-day," he declared. "Come to-morrow morning for the next lesson—that is, if you want to. The day after, you know, we go on the Wild Flower Picnic."

CHAPTER XXXVII

THE WICKED ROSE BUGS

"'ZEALOUS care brings big reward in rose growing,' our professor told us."

Billy was perched in the fork of an apple tree. The two girls and his mother were sitting on the grass which made a thick carpet beneath its branches.

"He used to say it over so often that the fellows nicknamed him 'Rosy,'" Billy went on.

"Oh!" exclaimed Mary Frances, "wasn't that awful!" but she and Eleanor giggled, and even her mother smiled.

"You didn't call him that, though?" said Eleanor.

"Not when he could hear me," laughed Billy. "But if I'm going to give you this lesson we must make a start. The subject, by the way, is—

HOW TO PLANT ROSES

Before you can make a list of the roses you wish to order, you must understand something about the state in which they will be when received, how far apart they may be planted, and—

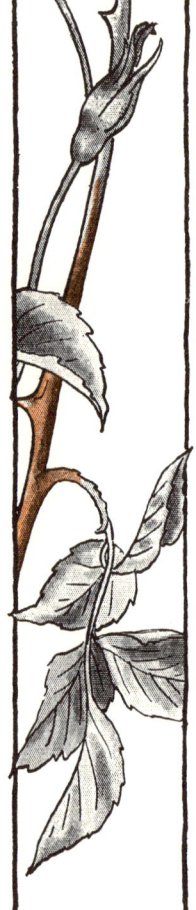

Where to Make Beds for Roses

Roses like warmth and air. They love to drink, but they do not like wet feet.

Knowing these things, you will select for your rose bed an airy, sunny place on the south side of a building or wall, if possible, where the ground is not so low that it will hold moisture long.

Having decided what is the best place you can offer your roses, you will want to know—

How to Make Beds for Roses

1. Do not buy too many plants for the space. Do not make the bed over five feet wide. If wider, you will tread on the soil and make it heavy.

2. Remember, roses are usually planted twenty-one inches apart. (Do not plant Wichuraiana or Rugosa roses in the bed.) Alternate the plants, as shown in the following diagram:

```
(1)    (2)    (3)
   (5)    (4)        This saves garden space, and gives
(6)    (7)    (8)       room for the roots.
```

3. To be beautiful, roses must have plenty of good food. So *dig deep;* eighteen inches is a good depth. Fill this space with a mixture of soil and well-rotted stable manure. It is best not to let the **roots** of the roses touch the manure. Sprinkle a

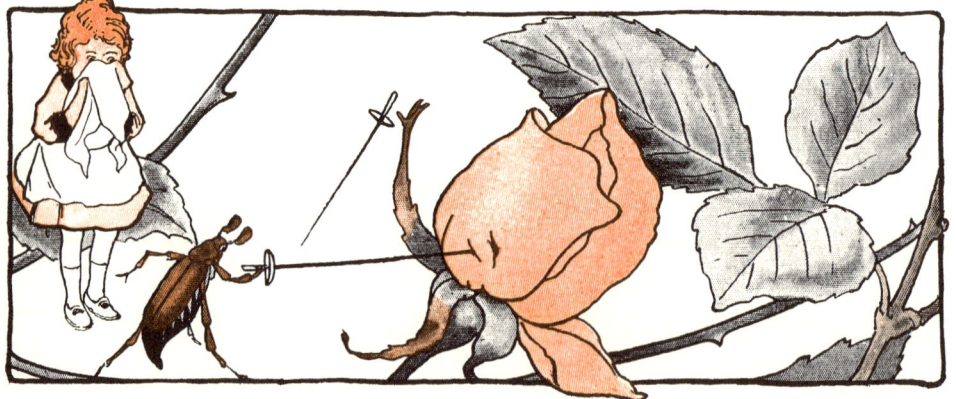

The Wicked Rose Bugs 213

little soil over the manure before putting the plant into its place. If the ground is very damp, dig deeper than two feet and throw in a basket of stones, through which the water will drain.

4. Roses are received from the dealer either growing in pots, or dormant (dry), or with little balls of earth around the roots wrapped in damp moss.

The young inexperienced gardener will do best with the potted plants, but if the plants are dry and dormant (dormant means *sleeping*), it is well to soak the roots before planting. Never expose damp roots to the air. Keep in water or damp earth until planted.

How Deep to Plant Roses

Unless grown in pots, spread out the roots and pack the earth firmly about them, putting the plant deep enough to bring earth three inches over the "bud" or graft.

The Best Time to Plant Roses

depends on where you live.

In general, Spring is the best time, but in the South and on the Pacific coast, Autumn is best.

Some of the *hardiest* sorts will grow well, when set out in the Fall, even in places where the winters are severe.

Now, the bushes are planted, and we will think about—

Caring for Roses

The chief cares for roses are:
1. Cultivating, or stirring the soil.
2. Feeding.
3. Destroying insect enemies.
4. Pruning.

You already understand the importance of cultivating and the importance of feeding the plants.

Fertilizers

Two of the best foods for roses and easiest to use, are bone dust and dried sheep manure, which you can buy at the seed store. These you may dig into the soil as you cultivate, being sure not to let the fertilizers directly touch the roots.

Enemies of Roses

1. Rose Bugs.
2. Aphids.
3. Rusts and Mildews.
4. Borers and other chewing insects.

There are several different kinds of beetles, called rose bugs, which come up out of the ground where they have spent the winter, just at the time of the most abundant and beautiful blooming.

In the Middle Atlantic States they stay in a place about two weeks.

The Wicked Rose Bugs

The best way to rid a plant of these enemies of roses which "eat them alive," is to hand-pick them, throwing them into a can of kerosene.

There is a patent preparation which is good. Write your dealer for information as to this.

Treat for other insects as you have already learned.

If your parents think you may be trusted to handle a poison, spray in the early Spring with "Bordeaux Arsenate of Lead" to prevent mildew and rust. In summer, use Flowers of Sulphur.

Now, as to—

Pruning Roses

Prune rose bushes in the early Spring, just when the plants *begin* to show green, which means that their sap is beginning to flow. Use pruning for cutting the stems back.

Remember these principal rules:

1. Hybrid Perpetual Roses should be cut back about two feet from the ground.
2. Cut back Hybrid Tea Roses more sparingly, that is, farther from the ground than Hybrid Perpetuals.
3. Cut back Tea Roses only a short distance.
4. Cut only the dead wood from the other kinds.

Pruning cuts off the ends of the branches and causes the plant to throw out strong joints from the eyes along the canes, which will bear flowers.

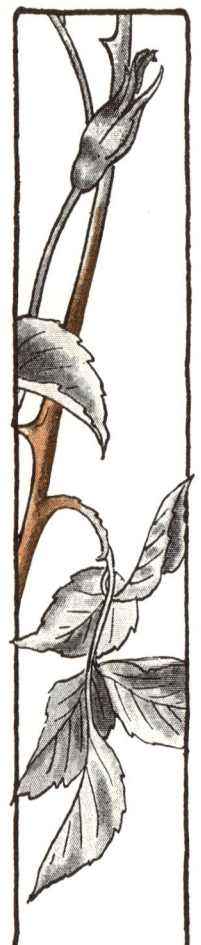

"My," exclaimed Mary Frances, as Billy closed his book suddenly and jumped to the ground. "Is that all about roses?"

"No, dear," answered her mother. "No, that is just a 'first beginning,' as you used to say when you were little."

"Speaking of insect enemies, I see the wicked rose bugs have eaten into the hearts of the most beautiful roses we own," went on her mother.

"Come," cried Mary Frances, "let's go see if we can find them—and drown them in kerosene."

"Oh, but I'm afraid of them!" shuddered Eleanor.

Mary Frances laughed. "They won't hurt you!" she said, running ahead. "I bet I can catch the first hundred!"

CHAPTER XXXVIII

THE FAIRY WOOD NYMPHS

JUST as the family had planned, they started on the walk in the woods the next morning.

Mary Frances and Eleanor were walking with their mother, while Billy and his father followed with the lunch baskets.

"Be careful where you step!" called Billy suddenly; but it was too late, for with a cry of pain, his mother fell upon the thick undergrowth.

Billy and his father came running.

"Oh," cried Mary Frances, "oh, dear! I ought to have told mother. I remember tripping over the vines here. Are you much hurt, Mother dear?"

"Not much," she replied, but as she made an effort to move, she sank back with a little sigh.

"It isn't a bad sprain, dear," said the father, examining her ankle, "but you ought not walk another step."

"Oh, the poor children will be so disappointed!"

"That's just like mother!" exclaimed Mary Frances. "Never to think of herself first!"

"I know what you and I can do, Father," said Billy. "Let's make a 'sedan chair,' and carry mother home."

"That's a good idea, Son—we'll leave the girls and the lunch; and if the doctor says she may come, I'll drive mother out late in the afternoon after she has rested."

"Oh, no, let us go with you!" cried Eleanor and Mary Frances together.

"It will make me so much happier, girls," said the mother, "if you will stay and try to enjoy yourselves. Billy will be back soon, and maybe you can have a bunch of wild flowers ready to take home when you come this afternoon. I'm not hurt seriously, but I think a hot-water bath and bandage for this ankle will prevent further trouble."

"All right, Mother dear," said Mary Frances, kissing her. "If it will make you happier, we'll stay."

"I'd eat lunch right over there," suggested Billy, pointing out a lovely green spot near a spring.

"Trust Billy to think of pleasant 'eats,'" laughed

Mary Frances, as Eleanor and she picked up the lunch baskets, and Billy and his father started off with the mother comfortably seated on the "sedan chair" which they made with their hands.

"We'll wait for you, Billy," called Eleanor.

"Better not," said Billy, "because I may be late—I may stay to dinner at home."

"We'll wait a while, any how," called Mary Frances. "Good-bye!"

"Good-bye!" called everybody.

* * * * * * *

The girls felt quite lonely and sad as the other three disappeared from sight.

"Oh, dear," sobbed Mary Frances, "I just pretended to be cheerful because I knew how sorry mother was to disappoint us."

"My, but you were brave," replied Eleanor. "Indeed, I felt just like crying, but when I saw how you were behaving, it made me feel ashamed."

"Well," said Mary Frances, drying her eyes, "let's set the table—Billy will be back sooner or later, and I don't want him to see I've been crying!"

So they spread their lunch cloth and paper plates.

"If we only had some flowers for a centerpiece!" exclaimed Mary Frances.

"Let's go gather some!" suggested Eleanor.

"All right!" Mary Frances sprang up.

"What can we put them in?" asked Eleanor practically.

"Oh, I know!" cried Mary Frances running to one of the lunch baskets. "Let's drink this milk, and use the bottle for a holder."

"Lovely!" said Eleanor. "My, I didn't know I was hungry!"

"Neither did I—let's take a sandwich and start."

Mary Frances led the way. "I've often walked through this path," she said, "and I've always found some flowers."

"Oh, dear, what was that?" cried Eleanor suddenly.

"Nothing at all," answered Mary Frances, "or maybe a bird flying about among the leaves."

"It isn't a bird!" declared Eleanor. "It's not a bird!" pointing down among the whirling leaves. "Hush! Do look carefully, Mary Frances, and listen!"

The Fairy Wood Nymphs

They stood still.

> "Wild carrot, toad flax,
>   Buttercup and daisy,
> Do you love them well as I?
> If not, you'll be crazy."

Although the voice was very thin and piping, they heard every word distinctly. "That's not a bird," whispered Mary Frances.

"Crazy, crazy, crazy, crazy, crazy," sang the voice.

Still the girls didn't see anything among the leaves where the voice seemed to come from.

> "Tinkle Bell,
>   In a dell,
> Dearly loved
>   A daisy.
> Do you love one
>   Well as she?
> If not, you are——"

"What?" asked the little piping voice.
All the leaves stopped whirling.

"What?" again asked the little voice.

"Crazy," replied Mary Frances, laughing softly. "But we're not crazy. We dearly love daisies, and wild carrot, and buttercup and—well, yes, we love toad flax, too."

"Oh, I'm so glad, because we can be friends."

At that the leaves began to whirl and dance furiously, and out of the midst of them leaped a little fellow not anything like as large as Mary Marie, Mary Frances' doll.

He was dressed in forest green from the tip of his pointed cap to the toe of his pointed boot. His coat and tiny knickerbocker breeches were made of green leaves. Even his hair and beard were yellowish-green as though made of very fine grass. For buckles on his shoes he wore tiny dew drops which glistened like diamonds. The buttons on his coat were of the same. At the end of his peaked cap dangled a tiny wild fringed gentian.

"Flower lovers are always friends," said he, bowing. "Young ladies, it gives me much pleasure to introduce myself. I am Jack-in-the-Pulpit!"

Mary Frances wanted to ask him how he hap-

The Fairy Wood Nymphs

pened to be out of the pulpit, but she suddenly thought he might not like the question, so she said:

"Why, how do you do, Mr. Jack? We are pleased to know you;" and she and Eleanor both smiled.

The little fellow was delighted.

"You really are glad—that I can see. There are lots of human people who come into the woods who never listen or look when we call."

"Why," asked Eleanor looking round, "are there more of you?"

"Oh, my, yes," nodded the little fellow. "Lots and lots more, only the others are very busy getting flowers ready for next Autumn and Spring—that is, all but one. Her name is Bouncing Bet."

At that the leaves began to bounce and to whirl again, and out of their midst sprang a tiny little lady. She was so beautiful that both the girls exclaimed, "Oh, isn't she lovely!"

She certainly was lovely, in a gown of queen's lace over wild rose petals. On her feet were tiny lady slippers; on her head a lovely violet. Her hair

was of yellow-white thistle-down. When she spoke, her voice sounded like a laughing bell.

"So you've found them at last, Jack," she laughed. "You've found human beings who can hear us and can see us. Let's tell what we can do for them."

"Yes," said the little fellow in green, taking Bouncing Bet's hand and speaking to the girls. "Please be seated."

As the girls sat down on the grassy slope, Jack began to speak:

"We know you are wondering whether we are really the flowers, 'Jack-in-the-Pulpit' and 'Bouncing Bet.' No, we are the fairies of those flowers. Every kind of flower has its fairy. They try to talk with the human beings they see, but very few can hear them or see them. Now, that you can see us and hear us, we would like to take you with us into Fairy Flower Land——"

"And tell you all we can in one short afternoon about wild flowers," finished Bouncing Bet. "Jack, lead the way."

CHAPTER XXXIX

Good and Bad Weeds

AT that, the little fellow picked up a tiny stick, which he used as a cane, and started ahead, Bouncing Bet following with a happy hop-skip-and-jump step.

Mary Frances and Eleanor were surprised that they had to hurry to keep up to the tiny little beings.

At length they came to a high hedge.

"Touch me with your hand," said Jack to Mary Frances, holding out his arm.

"Touch me with your hand," said Bet to Eleanor.

"Now, when I say 'three,' all jump," commanded Jack.

"One, two, three!" Over the top of hedge they went as though they had wings, and found themselves in the midst of a wonderful garden.

"Oh," cried Mary Frances, "I never, never saw so many wild flowers blooming at once."

"This is a fairy garden," answered Bouncing Bet,

"and the fairies keep it for just such friends as you, who are anxious to learn about wild flowers."

"But we can tell you only the shortest flower stories to-day." Jack caught up the conversation. "Just take a seat please, and I'll begin."

The girls sat on a pretty rustic bench under a tree, and Jack and Bet leaped upon a branch in front of them. Then Jack began:

"Good and Bad Weeds"

"Of course you know that all the flowers cultivated in your gardens have come from wild flowers.

"Through years of care, the wild flowers have improved so that it would be almost impossible to trace each of the plants in your gardens to the wild flowers from which it was started.

"There are many hundreds of wild flowers, but none more beautiful than those growing in America. There are many different kinds which were growing here when America was discovered, but the seeds of many more were carried over from Europe in grain for the colonists.

"Some of the wild things are most helpful to

Good and Bad Weeds

human beings; such as mint, and dock, and dear old dandelions, and other 'weeds' which may be eaten. From 'weeds' also come some of the most wonderful of *medicines. Perhaps you have tested the medicinal effects of mustard, catnip, and boneset."

"I tried catnip on our Jubey," said Mary Frances. "It did her lots of good."

"I've had mustard plasters, and mustard baths, and boneset tea when I've been ill with chills," Eleanor added.

"Just so! just so!" nodded Jack-in-the-Pulpit; "so you see, many 'weeds' are not useless plants, but are very valuable. The Indians knew that."

"My, I hadn't any idea weeds were valuable," said Eleanor.

"I always knew about mint and catnip," Mary Frances replied, "but I didn't know other weeds were of so much help."

"Of course there are many weeds which seem of no value at all. They steal the food of valuable

---

* For information concerning weeds used in medicine, send for Farmers' Bulletin No. 188, which may be had free from the United States Department of Agriculture.

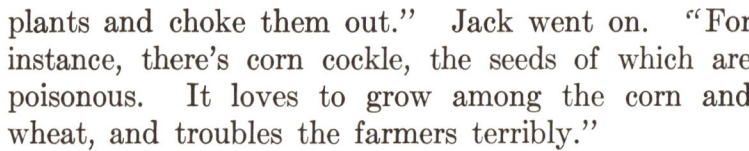

plants and choke them out." Jack went on. "For instance, there's corn cockle, the seeds of which are poisonous. It loves to grow among the corn and wheat, and troubles the farmers terribly."

"I think the flowers are quite pretty," Mary Frances ventured to say.

"Oh, you know them when you see them?" asked Jack. "That's good, because we can go on with our story faster if you know some of the wild flowers. You would like to gather some out of our fairy garden, wouldn't you? Well, you may take some of all that are in bloom at this time of year, after we finish telling you what we so much want you to learn about our dear flowers."

"Now, it is Bet's turn," he went on, turning toward the dainty little fairy, who began to bounce happily up and down on the branch of the tree.

The girls were delighted with her dancing. At length she stopped and began to talk in her musical voice.

"I am going to talk a little about the flowers," she said, "and shall mention only the ones known by most people, because we have such a short time

Good and Bad Weeds

for your lesson. I shall just mention them, and if you do not know them, please interrupt me, and Jack and I will take you through the garden to show them to you. Do you know the—

Daisy (Other names: Ox-Eyed Daisy, White Weed)	This charming gold and white, wheel-shaped flower, which is a troublesome weed to the farmer, blooms everywhere afield from May to November, from Canada to the southern States, and to the Mississippi River. It is perhaps the best known wild flower in the Eastern United States.
Great Mullein (Other names: Velvet Dock, Aaron's Rod, Flannel Leaf)	Almost everywhere this tall rod, bearing yellow flowers, which resemble huge buttercups, may be seen from June to November. Its velvety leaves, which grow in rosettes on the ground, are soft to the touch, but if sheep or cows try to eat them, the down upon them becomes splinters in the tongues of the animals. That is one reason it grows so widely—the down saves the leaves from harm. This same down is sometimes used by humming birds to line their tiny nests, which are no larger than a large thimble, yet hold two humming-bird babies. The seeds of the great Mullein are eaten by gold-finches, or they would scatter yet more abundantly. The great Mullein is a native of Europe.

"My winter coat is made of velvet dock," said Bouncing Bet.

"Mine is made of flannel leaf," Jack added.

"Yet they are both made of the leaves of the great mullein," laughed Mary Frances.

"Good," laughed Bouncing Bet. "Jack, we didn't catch her."

"Now comes a wild flower with a charming name," she went on. "It is the—

Butterfly Weed (Other names: Pleurisy-root, Orange-root)	This bright orange milk-weed is found blooming nearly everywhere in the United States except the far West, from June to September. It is greatly loved by butterflies because in its small deep blossoms they find sweet nectar, which even the long tongues of bumble-bees cannot reach. The pollen lies deep, too, and adheres to the long legs of the butterfly. The stem has very little milky juice, and the seed pods are not so interesting as those of the Common Milk-weed.
Common Milk-weed	This plant grows in the northern, eastern and middle western part of the United States and is most interesting because of the white milky juice in the stems, and because of the fluffy down in the seed pods. When I tell you about Seed Babies with Wings, I'll tell you more about this milk-weed down.

Just as Bet finished speaking about the milk-weed, there sounded a silvery clock.

Good and Bad Weeds

One! Two! Three! it chimed.

"Oh," exclaimed Jack. "Oh, can it be possible that it is three o'clock! Bet, you must stop talking and give me a chance!"

"Oh, dear," sighed Eleanor. "Oh, must she stop talking? I am so anxious to learn more about the wild flowers."

"Do you know all I've told about, when you see them?" asked Bouncing Bet.

"No," replied Eleanor. "Do you, Mary Frances?"

"Not all," Mary Frances shook her head.

"Come then," cried Jack and Bet, jumping from the tree. "Come," and they led them among the flowers, and pointed out to them besides the ones mentioned: Wake Robins, Trailing Arbutus, Lupines, Forget-Me-Nots, Columbines, Heather, Laurel, California Poppies, and hundreds of other wild flowers which were in bloom in the outside meadows and fields and woods.

"I'm so sorry we haven't time to tell you the story of each one," said Jack. "Some time next year, please come again and we'll tell you."

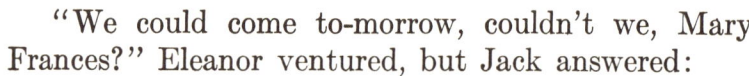

"We could come to-morrow, couldn't we, Mary Frances?" Eleanor ventured, but Jack answered:

"No, not to-morrow. Only once a year can flower fairies talk with human beings. It must be to-day. So now, just as quickly as possible, I am going to tell you something about how plants are related to each other, but please be more comfortable. Do take a seat in the grape-vine swing."

Then the girls noticed a hammock nearby, formed by the interlacing of growing grape vines.

It was wonderfully comfortable, and they leaned back contentedly as Jack took his place in a little green lily-shaped flower growing close by, and Bouncing Bet pranced around on the lawn near him.

"Jack's in his pulpit now," she said. "Hear him speak."

CHAPTER XL

Bouncing Bet and Her Friends

"YOUNG ladies," began Jack-in-the-Pulpit, "Bouncing Bet and I have arranged a little play for you. It's to be this way: after finishing a few introductory remarks, I will call the names of various flower families. Bet has been around to see certain members of each family, and although they are very busy, they have promised to come when she calls—that is, the fairy of each flower or plant that she calls will come to this grassy slope which is to be the stage for our play."

"How perfectly lovely!" cried the girls.

"But they will have little time to talk," warned Jack. "So," he went on, "let me tell you a few facts about—

Plant Families

"It may surprise you to learn that certain plants belong to certain plant families.

"You know that certain animals belong to certain

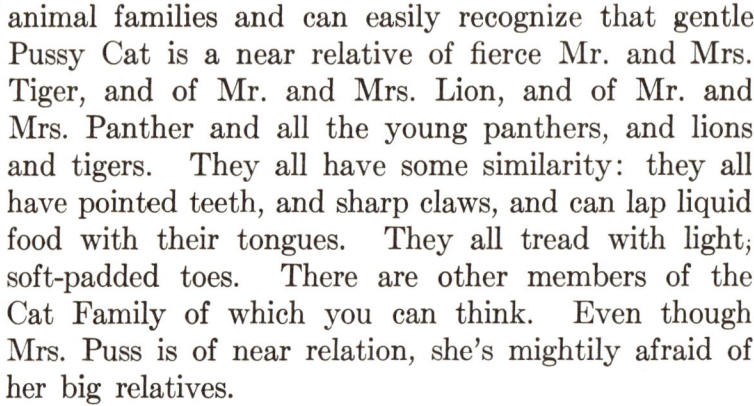

animal families and can easily recognize that gentle Pussy Cat is a near relative of fierce Mr. and Mrs. Tiger, and of Mr. and Mrs. Lion, and of Mr. and Mrs. Panther and all the young panthers, and lions and tigers. They all have some similarity: they all have pointed teeth, and sharp claws, and can lap liquid food with their tongues. They all tread with light, soft-padded toes. There are other members of the Cat Family of which you can think. Even though Mrs. Puss is of near relation, she's mightily afraid of her big relatives.

"Now, I wonder if you know that faithful Mr. Dog is own cousin to terrible Mr. and Mrs. Wolf. Indeed, I may be mistaken, perhaps he is their own brother, they are so much alike in some ways.

"Just as animals belong to certain families so do plants. They resemble each other in certain points which you may not notice at first, but which you would readily see if pointed out to you."

Jack drew quite a long breath.

"Now we are ready for the play, Bet," he announced, and Bet bounced down to the grass-carpet stage.

Bouncing Bet and Her Friends

Said Jack, "The first plant family called upon will be the Rose family.

Bouncing Bet blew a long musical whistle by using two fingers at her tiny mouth, and out from some shrubbery stepped a dainty little lady dressed in pink rose petals.

"My name is Rose," she said, smiling and throwing the girls a kiss; "and I'll introduce some of my cousins in the—

Rose Family

"*Cherry*," she called. Out stepped a red ripe cherry with a white cap trimmed with green leaves. Of course, the legs were very tiny, nearly like pins. Cherry smiled and bowed and took a place beside Rose.

"*Peach*," Rose called, and out stepped a beautiful peach, with a pink cap, trimmed with green leaves.

"*Strawberry*," called Rose, and surely enough, out came a red ripe strawberry with a white cap trimmed with green leaves.

"*Blackberry*," called the little Rose lady once more, and before the word left her mouth, a big

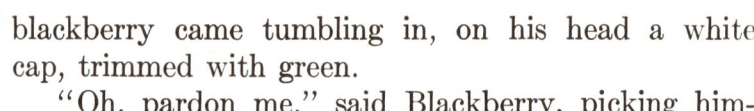

blackberry came tumbling in, on his head a white cap, trimmed with green.

"Oh, pardon me," said Blackberry, picking himself up. "I was afraid I'd be late."

Rose smiled and motioned the blackberry into place beside the strawberry.

Once again Rose called a name.

"*Apple*," she called, and roly-poly, "head-over-tin-cups," came a round rosy-cheeked apple into their midst.

"Excuse me," puffed Apple. "Please excuse my manners, Cousin Rose, but I am so fat that hurrying gets me all out of breath," and he fell in line.

"That will do," interrupted Jack-in-the-Pulpit, "that will do for the Rose family; we will now—"

"Excuse me," interrupted Mary Frances, "but may I ask—if all these are members of the Rose family?"

"There's no mistake," replied Jack. "Now, if you stop to think, you'll realize how very much the blossom of the cherry, and the strawberry, and the blackberry, and the peach, and the apple resemble a wild rose."

Bouncing Bet and Her Friends

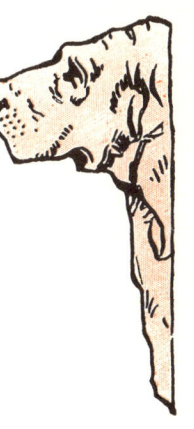

"Oh, I do!" said Eleanor.

"And I remember also," added Mary Frances, beaming, "that the seed pods of the roses look like fruit."

"Good!" cried Jack, dancing around.

"Good!" cried Bet, bouncing around, and all the members of the Rose families who were present formed a "ring-around-a-rosy," and danced around and around, and at length formed into line near the bush through which they had come.

"Their caps are their blossoms!" exclaimed Eleanor.

"They are," said Bouncing Bet. "Oh, you will always be on the lookout now to find other members of that family, for there are many more. I wanted to call *Bridal Wreath*, but there wasn't time."

"No time, indeed," interrupted Jack. "Now, Bet, call the Night Shade family. They are not so pretty as the Rose family," he whispered, "but just as useful." Bouncing Bet blew upon her fingers.

"Indian file," she called, and out filed several members of the—

NIGHT SHADE FAMILY

There were:

Common Night Shade, a tiny round black pill-like berry with a tiny white cap.

Sand Burr, in a buff coat full of prickles. And what do you think? There was—

Common White Potato, with a ridiculously small bell-shaped green and white cap.

"Oh," Mary Frances could not help exclaiming; "is White Potato a member of the Night Shade family? I thought night shade was poison!"

"I ain't poison—I ain't! Not after I'm cooked!" growled Potato. "You've ate up enough of my brothers and sisters to know that!"

"Hush!" admonished Bouncing Bet. "Keep still! That's terrible grammar, even though you are a common 'Tater,' you ought to speak more correctly than that."

"Excuse me, but we've fed hundreds and thousands of people, and that's more than any of the rest of you can say, even if you don't like my grammar."

"Mercy!" cried a *Tomato,* running in. "Did you forget me?" He was dressed in a bright red, and

wore a tiny yellow cap trimmed with green. "I belong to the Night Shade family, too, and I have fed hundreds and hundreds of people."

"Oh, you Love Apple!" broke in Potato. "Your relatives haven't fed people as long as mine have."

"That must be so," said Mary Frances. "I remember that my grandma told me that when her mother was young, tomatoes were called love apples, and were thought to be poisonous. Grand-mothers raised them in their gardens, though, because they were pretty."

"Poisonous!" Tomato's face turned redder than ever. "Poisonous! Well, I should say! But then, you know how good we are, and that we are excellent for people who eat too much meat."

"Indeed we do know, don't we, Mary Frances? We have some of you in our lunch basket," laughed Eleanor. "Mary Frances has a lot of you growing in her garden, too."

"Has she any of my brothers and sisters growing in her garden?" asked a new voice.

The girls saw the funniest, fattest brown fellow waddling along.

"Hello, Humpty Dumpty!" cried out Tomato.

"Nonsense," declared the new-comer, "I'm not Humpty Dumpty! I can prove it; I can fall and you can pick me up again. See?"

With that, over he went, smash!

The other Night Shade people all ran to help him up.

"How's that, young ladies?" said he when they had set him on his tiny legs. "Doesn't that prove I'm not an egg? Humpty Dumpty, indeed!"

"Oh, you *Egg Plant!*" cried Potato. "Welcome, cousin. You're another useful member of the Night Shade family."

"Perhaps 'you-all' don't like me as well as those other Night Shades, but some folks do."

"Who's that?" asked Eleanor.

"It looks like Lucinda Marguerite, my colored paper doll," replied Mary Frances, laughing.

No wonder she thought so, for the owner of the new voice looked like a little darky, dressed in green, with a long-pointed white cap.

"Some folkses likes me bettah than food," went on the speaker. "You can just put that in your pipe an' smoke it!"

Bouncing Bet and Her Friends 241

"*Tobacco!*" guessed Mary Frances.

"Oh, how funny!" cried Eleanor, and they burst into gales of laughter.

"I didn't know tobacco had such a pretty blossom," said Mary Frances, examining the pointed cap more carefully.

"That will——" Jack-in-the-Pulpit began.

"Wait a minute, wait a minute," cried a new voice, and in danced a beautiful little lady, dressed in a fluffy-ruffly skirt made of flower petals.

"Guess quickly," smiled Bouncing Bet. "Quickly!"

"*Petunia*," guessed Eleanor. "We have them in a window-box at home."

"What a pretty member of the Night Shade family," said Mary Frances.

"Fall in line," Jack commanded, leaning far out of his pulpit, and pointing out a place where the Night Shade family took their position.

CHAPTER XLI

BUTTERCUP AND DAISY FAMILIES

"THE next family," announced Jack-in-the-Pulpit, "will be the—

BUTTERCUP FAMILY

At the moment Bouncing Bet whistled, in danced the family headed by little Buttercup.

"My name's little *Buttercup*," she sang.

You can imagine how lovely she looked dressed in shiny yellow, trimmed with green.

Then she introduced the others:

"This is *Columbine;* this, *Marsh Marigold;* this *Larkspur*," she said, "and this is *Cowslip;* and this, *Pæony*."

All the beautiful flowers bowed and smiled and threw kisses as they danced to the place Bouncing Bet pointed out to them.

"Aren't they lovely," murmured Mary Frances. "I've always loved buttercups, but I hadn't any idea there were so many beautiful members of their family."

Buttercup and Daisy Families 243

"Oh, there are many more," spoke Jack, "but our time is shortening, and as Daisy wants very much to greet you, I shall call for some members of the very large—

Sunflower Family (Composite Family)

Such a number of flower people came dancing and running in that it was difficult to see who was who, with the exception of the big Sunflower who led them.

"I'm *Daisy*," called a charming gold and white flower fairy. "And I love everybody, no matter whether everybody loves me or not."

"Oh, we love you!" shouted Mary Frances and Eleanor. "You are a dear!"

"I hope you love all the Sunflower family," spoke up a big *Chrysanthemum*.

"Oh, please love me!" "And me!" "And me!" "And me!" begged *Dahlia*, and *Goldenrod*, and *Aster*, and *Cosmos*.

"And me!" said the *Bachelor's Button* in a deep masculine voice.

"And me!" repeated a dudish-looking *Dande-*

lion, at whose comical dress the girls couldn't help smiling, for he was rigged up in the height of an old-fashioned style, with a high collar and a knotted green tie; with "pumps" on his feet—and he carried a grass-blade cane!

"I know they love me!" There stood *Black-eyed Susan*, with arms akimbo.

"We've loved you for years!" declared the girls.

"Here comes that *Everlasting Flower!*" exclaimed Dandelion.

"What a way to speak!" whispered Eleanor; but the speech of Dandelion was soon explained when a crisp Strawflower, or "Everlasting," came stiffly in.

"Everlastingly late," said the new-comer dryly, "but nothing like so common as some flowers," glancing at Dandelion.

"Don't disgrace the family by quarreling," warned the big Sunflower.

"It's so hard to keep such a big family straight," he said with a sigh, yet he went on proudly, "You see, ours is the very largest flower family. There are from 11,000 to 12,000 members of the Sunflower or Composite Family.

Buttercup and Daisy Families

"I wonder how many different kinds of plants are known," said Mary Frances to Eleanor.

"About 120,000," answered Jack, who overheard from his pulpit. "I wish we could show you all the different flower families, and tell you about them, but as we haven't time, we will explain about just a few more. Bet, will you begin?"

Then Bouncing Bet began to speak in her sweet musical voice.

"The *beans* and *peas* you eat belong to the same family as the *clover*. It is the *Pulse* family. The *cranberry* and the *honeysuckle* and the *rhododendron* and *trailing arbutus* are of the *Heath* family."

"And may I ask," interrupted Mary Frances, "to what family you belong?"

"And Jack?" added Eleanor, eagerly.

"Thank you for the questions, dear children," smiled the delighted little fairy. "I will tell you: *Jack-in-the-Pulpit* belongs to the *Arum* family. Calla lily and——"

Here the fairy looked at him and giggled. "Shall I tell them, Jack?" she asked.

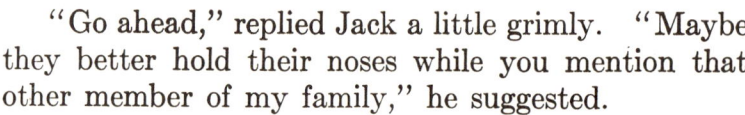

"Go ahead," replied Jack a little grimly. "Maybe they better hold their noses while you mention that other member of my family," he suggested.

"Well, the beautiful white calla lily and—and—" Bet hesitated.

"Say on," said Jack, "or I'll tell, myself."

"Well, Skunk Cabbage, then," said Bouncing Bet, "*Calla Lily* and *Skunk Cabbage* belong to Jack-in-the-Pulpit's family."

"Mercy!" Mary Frances exclaimed before she knew it.

"Oh," gasped Eleanor.

"I beg your pardon—indeed, I do!" said Mary Frances to Jack.

"Oh, never mind," he replied, "I must say we are not very proud of that branch of the family, but they have one thing about them which is very interesting. They are the very first flowers in the Spring—oftentimes blooming in February. There are other members of the *Arum* family, though, of which we are prouder."

"He'll tell you about them later," smiled Bouncing Bet.

Buttercup and Daisy Families 247

"Your family isn't the same as his, then?" queried Eleanor.

"No," she replied, "I belong to the *Pink* family."

"Oh," asked Mary Frances, "are all your family pink in color?"

"Oh, no," Jack answered her. "She's all dressed up in her Sunday-go-to-meeting clothes. She just borrowed that 'queen's lace' gown. *Queen's* lace belongs to Wild Carrot, you know, and *Wild Carrot* belongs to the *Parsley* family. Run, Bet, and take off your party clothes. Dress in your own clothes; then they'll recognize you."

Bet bounced away, laughing, and returned almost immediately in her every-day dress of—you know, calico-and-gingham-like petals.

"Now we know you, Miss Bet," cried Mary Frances; "but even your every-day dress is light pink! Are you sure all your family doesn't wear pink all the time?"

"Oh, no," answered Bouncing Bet, "you'll soon see that that is not the case when I mention my cultivated cousin, *Carnation;* and another cousin, *Sweet William.*"

"And you'll be glad to know also," laughed Jack, "that among her relatives is *Dusty Miller*."

"Now, Jack," laughed Bet, "that's an old joke of yours! Please go on and tell something about some other members of your own family."

CHAPTER XLII

Water Babies

JACK cleared his throat and began:

"Well, I don't want to seem to be too proud or conceited, but to me it is quite a pleasant thing to think that the roots of Jack-in-the-Pulpit, or *Indian Turnip*, which is my other name, have been used as a medicine many a time; and that the roots of my cousin *Calamus*, or *Sweet Flag*, are valuable as a tonic. Some of the *Arum* family like dry soil and some like damp, marshy places. I do not like very dry places myself, and Cousin Calamus Sweet Flag likes his feet wet all the time."

"Isn't it wonderful," Mary Frances leaned forward in her interest. "Isn't it wonderful, how plants growing side by side are so different?"

"They eat the same things, yet are so different," smiled Bouncing Bet. "For instance, isn't it surprising that an onion and a lily may grow side by side? By the way, the *Onion* and *Lily-of-the-Valley* and *Tiger Lily* and *Day Lily*, and *Hyacinth*, and *Dog-toothed*

Violet, and *Solomon's Seal,* and, yes, *Asparagus,* all belong to the same family."

"Oh," murmured the girls, "to think that the onion and the lovely Lily-of-the-Valley are cousins and belong to the same family!"

"Yes, and Onion is cousin of *Easter Lily,* and *Tulip* too," Bet added.

"What about Water Lilies?" asked one of the girls.

"Now," answered Bouncing Bet, "you've mentioned another member of the same family as the onion, for by this time, no doubt, you have guessed that I am naming members of the *Lily* family. *Water Lily* is one of their greatest beauties. How she ever manages to be so fragrant, so lovely, living in mire and slime, only her Maker knows. She is our dearest Water Baby."

"Oh, please tell us of more Water Babies," begged the girls.

"There's a whole family of big water babies, that you know well," Jack broke in. "That is the *Cat-tail* family."

"How interesting!" cried Mary Frances. "I thought cats didn't like water."

Just then the silvery bell of the fairy clock struck the half-hour and Jack turned toward all the fairy flower folks who were present.

"Time's up! Thank you, kind friends," said he, "and now, after a dance, you may go."

With that, the sweetest music the girls had ever heard began to play, and the fairies began to dance, keeping time perfectly with their tiny feet.

"I'm afraid it's a dream, and that I'll wake up," whispered Eleanor to Mary Frances.

"So am I!" Mary Frances whispered back, and took hold of her little friend's hand.

Suddenly the music stopped and every fairy except Jack and Bet disappeared.

"It was so beautiful," said Mary Frances, still speaking in a whisper, "that we can never thank you."

"We're so glad you enjoyed our little surprise," Jack replied, "for it shows how you love us flowers. Now I want to tell you something about the way in which we grow, and how to feed us. You have a garden, and I feel certain you would like to hear about that."

"I've studied quite a little about seed-babies," replied Mary Frances. "I love the little things dearly."

"Good," cried Bet; "you'll love them even more after you've heard what Jack is going to tell you."

"Do water babies grow in the same way as other plant babies?" asked Mary Frances.

"In quite the same way," replied Jack. "I'm going to show you how the roots of plants take up the food needed, and how the leaves help make that food right for their digestion."

"Why, I thought—" began Eleanor.

"Yes?" asked Jack, expectantly.

"I thought that plants breathed with their leaves."

"Well, they do breathe with their leaves too, but they also breathe with their stem surface; or, in trees, with the surface of the trunk. In fact, they breathe all over."

"I know," said Eleanor, "that I've been taught to wash the leaves of house plants in order that the leaves might get air."

"Very wise, indeed," said Jack. "Air is very,

very important to the leaves, as you will see when I have told you about their way of growing."

Just then he took a tiny silver bugle from his shoulder and blew a long note.

Four little elves appeared. They were dressed in light brown and dark brown leaves. On their heads, each wore a cap of a different color. One was red; one was yellow; one, tan; and one, pink. They all stood "attention," looking at Jack.

"Bring in the magic tree," said Jack, and off ran the elves.

In a moment they returned, half carrying and half dragging a plant which looked like a tiny tree. It was growing in a glass tub, which, although small, seemed a heavy burden for the little fellows.

"Oh!" Mary Frances sprang up. "Oh, please, let me help," she begged as she stooped down to take it.

"Better not, better not," warned Jack. "That is a fairy tub and will go to pieces if you touch it."

By that time the little elves had it in place, and they smiled their thanks to Mary Frances as they

wiped the perspiration from their foreheads with tiny handkerchiefs made of colored Autumn leaves.

Jack jumped down from his pulpit.

"That will do, attendants," he said. "Thank you," and the little elves ran away.

"We have here," he continued, "a fairy view of the way in which plants grow. Come, Bet!"

With that, both the little fairies sprang to the top of the tub, and a wonderful thing happened.

The tub and the tree began to grow so fast that before you could count three, they were as high as the girls' knees, and before you could count seven, the top of the tree was even with Eleanor's head.

"That's tall enough, tree," cried Jack, and both tub and tree stopped growing.

"Can you see, young ladies," he asked as he bent over the side; "can you see the roots of the magic tree through the glass?"

The girls could see them plainly.

"Did you notice how they pushed their way through the stones and pieces of rock, and even moved them as they grew!"

"I did!" answered each of the girls.

"I thought it wonderful," continued Mary Frances, "but I supposed it was a fairy way of growing."

"No," Jack shook his head; "that is the way all plants grow, whether small or large, only they grow slowly. Notice the smallest roots. They are hollow and have very thin delicate coverings."

"You will see why in a minute," he went on, "but now I wish to call your attention to something else. In between the stones and sand you will notice decaying leaves and——"

"Humus!" cried Mary Frances jumping up in excitement.

"Good!" he said. "Humus soup is what the plants eat. The tiny roots draw it up through their thin walls. In the humus soup is not only decaying vegetable matter, but very tiny bits of mineral matter, too —like pepper and salt for the plant, maybe."

The girls laughed.

"Listen!" he went on earnestly; "for any plant to produce one pound of dry matter, the roots must take up from 300 to 500 pounds of water."

"Oh, now, I see why plants must have water," said Mary Frances. "Now, I understand why it is

so necessary to cultivate—to hold the moisture in the ground."

"To make humus soup," Eleanor added.

"Fine!" cried Jack, rubbing his tiny hands in glee. "It's splendid to teach such interested persons. It took human beings many, many years to find these things out. If only their eyes and ears had been open to us fairy folks, it wouldn't have taken so long."

"Now, human people, in growing garden plants, want to give them the best kinds of food," he continued. "So, after studying to find out what is in the soil that plants need most, they have gathered those things together from various places, and have made Commercial Fertilizers.

"They are to be had in a powdered form, and are very concentrated plant food. Nothing is better to use, however, than barnyard manures."

"One of the best commercial fertilizers is Nitrate of Soda." (See Chapter LVIII entitled, "Some Hints on Growing Vegetables.")

CHAPTER XLIII

How Plants Grow

"WHAT becomes, please, of the humus soup after the plant roots take it up?" asked Mary Frances thoughtfully.

"It's a wonderful story," Bouncing Bet spoke in her sweet voice. "You see, the plant food soup is carried up into the larger roots, into the sapwood of the tree, into the branches and into the leaves; and the leaves——"

"Give us shade!" Eleanor did not realize that she had interrupted.

"They do," smiled Bet. "But that is not their work."

"Oh, do leaves work?" Eleanor was surprised.

"They work very, very hard," Bet replied. "They do such wonderful work that a leaf has been called a leaf factory, or a leaf-mill."

"You think that leaves do not resemble the factories or mills you have seen," went on the fairy. "It is not in appearance that they resemble mills and

factories, but in the work they do; for they manufacture starch. I suppose there is really no starch in the whole world that leaves have not made."

"Oh," exclaimed Mary Frances; "even the starch in our dresses—is that made by leaves?"

"Yes," Bet smiled, "even that; and the starch in your bread and the——"

"Tell them the story, Bet," said Jack, who was much interested.

"All right," answered the little fairy, turning to pick a leaf from the magic tree. "Please do not interrupt, and I will tell you about—

The Leaf-Mill

Nothing can grow without the right kind of food.

Plants cannot use the "plant-food soup," just as it is taken up by the roots, to make new growth.

The leaves must first turn the liquid food into *starch*, which is the right kind of food for the plant.

A leaf has been called a leaf-mill, because it has many tiny grinding stones.

These tiny grinding stones are the green grains in the cells which form the leaf. They are called *chlor-o-phyll* bodies.

The leaf-mill grinding stones are turned by sunshine power. Without sunshine they cannot work.

How Plants Grow

By the leaf-mill grinding stones, a gas from the air (carbonic acid gas) is mixed with the plant food soup sent up by the plant's roots, and starch is formed.

While doing the work of manufacturing starch, the leaf-mill throws off into the air another gas, called oxygen. Oxygen is needed by all animals; carbonic acid gas (or carbon dioxide) is needed by all plants whose leaves make starch.

But even the starch must be changed before the plant can use it to make new growth. It must be made into sugar!

So the leaves act as stomachs, and digest the starch they have made for the plant's use. In them, in some wonderful way, the starch is changed into sugar, and some mineral matter from the humus soup is mixed with the sugar. This combination forms a perfect food, ready for the plant to make into new growth.

"Isn't it a wonderful story?" asked Bouncing Bet, as she finished speaking.

"It's the most surprising garden story I've yet heard," declared Mary Frances.

"I'll never, never think of leaves again as just 'for shade,'" declared Eleanor. "But I'm glad they do give shade," she added.

"Trees give a great deal of shade," said Bet, "because they expose as large a surface of leaves as possible to the sun. On a large tree, nearly half

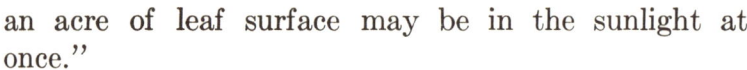

an acre of leaf surface may be in the sunlight at once."

"And the sunlight turns the grinding-stones of the leaf-mill," said Mary Frances softly.

"And they make food for the tree," Eleanor whispered.

"Sometimes a plant does not need for immediate use all the food the leaves have made," Bet continued, "so it stores it away for future use: sometimes, in roots; sometimes, in leaves; sometimes in other parts of the plant—as in the grains of wheat."

"I wonder how the storage places look," said Eleanor.

Bet laughed. "You've often seen some of them," she said. "When you eat turnips and beets, you are eating the food stored in the roots of these plants. When you use onions, you are using food stored in leaves."

Mary Frances thought the fairy had made a mistake, and Bet seemed to read her thought.

"Oh, no," she laughed, "I'm not mistaken. You see, the bulb of the onion is made up of the thickened

How Plants Grow

lower ends of the leaves, the top green parts of which have dried off."

"It is interesting," she went on, "to see how quickly the plants which have stored food begin to grow when put into the warm place. It is because of this fact that bulbous flowers are the first to bloom in the Spring. They do not have to make food to begin to grow, for their food is ready for use, and just a little warmth and moisture will start them."

"Oh, I see why crocuses, and hyacinths, and tulips bloom so early," said Mary Frances.

"Yes," nodded Bet, "and it is an interesting experiment to make a carrot hanging basket. Cut the top off a large carrot and scoop out a hollow. Fill the hollow with water, and hang the carrot in a warm room. The beautiful green leaves will soon grow, using the material stored in the root for food."

Just at this point, Jack stepped forward.

"I'm sorry," said he, "to interrupt such an interesting lesson, but as we have so little time, by your leave, Bet, I will commence my story about some of our most peculiar relatives—if the young ladies would njoy hearing about them."

CHAPTER XLIV

A Wicked Innkeeper

"INDEED, we would enjoy hearing about them," declared both the girls.

"Before I begin to tell you about our peculiar relatives, some of which kill, some of which steal——"

"Oh!" gasped Eleanor.

"Oh!" muttered Mary Frances.

Just at that moment out of the bushes ran the tiniest, littlest bit of a dog that ever lived.

At first the girls didn't see him, he was so small.

He ran right to Jack, and put a tiny bit of paper in his hand.

"For pity's sake, Bet," Jack exclaimed, "I forgot to send back the magic tree and here's the Queen's messenger with a command from Her Majesty! Oh, oh, oh!"

"Will it be all right if he sends it back immediately?" Bet asked of the tiny dog, whose head she was patting.

A Wicked Innkeeper

The dog wagged his tiny tail and stood on his hind legs. Bet bent her ear to his mouth.

"It will be all right," she said aloud, "if you return it this minute."

"Attendants!" shouted Jack. "Attendants!"

Out ran the tiny elves.

"Take back the magic tree!" commanded Jack, "and apologize to Her Majesty for keeping it over time."

He took a little box out of his pocket. Opening it, he shook out a shining powder, and before the girls could see how it came about, the tiny tree just as they first saw it, growing in the little tub, was before them. The elves sprang to its sides. The little dog ran on before; and elves, dog and tree vanished from sight.

"I wouldn't have had it late for anything!" Jack spoke sadly.

"You were teaching us so kindly," said Mary Frances; "that was the reason you forgot. Oh, I'm so sorry."

"If you appreciate my lesson so much," Jack said, smiling, "the Queen won't mind at all."

"How glad we are!" cried the girls.

"And now," Jack went on happily, as Bet danced around; "now, I will begin a story about one cousin—

A Wicked Innkeeper

As you know, plants hang out signs to attract Mrs. Bee and Mrs. Butterfly and other insects to the feast they have spread—the pollen and the nectar feast. The signs are the attractive colors of the flowers.

One flower that hangs out a very pretty little white sign is the Sundew. The sign seems to say to the passing fly or gnat, "Come, rest upon one of my pretty, sparkling leaves, and take a meal at my pretty white blossom-table. Stop at Sundew Inn."

The little fly is charmed with the cordial invitation, and lights down upon one of the leaves which glisten all day with a substance that looks like dew.

In a moment, he knows his mistake, for the sparkling drops are a sticky fluid which holds the little fellow fast, and the tiny hairs on the leaf's surface bite him like so many mosquitoes!

The leaf rolls up a little, and more of the sticky fluid pours upon him. It is the digestive fluid of the plant. The wicked Sundew Innkeeper is eating up his guest!

"Just like the Spider and Fly in the old story," said Mary Frances, repeating the lines:

A Wicked Innkeeper

" 'Will you walk into my parlor?'
Said the spider to the fly,
'Tis the prettiest little parlor
That ever you did spy.' "

"Exactly!" agreed Jack. "The sundew invites the fly for the same reason that the spider does—because it needs it for food."

"Oh," shuddered Eleanor, "do plants eat animals?"

"Not if they can help it," replied Jack. "Many, many years ago, when the sundew's great-great-great-great-grandparents were unable to find the kind of food they needed, they developed this method of getting nitrogenous food, to keep from starving."

"Oh, I see," said Mary Frances, looking wise.

"Is the sundew the only plant which eats insects?" asked Eleanor; "and does it grow around here?"

"It grows in every section of this country," replied Jack, "and also in Europe and Asia."

"The Pitcher Plant, which is found in soggy marshes, eats insects, too," he went on; "only it manages in a different way. Its leaves are shaped like vases or pitchers, and are usually half filled with

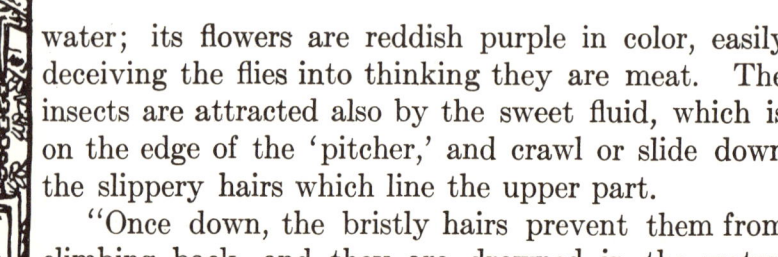

water; its flowers are reddish purple in color, easily deceiving the flies into thinking they are meat. The insects are attracted also by the sweet fluid, which is on the edge of the 'pitcher,' and crawl or slide down the slippery hairs which line the upper part.

"Once down, the bristly hairs prevent them from climbing back, and they are drowned in the water. The plant eats the soup which their bodies make. The form of Pitcher Plant which grows in the western states has vases large enough to drown small birds and field mice."

"It isn't a pretty story," commented Mary Frances.

"Not a bit," agreed Eleanor.

"It would make us ashamed, wouldn't it, Jack," Bouncing Bet was speaking, "if anybody but Mother Nature had invented that way of keeping things moving?"

"She must have had good reason," replied Jack.

CHAPTER XLV

Uninvited Guests

"So much, then, for the disrespectable murderer branch of the family," he continued. "Now I will tell you about some of our thieves We don't approve of them any more than you would approve of a cousin who turned out to be a thief, but—well, I shall begin by telling you about—

Dodder

No plant would invite such a miserable pauper as a visitor. It's worse than any beggar you have ever known, for a beggar at least digests his own food.

Not so with dodder. It is too lazy to do even that! It has therefore, no leaves. It doesn't need them. It starts out as an honest plant baby, but soon "goes wrong," reaching out long tendrils by which it takes hold of any convenient plant neighbor. It sends little leg-like suckers down into the stem of this plant neighbor. It lets go of the earth with its roots, and drinks the life-blood, or sap, of its host, the plant on which it has seized hold.

The disgracefully lazy dodder does no work at all except to make flowers and seeds. The flowers are tiny, star-shaped, of a

yellowish, greenish or white color, and each flower makes four seeds to go on to make more thieving plant babies!

"Isn't it disgraceful!" exclaimed Bet. "Jack and I never want to associate with plants that murder and steal——"

"Not if we can help it," said Jack, "we don't."

"You'll be sorry," he went on, "to learn that Indian pipes, too, are uninvited guests, living on food in other plant roots."

"Oh," said Mary Frances regretfully. "I always thought them so pretty!"

"Well, they are pretty, and dodder, even, is pretty in a way, because of its yellow color, but both are—

Parasite Plants

Parasite means "eating at another's table."

Parasite plants are those which fasten upon other plants and steal their food.

Real parasite plants lack all green color, for since they steal food already digested, what need have they for green matter (chlor-o-phyll) by means of which a plant digests its food?

There are also some half parasites, which, while living partially upon stolen food, get some food for themselves.

Uninvited Guests 269

The pretty waxy Christmas mistletoe is a half parasite. You notice that it has some green coloring or chlor-o-phyll, which it uses to digest the nourishment it gathers from the air.

"My," exclaimed Eleanor, "I'm glad it doesn't steal all its food. That shows it's trying to help itself. It isn't such a 'piggy' as some plants!"

"Oh, not every parasite plant destroys the plant whose food it takes. Not very long ago, human beings found out that the very tiny parasite plants which fasten themselves to peas and beans and other similar plants (called Legumens) are very beneficial to them. They do steal some predigested food, but in return they give to them a much more valuable food, which they have taken from the air. This valuable food is nitrogen.

For this reason, these parasitic plants, or nitrogerms, have been gathered and grown, and are now sold under the name of 'Cultures for Legumens.' When applied to peas, beans, clover, etc., they cause them to grow very rapidly, and give very abundant crops."

"How wonderful!" said Mary Frances.

Just then the fairy clock chimed four.

CHAPTER XLVI

How Seed Babies Travel

"COME," cried Bouncing Bet. "Now, I am going to tell you a wonderful, true fairy story. You never realized, did you, that plants travel? I mean that they travel without the help of human beings."

"No," the girls shook their heads.

"You can't deny that they spread from place to place, can you?" asked Bet.

"Indeed, I can't," said Mary Frances; "the dandelions have spread all over our land within a short time."

"And I'll tell you how they did it," Bet went on. "But first I'll tell you—

Why Plants Travel

If the seeds of a plant always fell on ground nearby, the space would soon become choked up, and the new seed babies would have no chance to live; so, many plants have been provided means of sending their seed babies a long distance from the mother

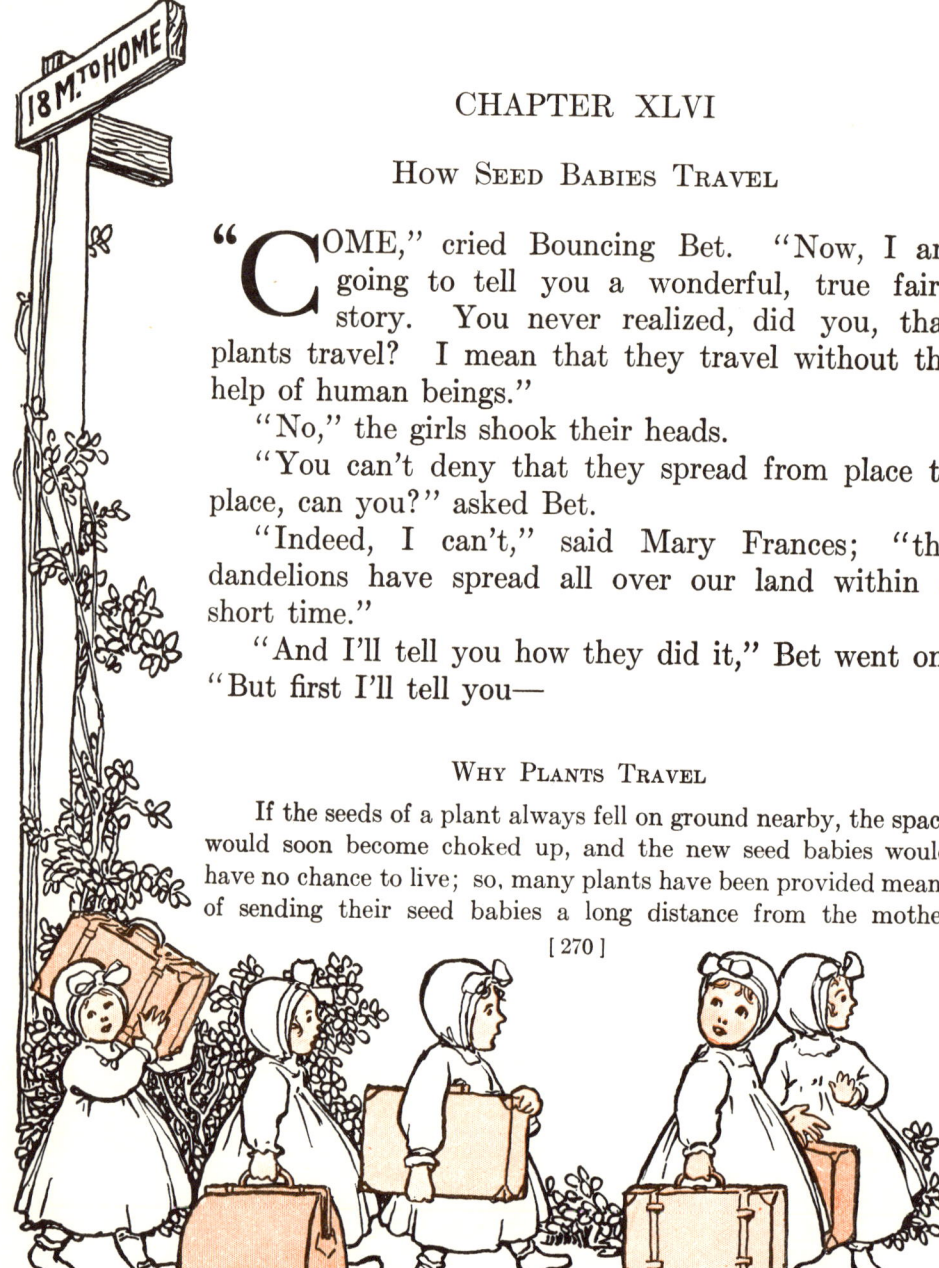

How Seed Babies Travel

plant, and in this way they have spread or traveled from place to place, until some cover very large areas.

How Plants Travel

Seed Pods with Burry Coats

Did you ever think, when you pick "beggar lice" and "sand burrs" off your clothing and throw them down on the ground, that you are helping the plant mother do just what she wanted you to do with her seed baby?

She put "stickers" all over the coat of her seed baby so that it might catch hold of your dress, or of the fur of your doggie, or your cow, and be dropped in a new place where the seed baby could grow with better chances than at home near her.

When you make burr baskets out of the sticky burdock seeds, unless you burn them, you are helping the burdocks to travel.

Pods which Shoot Seeds

The mother plants of the "spider plant," and of the pansy, and of the violet send their seed babies to new homes by using seed pods which burst open and shoot the seeds far and wide in all directions.

Tumble Weeds

Some mother plants actually carry their seed babies to new places.

The "tumble weeds" of the West dry up in Autumn, and are

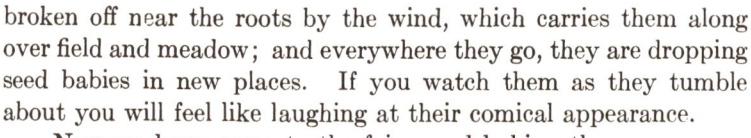

broken off near the roots by the wind, which carries them along over field and meadow; and everywhere they go, they are dropping seed babies in new places. If you watch them as they tumble about you will feel like laughing at their comical appearance.

Now we have come to the fairy seed babies, the—

Seed Babies with Wings

You've seen them often—seed babies flying about on the wings which their plant-mother gave them. Sometimes you have helped them start to fly.

Oh, yes, you have.

Don't you remember when you pulled the fluffy head off a dandelion, and blew it to "see what time it was?"

Of course you didn't know it, but you sent scores of dandelion seed babies floating off in the air on their fairy wings. Perhaps the wind took one up where you left off blowing, and landed it such a distance away from its old home that it might have seemed like hundreds of miles to the little thing.

Milk-weed seed babies fastened to their beautiful silky down, which is so light it floats along like a fairy's feather, actually travel on the "wings of the wind."

Some trees, too, give their seed babies wings. Haven't the winged seeds of the maple fooled you into thinking they were birds or insects of some kind? It has amused you, too, to notice how far the wings of these seed babies have carried them on the wind.

"Haven't the plant mothers provided wonderfully for their seed babies' welfare!" exclaimed Mary Frances.

"Yes," replied Bet; "back of the plant mother is another mother—Mother Nature. Oh, but she is wise!"

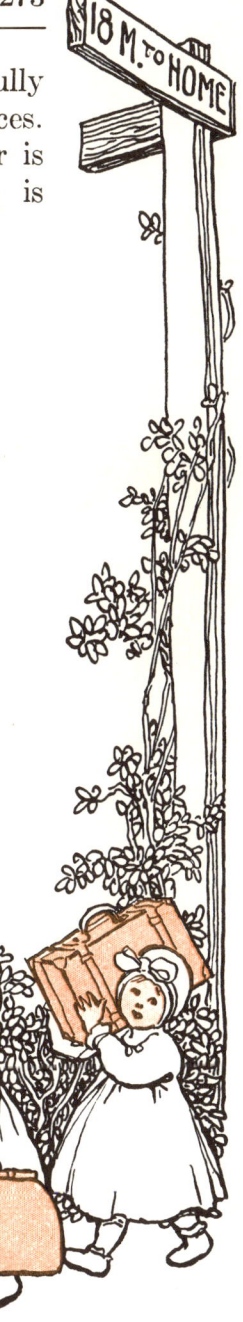

CHAPTER XLVII

Have a Seat on a Toad Stool

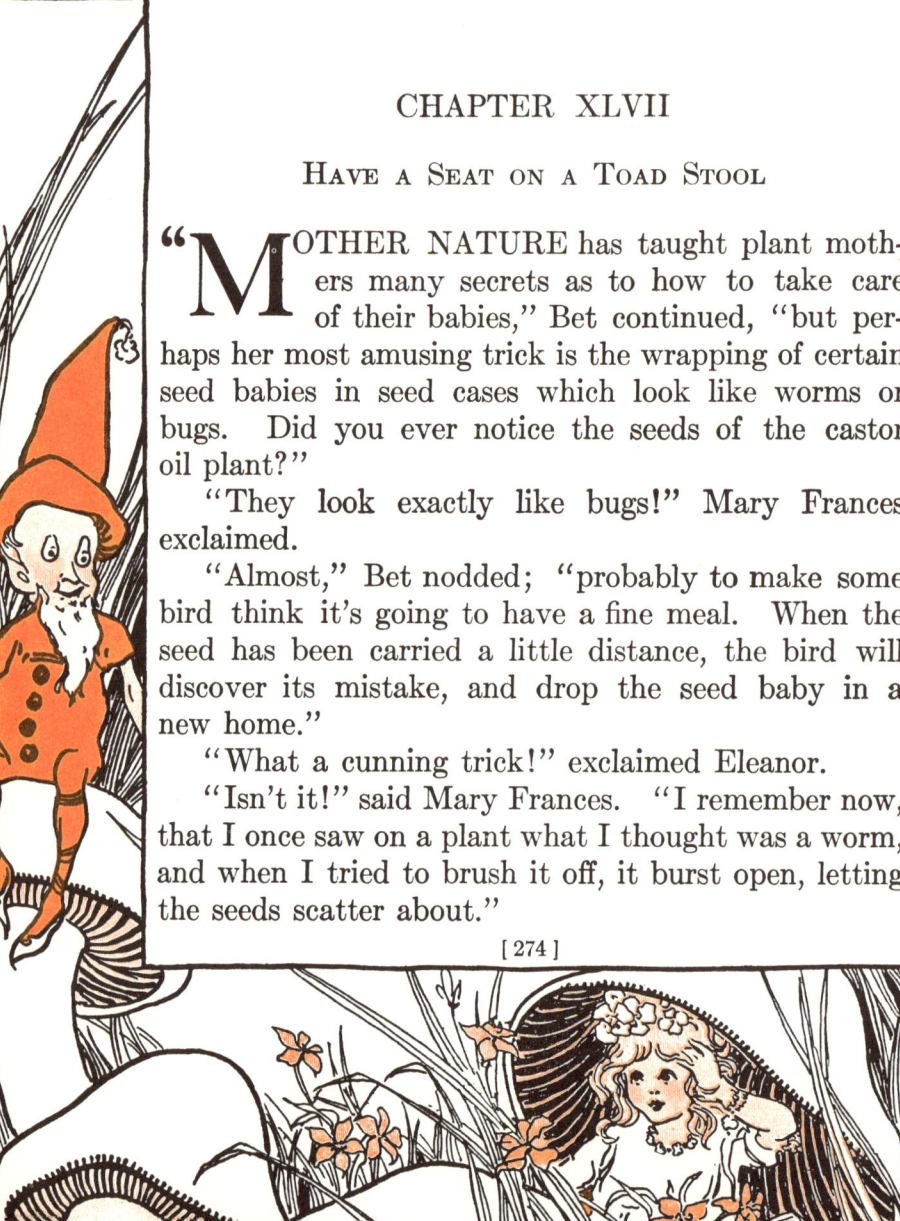

"MOTHER NATURE has taught plant mothers many secrets as to how to take care of their babies," Bet continued, "but perhaps her most amusing trick is the wrapping of certain seed babies in seed cases which look like worms or bugs. Did you ever notice the seeds of the castor oil plant?"

"They look exactly like bugs!" Mary Frances exclaimed.

"Almost," Bet nodded; "probably to make some bird think it's going to have a fine meal. When the seed has been carried a little distance, the bird will discover its mistake, and drop the seed baby in a new home."

"What a cunning trick!" exclaimed Eleanor.

"Isn't it!" said Mary Frances. "I remember now, that I once saw on a plant what I thought was a worm, and when I tried to brush it off, it burst open, letting the seeds scatter about."

Have a Seat on a Toad Stool

"I wonder if that wasn't this plant?" Bet asked as she held up a dried flower head, out of which a worm seemed to be crawling.

"That's it!" cried Mary Frances. "What is the plant called, please?"

"It has a very long name," Bouncing Bet replied; "too long for you to remember, I fear; but it means a 'coiled worm,' and shows how perfectly one plant mother has performed this comical trick."

"I suspect all plant mothers have some trick," Mary Frances ventured.

"That leads me to tell you about one kind of plants we've not yet mentioned.

They are the—

Plants without Flowers

If plants have no flowers, you will ask, how can the new baby plants grow? Can there be seed babies without flowers?

No, flowerless plants do not bear seeds, but they do have plant babies, otherwise we would not have ferns, mushrooms, and many other important plants.

The plant babies of flowerless plants come from spores, not seeds.

Did you ever gather Christmas ferns? They are the ones

which cheer you so with their beautiful green color in the woods when so many other things are asleep in winter.

On the back of the fern leaves, perhaps you have noticed little brown rusty-looking spots.

In these spots or spore-cases are the spores. When the spore cases are ripe, they burst open and throw out the spores which look like a fine dust.

Each grain of this dust must live in a moist, warm place, and pass through several changes before a baby fern can grow.

Mosses grow in a similar way. So, also, do—

Mushrooms or Toad Stools

Mushrooms are flowerless plants, and they do not grow from seeds, but from spores.

The spores fall from the pretty gills on the under side of the umbrella part of the plant.

Of course, since they have no green color, you know that mushrooms do not make their own food. They, like most other—

Fungi,

live on dead vegetable matter.

Mushrooms grow by means of thread-like feeders which they send down into the dead material which they use.

It is a good thing that fungi use dead trees and leaves and other dead matter for food; otherwise, these things would keep on piling up!

Have a Seat on a Toad Stool

I wish to tell you of one kind of fungus, though, which lives on living material in trees. It is called the—

Bracket Fungus

Perhaps you have thought the bracket-like shelves you have seen on some tree, pretty.

You did not know, then, that some spores of the bracket fungi had fastened into a wound in the bark, and had sent long threads down into the living part of the tree.

The poor tree cannot help itself, and after a while it will die of starvation because the bracket fungi have used up all its food material.

So do be careful never to injure the bark of a tree; for wherever it is torn, it leaves an open wound—just as when you scratch your finger or your arm.

There are other fungi which you've seen oftener than toad stools. They are—

Molds

You've often see the mold which comes on bread which has been left in a rather dark, warm, moist place.

The mold comes from the thousands of germs in the dust in air. These germs settle down and use anything possible for food, and send out spore-dust to make more germs.

While they are growing and making spore cases, they appear as molds and mildews.

The germs in the dust are too tiny to be seen without a microscope, and their near relatives—

Bacteria

are about the tiniest of living things.

They grow everywhere. Some do us harm and some benefit us wonderfully.

Cheese is made out of milk by one of the good kind; another kind makes vinegar; some other kinds fasten themselves to the inside of our mouths and bodies, bringing disease, like typhoid fever and consumption.

When we keep our bodies and mouths and teeth clean, we help our blood to destroy such bad bacteria.

Sunlight destroys bad germs.

Fresh air destroys bad germs. You should have plenty of fresh air both day and night.

"Pshaw," said Jack, as Bet finished speaking; "toad stools are meant for fairies to sit on, and mushrooms for human beings to eat. What kind of nonsense are you trying to teach, anyhow, Bet?"

The girls laughed, for they saw Jack wink as he spoke.

"Come," said he, "you've been standing too long—come, have a seat on a toad stool?"

HAVE A SEAT ON A TOAD STOOL   279

With that he ran toward a beautiful white mushroom, and Bet followed.

When they were seated, Mary Frances asked:

"What is the difference between a mushroom and a toad stool?"

"Well," Jack replied, "I guess there isn't really any difference, although some people think that toad stools, if eaten, poison people and that mushrooms are harmless, but some mushrooms are very poisonous, so do not try to use any you gather, unless some grown people know them to be harmless, for some of the most beautiful would kill you the most quickly."

"I've eaten mushrooms," said Eleanor, "but they were canned ones."

"Oh, they are safe enough," Bet smiled.

Then the fairy clock struck the half-hour.

CHAPTER XLVIII

Some Ways to Rid of Weeds

"FOUR-THIRTY!" exclaimed Jack, "and we have only until five o'clock."

"My, you'll have to talk fast," said Bouncing Bet, "in order to tell all you want to."

"One quarter of all I want to, you mean, Bet," Jack replied.

"I'm afraid my brother and father and mother will come look for us," said Mary Frances.

"No," Bet shook her head, "not until five o'clock."

"I suppose fairies know," Eleanor whispered.

Jack began to talk rapidly:

WEEDS

To the little plant baby which you love and wish to grow, weeds are like terribly hungry beasts who steal their food, and choke them to death, and say:

"Get out of here! I'm a piggy-wig, and I want everything myself!"

So unless you want your favorite plants to die, you will kill the weeds in your garden.

Some Ways to Rid of Weeds

Even if some of your plants do live through the fight, they are weak and poor from the lack of food, and the hard work they have been through.

Someone has said that weeds are plants that are not wanted, and people often find that the less they are wanted, the harder it is to get rid of them.

You see, most weeds have grown in spite of everything, and have accommodated themselves to such unpleasant surroundings that when they find themselves in splendid surroundings, as in your garden soil, they begin to grow 'with a vengeance.'"

"I know!" Mary Frances laughed.

"Well, we fairy folk want to help you as much as possible with your garden. I am going to tell you about—

Some Ways to Rid of Weeds

Of course, one of the best ways is to pull the weeds, never allowing them to go to seed. That's best for annual kinds.

But the perennial kind must have the roots destroyed, so deep digging or ploughing in the Fall is a great help.

Cleaning off the growth and burning it in the Fall kills many seeds which might "winter over," and come up in the Spring.

Salt is often used to kill grass in paths and garden walks.

Some of the commonest weeds found in the garden are—

Lamb's-quarters, or *Pigweed*, which is usually very unwelcome in the garden, but which some people use for "greens."

ROMAN WORMWOOD

BEGGAR-TICKS

Roman Wormwood, or *Hogweed,* which, from its name, you can see is troublesome everywhere.

Beggar-ticks, or *Stick tights.* I guess you know them—

Their seed babies, I mean. Didn't you get them all over your dresses and stockings one day in the woods?

Smartweed and *Knotweed* and *Lady's Thumb* all resemble each other in appearance.

Plantain and *Rat Tails* (Rib Grass, English Plantain) are cousins in the same family.

Pepper Grass and *Shepherd's Purse* are cousins, too, and both belong to the Mustard family. You've often eaten pepper grass seeds, haven't you?

Field Laurel, or *Sour Grass,* has leaves with a pleasantly sour flavor.

"Excuse me," said Mary Frances, as Jack paused, "but you didn't mention that if you 'cultivate' your garden, it will kill weeds."

"I'm so glad you said that!" Jack replied. "It is

Some Ways to Rid of Weeds

the best way to keep weeds out of your garden; but I was speaking of where they had 'gotten a start.'"

"They're hard to pull sometimes," remarked Eleanor. "I'll tell you how I know. We have just the tiniest lawn, and father gives me an ice-cream cone for pulling five cents' worth of weeds."

"Isn't that lovely of him!" Jack exclaimed.

"Sometimes," he went on, "it is not only for the sake of the plants you want to have grow that you destroy the weeds, but to protect yourself. For instance, you wish to kill out all poisonous plants; such as—

Poison Ivy

The leaves of poison ivy, if touched, will provoke a painful, poisonous rash on the skin of most people. This is caused by the irritating, acrid juice in the leaves. This juice probably protects the plant—for instance, no cattle will enjoy eating it.

Thousands of cases of ivy poison could be avoided if everyone knew the plant.

Remember, the poison ivy vine

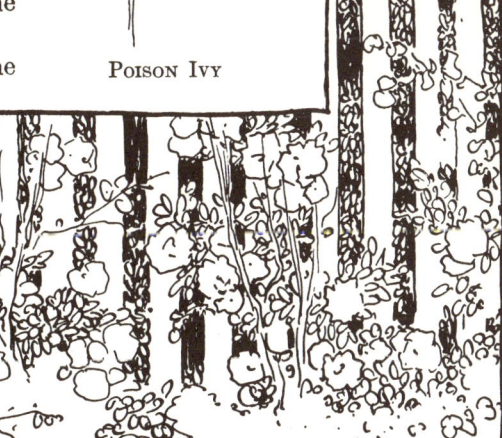

Poison Ivy

has three leaves on a stem, while its harmless and beautiful cousin, Virginia Creeper, which resembles it so much, has five leaves on a stem.

Jack stepped forward and showed the girls the difference in the leaves, just as they are pictured here.

They examined them carefully.

"I think I'll never mistake poison ivy for that other plant," said Eleanor.

"I hope not," Bet chimed in, "for I am so fond of—

Virginia Creeper

This plant is a native of America, growing everywhere from Canada southward even to Cuba. It makes a charming decorative vine on wall and fence.

It will soon repay one for the trouble of carrying a root home from the woods, for it easily takes root in a new place, and everyone is delighted with its magnificent brilliant red foliage in the Autumn.

"That sounds like a book, Bet," exclaimed Jack. "I think the most interesting thing about Virginia Creeper is the tiny hand-like 'clingers' with which it holds on to the wall or fence."

Some Ways to Rid of Weeds

"I was going to tell that, Mr. Jack," Bet replied; "but, never mind, I want to tell about—

Some Ways in Which Plants Protect Themselves

You remember that I told you that the "velvet" fur of the great mullein keeps animals from eating the leaves?

Well, perhaps you've never thought of it, but the prickles of the rose and blackberry and the thorns of some trees prevent their being destroyed many and many a time.

"Indeed, I know," laughed Mary Frances. "No one will ever see me try to pick a wild cactus!"

"Or nettles?" asked Jack, pretending to pick splinters from his hand.

"I hope your garden never has more weeds than we saw when we were over there in the moonlight last evening," he went on.

"Why, were you in my garden?" Mary Frances was amazed.

"It looked splendid," beamed Bet.

"We will come often," Jack added, "and if we never see more weeds than last evening, you'll be growing wonderful vegetables and flowers."

"Feather Flop—" Mary Frances began, then

she thought perhaps she'd better not mention the rooster.

"It's about time to say good-bye," Bet said, "but you need not feel sorry because we will—

>Come in the moonlight
>To see how your garden grows."

CHAPTER XLIX

Queen's Lace Trims Well

"How lovely that will be, Mary Frances!" exclaimed Eleanor.

"I shall come out some evening to see you, dear fairy folks," said Mary Frances, "even if you cannot talk with me. Maybe Eleanor will come, too."

"I don't believe you'll know us when you see us. I might come as Jack Frost," Jack answered.

"And I might seem a Luna moth," said Bouncing Bet. "But you'll know we are interested and are trying to help you."

"Come," said Jack, "we have a gift for you. Here is a package of wild flower seeds which we hope you will plant."

"Thank you, oh, thank you!" Both the girls were delighted.

"There's only one condition with our gift; you must never tell anyone about us! If you do, not a seed will grow."

"Oh!" The tears came into Mary Frances' eyes. "Not Mother?" she asked.

"Would the Queen let them tell her mother?" Jack turned to Bet.

"Yes," said Bet, "because her mother believes in fairies."

"Indeed she does!" Mary Frances was enthusiastic. "She knows all about the Cooking People."

"Yes," both Bet and Jack nodded.

"The Thimble People."

They nodded again.

"And the Doll People."

The Queen of All Fairies sent them, you know," said Jack to Bet.

"Of course," Bet replied.

"Now for my party dress," she suddenly sang out, and with "Excuse me!" ran away.

When she came back she was dressed in the queen's lace gown, only it was more gorgeous than before, for it sparkled with a thousand jewels.

She picked up her dainty pink skirt and began to dance.

"Isn't my dress pretty?" she asked.

"Queen's lace trims well," she laughed. "Come, Jack!" And together they danced in mid-air, treading on nothing.

"Good-bye, dear girls," they sang. "Good-bye, little gardeners! Good luck! Remember the fairies will be watching your gardens!"

Just then Mary Frances noticed a big soap bubble floating toward the little dancers. Nearer and nearer it came, and stopped in front of them.

Jack opened a door in the soap bubble, and in they stepped.

"Good-bye," cried Bouncing Bet, as Jack closed the door.

"Good-bye!" cried the girls. "Good-bye, kind, lovely fairy folks!"

Jack and Bet threw kisses to them until the bubble floated out of sight over the tops of the trees.

* * * * * * *

"Oh, Mary Frances," cried Eleanor after a short silence. "Oh, it was the most wonderful thing that ever happened to me!"

"Well, so this is where you girls were hiding!" Billy's voice made both the girls jump. "My, you

gave me a scare! Not a bit of lunch tasted, and not a sign of you!"

"Oh, Billy," exclaimed Mary Frances, "how you startled me! How's Mother? Could she—could she come?"

"Mother's all right," said Billy, "only Father thought best for her not to try to come, and sent me for you girls—Hello! I see you've been gathering wild flowers."

He had spied the flowers that Jack and Bet had let them gather.

"Gee! aren't they beauties! Did you find them near here? I don't wonder you forgot your lunch!"

"Oh, Billy—that reminds me—I'm awfully hungry!" Mary Frances said, "and I imagine Eleanor is, too."

"I'm—I am hungry," Eleanor spoke as in a dream.

"Well, then, since there are no fairies to bring the lunch baskets to us, let's go to the lunch baskets," said Billy, picking up the bunches of flowers and leading the way.

"You'll need a pail to put these flowers in water," he said.

When he spoke of fairies, Mary Frances put her fingers to her lips. Eleanor smiled and nodded.

"Let's spread supper!" said Billy.

"That will make us late getting home, I fear," Mary Frances parleyed.

"No, sir-ee!" Billy smiled, "Father's going to drive over for us!"

"Oh, isn't that fine!" cried the girls, opening the baskets.

They ate as only hungry children can eat.

"Here comes Father—just in time for dessert," cried Billy suddenly, and all ran to meet him.

They reached home before dark, and were welcomed by a smiling mother.

"Our wild flower picnic was a success after all," Mary Frances said, kissing her and giving her the beautiful flowers.

CHAPTER L

The Wild Flower Garden

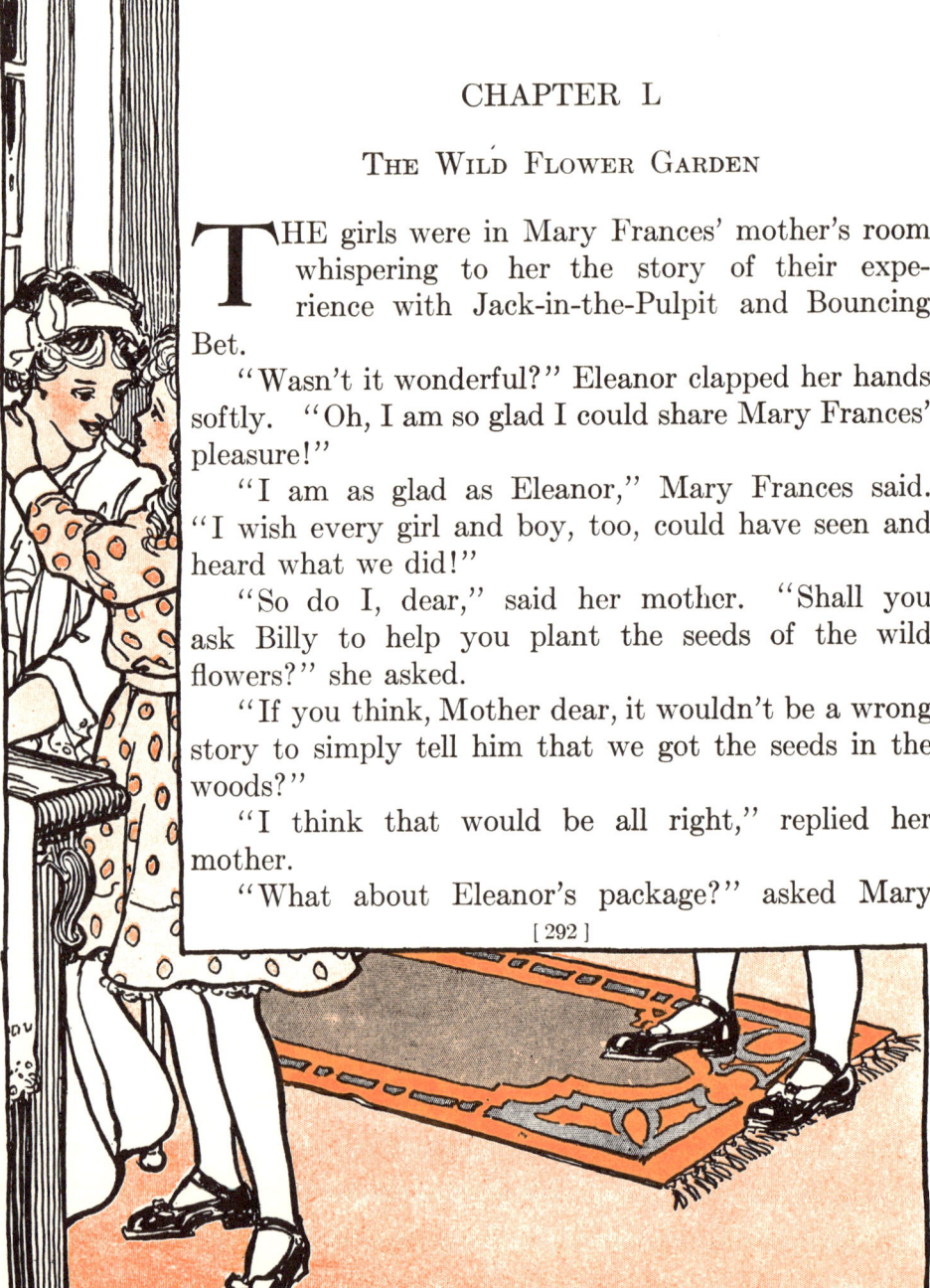

THE girls were in Mary Frances' mother's room whispering to her the story of their experience with Jack-in-the-Pulpit and Bouncing Bet.

"Wasn't it wonderful?" Eleanor clapped her hands softly. "Oh, I am so glad I could share Mary Frances' pleasure!"

"I am as glad as Eleanor," Mary Frances said. "I wish every girl and boy, too, could have seen and heard what we did!"

"So do I, dear," said her mother. "Shall you ask Billy to help you plant the seeds of the wild flowers?" she asked.

"If you think, Mother dear, it wouldn't be a wrong story to simply tell him that we got the seeds in the woods?"

"I think that would be all right," replied her mother.

"What about Eleanor's package?" asked Mary

Frances. "Shall she keep it until she goes home to plant in her own garden?"

Her mother hesitated. "I may as well tell you, girls. I have a wonderful surprise for you, myself."

"Oh, do tell us!" they cried.

"Sit down, then," she said, and they took their low chairs to her knee.

"This is my secret. Our dear old friend, Eleanor's father, has to go away on business—maybe he will be gone a year—and Eleanor is to come live with us."

"Oh, how lovely!" cried Mary Frances, throwing her arms about her friend's neck and kissing her.

Tears came into Eleanor's eyes.

"I'm so glad," she said. "I shall miss Father terribly, but if you and Mary Frances' father just adopt me for a while, it will be something like having my own dear father and mother. What about Bob? Do you know where he is to be?"

"Yes, dear child," smiled Mary Frances' mother; "that is another pleasant surprise. Bob is to go away to school with Billy."

"Oh, will he study gardening?" cried Eleanor.

"He will, if he wishes, your father said."

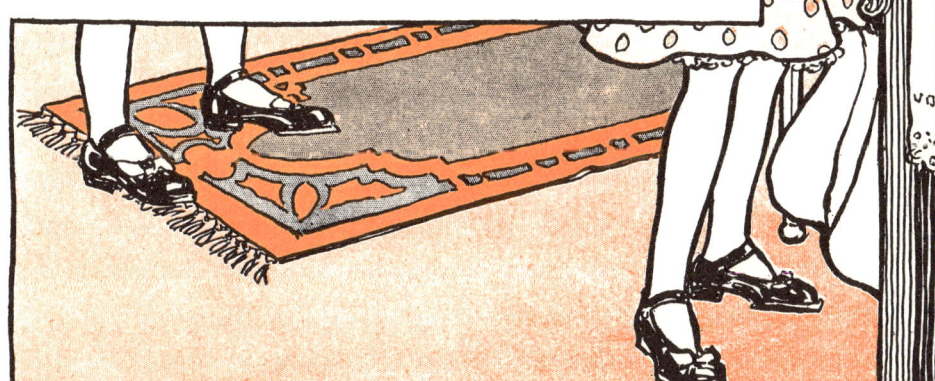

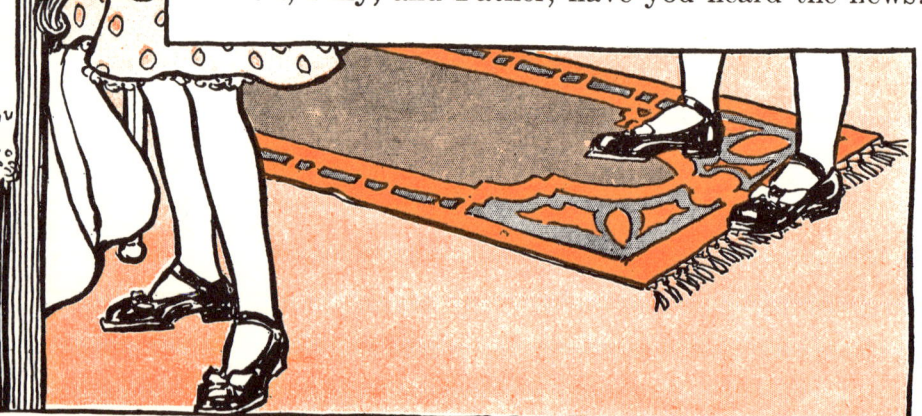

"Isn't that grand!" Eleanor was enthusiastic—then her face suddenly clouded.

"When will Father go?" she asked.

"Not until the middle of September, Eleanor. He and Bob are to come visit us the first of the month, and you are to be with us from now on."

"You're to be my sister!" Mary Frances laughed.

"And you may call me Mother, if you wish, dear," added Mary Frances' mother.

"Oh, it seems so cozy and lovely!" sighed the little girl.

"Well, now, my girlies, since the secrets are told, why not get Billy to help you plant the wild flower seeds?"

"All right!" they cried, jumping up and kissing her before they ran away.

"Oh, Billy! Billy!" they shouted as they saw him in the garden.

"Here come 'our twins'," laughed Billy, turning toward his father. "I wonder what's up."

"Hello, girls," he answered as they came near. "What can we do for you?"

"Oh, Billy, and Father, have you heard the news?

THE WILD FLOWER GARDEN

Of course you have! Eleanor is to be my sister, and yours, Billy, and she's to call Father, Father; and Mother, Mother; aren't you, dear?" said Mary Frances, kissing Eleanor, who smiled shyly.

"Whew!" exclaimed Billy. "Stop for breath, Mary Frances, can't you? If Nell were as bad as you——"

"Oh, Billy!" chided Eleanor.

"I guess all that Billy means to say," interposed his father, "is that we're all glad that such a good little girl is to come live with us."

"You'll have to live up to that reputation, young lady," laughed Billy.

"And now," Mary Frances produced the packages of wild flower seeds, "we want our brother to help us plant seeds."

"What kind of seeds are they?" questioned her father.

"Where did you get them?" asked Billy.

"We got them in the woods where we gathered the wild flowers," answered Mary Frances.

"No wonder I couldn't find you," Billy commented. "Where do you think they'd better be planted, Father?"

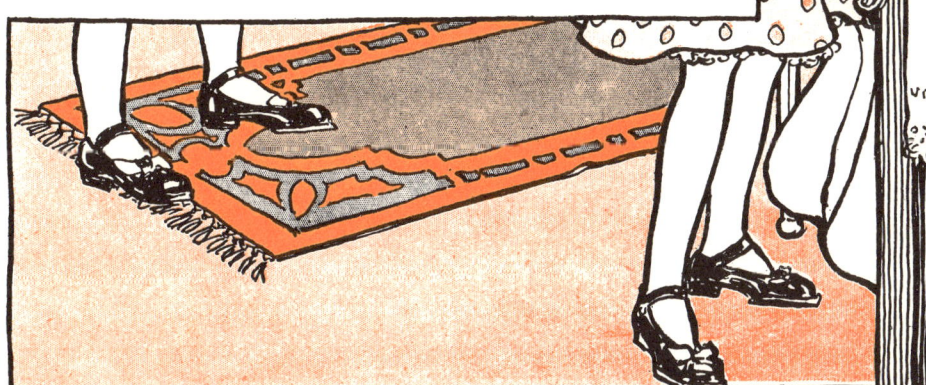

"Not near a garden of cultivated flowers," said his father.

"No," Billy remarked, "for we learned that the cross-fertilization or a mixture of pollen might bring very poor flowers in the garden if wild ones were planted too near, and might also fill it up with weeds."

"Down in this corner would be a good place, it seems to me," said their father, leading the way.

"I'll be with you as soon as I get my spade and fork," called Billy.

Everybody helped, and the bed was soon planted.

"I know they'll all grow for Jack——" Eleanor began.

Mary Frances pinched her arm, and Eleanor just caught herself in time.

"For Jack Frost will not get here soon enough to harm them," finished Eleanor.

"He'll not be here in time to harm the perennial kind," Billy said.

"No," his father took up the thought, "August is an ideal time to plant the seeds of perennials."

"We have a number of seeds ready for planting."

The Wild Flower Garden

Billy turned to Mary Frances. "Where are they, sister?"

"In the play house," replied Mary Frances. "Shall we get them?"

"Yes," said her father, "I have plenty of time now, and I will help Billy, if he will act as 'master of ceremonies.'"

"Father, I don't know such a heap." Billy's face colored.

"Well, son," said his father, "we'll all appreciate your telling us all you can of what you learned. I know a little theory on the subject myself. I only wish I could have had training and experience in gardening when I was a boy."

"It's the most interesting subject in the world, I believe," Billy said earnestly.

"Here are the seeds," cried Mary Frances, as she and Eleanor came with a number of packages.

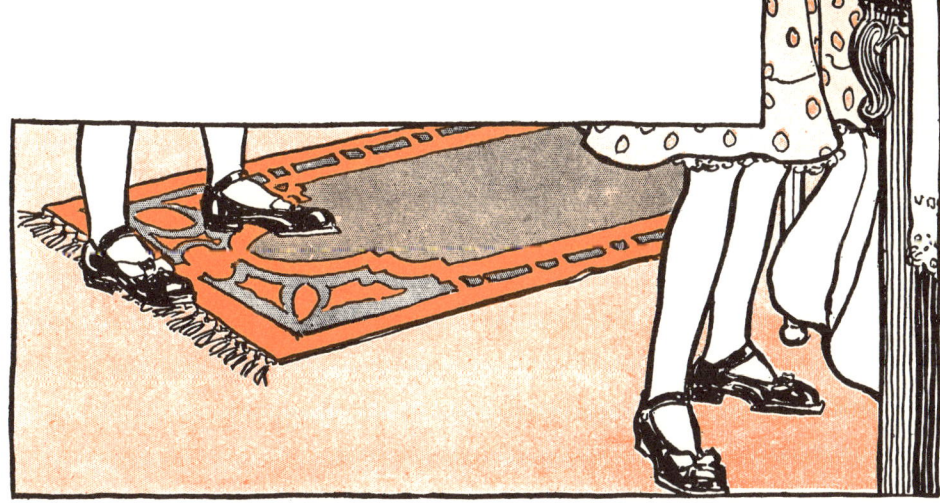

CHAPTER LI

Growing Perennials from Seed

"WE bought," said Billy, taking the packages in his hand, "only the seeds of the perennials which are easily grown. It's far better to buy the young plants of the more delicate kinds."

"I should think so. May we see what you have here?" asked his father, reading aloud the names on the envelopes which Billy gave him. They were—

Gaillardia	Oriental Poppies
Coreopsis	Baby's Breath
Iceland Poppies	Hollyhocks
Larkspur	Foxgloves
Bell Flowers	Columbines

"Of course," Billy explained, "all of these seeds could be started in the early Spring in a sunny window in the house, or in a hotbed, and transplanted to the open ground in June; but the advantage in planting them in July or August is that they will get a good

start before cold weather, and will bloom the next Summer."

"Oh, wouldn't they bloom in the coming Summer if planted in the house very, very early in the Spring?" asked Eleanor.

"A few, such as sweet williams and gaillardia, might," Billy answered, "but it would be quite uncertain."

"Do you make the seed bed in just the same way as for any other seeds?" asked Mary Frances.

"Yes, taking great pains to have it finely pulverized. Well, let's get to work! Father, please tell us what you think is a good place."

After pointing out a good sunny place, his father helped Billy make the seed bed, and the girls sowed the seed.

"Cover the tiny seeds with just a thin layer of soil," directed Billy, "but put a heavier cover on the larger ones. The rule is to cover a seed with three times its diameter."

"Next we press them down firmly," said Mary Frances, "and sprinkle with water very gently."

"Good!" her father praised her. "What a fine

little gardener you are! By the way, when do we see that play house garden of yours, dear?"

"Oh, Father, that's to be another surprise!" Mary Frances answered. "You're to be invited to a Garden Party—you and Mother, and other people, too."

"Won't that be fine! I hope you will not forget Aunt Maria," her father smiled.

"That's a part of the secret, Father; please, please don't guess any more! And please don't tell Mother, will you?" Mary Frances begged anxiously.

"Indeed, I shall not, little girl," he answered. "I think it is a delightful idea."

"The bed should be shaded from the hot sunlight," Billy went on irrelevantly, "until the plants are quite large."

They turned toward him.

"How's that best managed, son?"

"It can be managed in several different ways," said Billy. "For instance, brush may be laid over the bed, but that is not a very good method. A better one is to make a—

Cheese-cloth Shade Frame

Drive down several stakes on the border and in the center of the bed.

Make a cover of cheese-cloth to fit over the bed, and fasten it to the stakes.

You see, the cheese-cloth lets in light and air and rain, yet protects the little seedlings from the direct hot rays of the sun.

"We boys will drive down the stakes if you girls will make the cheese-cloth cover," volunteered their father.

"Sew we will, won't we, Eleanor?" laughed Mary Frances.

"Was that a pun?" asked Billy. "Why, Mary Frances!"

"She meant we will so," Eleanor tried to explain, but everybody smiled.

"You do not need to sew if the beds are narrow, for the cheese-cloth will be wide enough," Billy said, "nor if you use another method of shading the seed beds. I mean if you use—

Lattice Shade Frame

Instead of using cheese-cloth, laths are fastened to the upright stakes to form a "lattice."

"I think the cheese-cloth frame would be less trouble to make." Eleanor was much interested.

"All right, then," said Billy. "We'll expect you to have your part ready in time."

"Do you leave the cheese-cloth, or the lattice shade frame over them all winter?" asked Mary Frances.

"No." Billy shook his head. "After the little plants are about three inches high, you remove the frame, and let them grow with a will. By the latter part of September they will be well rooted, able to live over winter if covered with leaves when the weather becomes frosty, and sheltered from the north winds."

CHAPTER LII

THE MONEY THE CHILDREN MADE

"ELEANOR, if you're going to 'market garden' with Billy and me, you'll have to get up right away."

Mary Frances shook her little friend into wakefulness.

"Mar-ket—gar-den-ing?" yawned Eleanor, stretching. Then sitting up, "Oh, yes, I remember now, Mary Frances! How stupid of me! It's Saturday! My, I'm sorry I overslept!"

"Never mind, girlie, but hurry up and dress. Billy's already out in the garden putting things in the wheelbarrow."

They didn't take much time for making a fancy toilet, and were soon out in the play house garden with Billy.

"Hello, girls," he called. "Aren't these green peppers beauties?" holding some up.

"Green peppers!" said Eleanor. "Why, lots of those green peppers are red!"

[303]

"Oh, you're no Italian," laughed Billy, "or you would know that most green peppers turn red when ripe enough."

"What else have we to-day?" asked Mary Frances. "Of course we have our parsley, and lettuce, and tomatoes, and 'pot herbs.'"

"And cabbage, and carrots, and beans, and cucumbers," added Billy.

"And egg-plants!" Eleanor was proud to be able to add a name to the list.

"All the articles mentioned, Ma'am," said Billy, pretending to offer them for sale.

"I'll buy everything you have," answered Eleanor, "if you'll sell for a penny."

"'Said the piggy, "I won't!"'" Mary Frances misquoted, "and I don't blame Billy, for we've made lots of money this Summer."

"Yes, I know," said Eleanor; "from the times I've been out with you selling garden truck, you must have quite a fortune by now."

"Oh, say——" began Billy.

"What?" asked Mary Frances.

"Why, I was just thinking that since Eleanor

was always helping us so much, she ought to share in the profits."

"Wouldn't that be fine!" Mary Frances hugged her friend in delight.

"No." Eleanor shook her head. "If you divide among three, you won't make money nearly as fast."

"We've done so well that we won't mind going a little more slowly," said Billy. "Shall we tell what a pile we have in the bank, Mary Frances?"

"Oh, Billy, you know I'm crazy to tell her!"

"Well," Billy took a book from his pocket, "last Saturday night we had forty-four dollars and fifty-seven cents, and Mrs. Dailey owes us two dollars and nineteen cents."

"Oh, Billy, did you two make that much in this short time?" Eleanor could scarcely believe her ears.

"More than that!" Mary Frances exulted. "And we've paid Billy back the money we borrowed from his 'prize money' for seeds."

"Let me see. Forty-four and two are forty-six," said Eleanor. "You may have sixty dollars by cold weather!"

"More likely seventy, Billy?" asked Mary Frances.

"I've heard of counting dollars before they were hatched," Billy laughed.

"Is Nell a partner from now on?" asked Mary Frances.

"Yes," Billy said, "if she helps, she shares in the profits—but, gee, I wish Bob was here!"

"Well, you know he's coming soon!" said Mary Frances, "and, besides, you'll be together the whole school year!"

"Say, you girls get to work!" exclaimed Billy, and they flew to gather parsley, and tiny little red peppers, and thyme, and leeks, out of which Mary Frances made penny bunches of pot herbs, while Eleanor tied some three-cent and five-cent bunches of the parsley.

"Are we ready now?" asked Eleanor as Billy piled the wheelbarrow high with vegetables.

"No, indeedy!" Mary Frances exclaimed. "Now, it's my turn. Come on out into the front garden and help me gather my bouquets."

"Let me see the order book, Billy, please?" she asked.

"Oh, yes, Doctor Hopewell wants roses, larkspurs, and baby's breath; Mr. Courtley asked for sweet

peas. As we have only the perennial kind which have no odor, I shall put a sprig of lemon verbena with them. Aren't they beautiful?" as she began to gather them. "I just believe Mr. Courtley is going to give them to Miss Constance. Last Sunday she wore to church the bunch of tufted pansies he bought of me on Saturday."

"Nell, you gather yellow flowers to-day. Isn't that right, Mary Frances?"

He handed her a basket.

"In that," Mary Frances nodded. "You'll find scissors inside the play house door."

Eleanor was soon cutting perennial sunflowers and coreopsis.

"Billy, get some blue flowers to put with the coreopsis?" Mary Frances called after a minute, and Billy began to cut some eupatorium.

"Isn't this a charming bouquet!" exclaimed Eleanor as she arranged the blue and yellow flowers.

They all admired it, but they voted the pink roses, and larkspur, and baby's breath the most beautiful of all.

"Now, we're ready to start!" Billy led off with

the wheelbarrow, the girls following with baskets of the herbs and flowers.

"Have you planned to do anything special with the money, Mary Frances?" asked Eleanor.

"Well, for one thing, I shall save a good deal for seeds and plants in the Spring, and Billy says we'll plant bulbs in the Fall. That will cost quite a little."

"And we're planning to make a hotbed and a cold frame," broke in Billy, who overheard.

"And when we started gardening I borrowed quite a little sum for seeds from my savings account—with Mother's permission. I have to put that back," Mary Frances added.

"Money, like all good things," Billy looked wise, "should be taken care of!"

"Oh, you miser, Billy!" Mary Frances playfully shook her finger.

"Isn't it strange what funny ideas some people have of how things grow?" remarked Billy. "A city chap at school told me he had always thought that cabbages grew on vines and potatoes were picked off bushes!"

"Well, if he never saw them growing, how could he

know?" Mary Frances reasoned after they stopped laughing.

"That's right!" teased Billy. "Stand up for him."

By that time they were in the heart of the village, and had very soon sold everything, for the village people had become accustomed to look for the children.

"Every vegetable you bring is so fresh that we wait to buy of you," several said.

"Splendid luck to-day," commented Billy, on the way home.

"Have you saved the things your mother ordered?" asked Eleanor.

"Of course," answered Billy. "You don't suppose we'd neglect one of our first and best paying customers."

"Mother is a dear!" said Mary Frances. "So is Father! They must wonder why they haven't been invited to see our gardens."

"When are you going to ask them?" Eleanor inquired.

"Why, don't you remember? When we give our garden party."

"That's to be about the first of September, I believe," said Billy.

CHAPTER LIII

Mary Frances' Garden Party

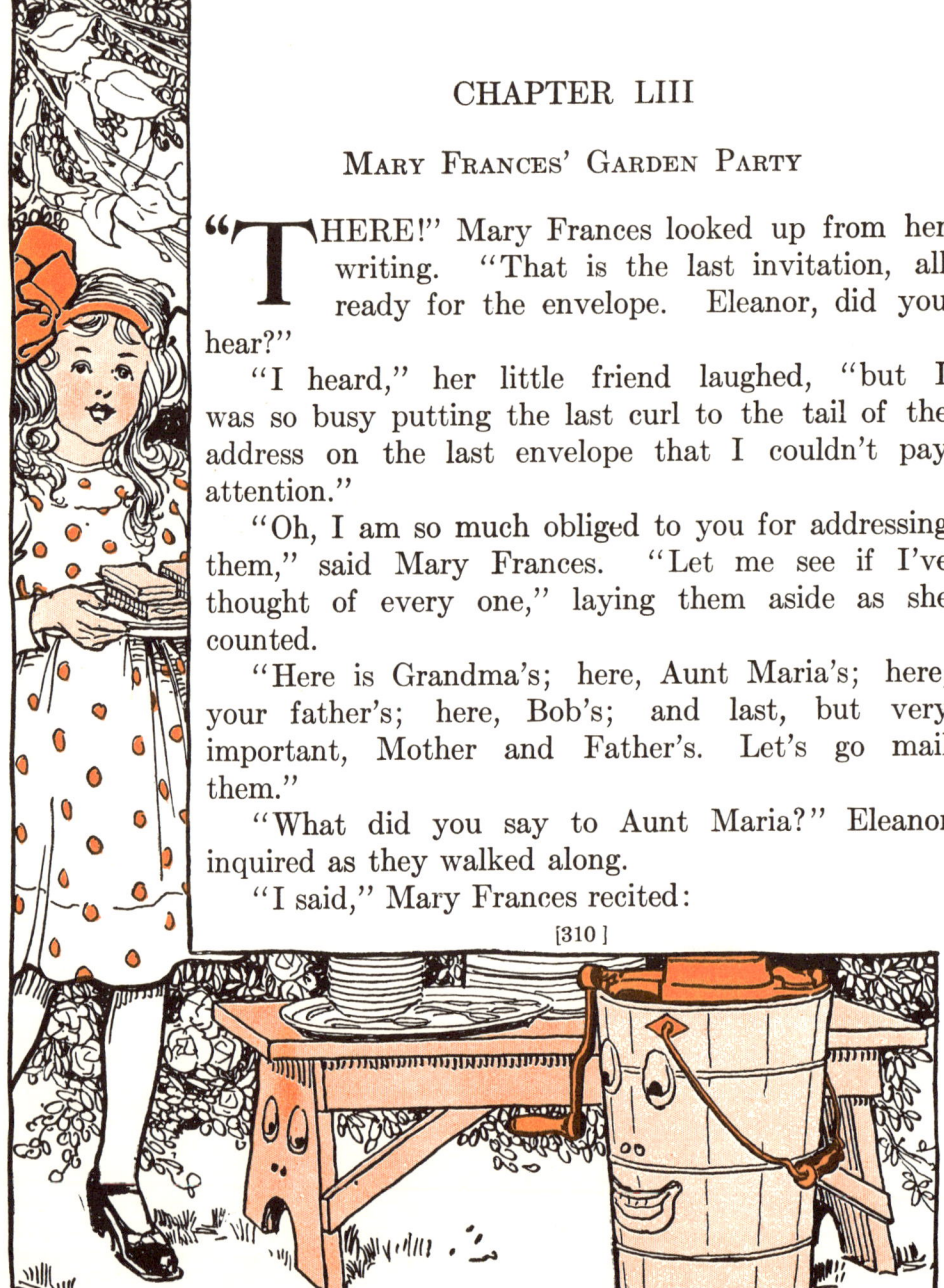

"THERE!" Mary Frances looked up from her writing. "That is the last invitation, all ready for the envelope. Eleanor, did you hear?"

"I heard," her little friend laughed, "but I was so busy putting the last curl to the tail of the address on the last envelope that I couldn't pay attention."

"Oh, I am so much obliged to you for addressing them," said Mary Frances. "Let me see if I've thought of every one," laying them aside as she counted.

"Here is Grandma's; here, Aunt Maria's; here, your father's; here, Bob's; and last, but very important, Mother and Father's. Let's go mail them."

"What did you say to Aunt Maria?" Eleanor inquired as they walked along.

"I said," Mary Frances recited:

"Dear Aunt Maria:—

"Please come to my Garden Party next Wednesday. We've been industrious enough this Summer to please even you!

"I don't want to tell you any more, for fear I'll spoil the surprise, but we won't have a bit nice time unless you are with us. I'll never forget how pleased you were with my cooking surprise.

"With love, which I want to give you in real hugs, and real kisses, "Mary Frances."

"Mary Frances, do you dare hug your Aunt Maria? I'd never dare, I'm sure. The very thought scares me! She always seems so cross."

Mary Frances laughed. "I used to feel the same way," she said, "but after I found out that she was cross just because she was afraid——"

"Afraid? Your Aunt Maria afraid!"

"Yes, afraid, and ashamed that somebody might think she was loving and kind. When I found that out, I felt different. I was sorry for her."

"I know she loves you dearly," Eleanor admitted.

"She's a dear old bear who growls just for fun, and

I hope she comes to the party. Grandma will come, I know, and——"

"So will Father and Bob," finished Eleanor.

"Oh, I can scarcely wait for Wednesday!"

They were at the post office by this time. On their way home they discussed their plans.

"Billy will bring the tables to the play house on Tuesday," said Mary Frances, "and we'll all do everything we can to get ready."

"What shall we have for refreshments?" Eleanor asked.

"Why, I think it would be lovely to have everything from our garden—of course, excepting the ice-cream," Mary Frances laughed. "I wonder how this would be:

Tomato and Lettuce Salad with Mayonnaise Dressing
Creamed Potatoes
Cucumber Relish

Sandwiches
Green Pepper and Cheese   Nasturtium

Ice-Cream
Spearmint Jumbles
Coffee

Mary Frances' Garden Party

"Oh, Mary Frances, that sounds perfectly wonderful to me!" exclaimed Eleanor, "but how can you manage to serve so many things?"

"It won't be hard to manage," Mary Frances answered, well pleased. "I've thought it all out carefully. We can have the mayonnaise dressing all ready for the salad the day before, and can make the sandwiches Wednesday morning if we wrap them in waxed paper."

"How do you make those sandwiches, Mary Frances?" asked Eleanor.

"Oh, I'm glad you asked that, for they are so good, Eleanor. Use—

For Twelve Green Pepper Sandwiches

3 five-cent packages cream cheese
2 green peppers, chopped very fine

Mix together and spread on well-buttered thin slices of bread. Cover each with another buttered——

"As if I didn't know that much!" exclaimed Eleanor. "How do you make the other kind?"

"Oh, the nasturtium sandwiches? Why, you use

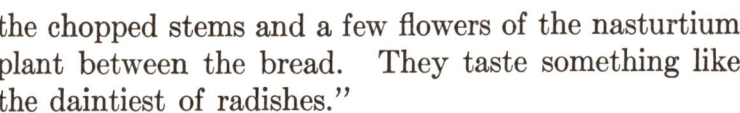

the chopped stems and a few flowers of the nasturtium plant between the bread. They taste something like the daintiest of radishes."

"I can make the sandwiches!" Eleanor exclaimed. "They are easy. Now, what about the potatoes?"

"They can be creamed in the morning and warmed in the oven just before serving."

"Oh, that's fine! What about the spearmint jumbles you mentioned?"

"I made up that recipe," Mary Frances confessed. "You see, I'm so crazy to have everything from the garden that I just had to be original."

"I'm wild to hear about this recipe!" Eleanor said. "Let's go into the play house and I'll write it down."

When they were seated, Mary Frances began:

"I looked all over the garden, Eleanor, and I couldn't think of a thing we could use in making candy, and I certainly think we need candy, don't you?"

"Indeed, I do!" Eleanor agreed.

"Suddenly I spied the spearmint growing with my other herbs. 'The very thing!' I thought, so I just made up a very simple recipe for—

Spearmint Jumbles

2 cups sugar
½ cup water
1 cup mint leaves

1. Wash the mint leaves.
2. Put the sugar in a saucepan. Add the water.
3. Stir sugar over the fire until dissolved.
4. Cook quite hard until the sugar begins to turn brown. Take from the fire. Add mint leaves, stirring hard.
5. Turn out on a buttered pie plate. Add 2 tablespoons butter.
6. Stir hard until candy falls apart or crumbles into small pieces.

"My, but you are smart, Mary Frances!" declared Eleanor. "I wish I could do such things—but what if some people don't care for spearmint flavor?"

"We could make some fudge." Mary Frances met the suggestion, "but I think everybody ought to think it good this time because it's from our garden. I didn't like to plan for ice-cream even because it didn't grow there."

"Don't you wish it did!" cried Eleanor.

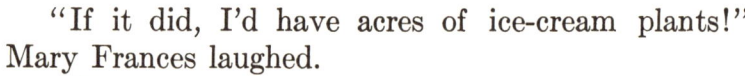

"If it did, I'd have acres of ice-cream plants!" Mary Frances laughed.

"We'll cook everything right here in the play house," she continued; "that little stove will do all that we want."

"Oh, won't it be too grand for anything!" Eleanor hugged Mary Frances in enthusiasm.

. . . .

So when Tuesday came, they set to work, and carried out their plans.

"Who's to serve the feast?" asked Billy, as he arranged the plates according to the girls' directions.

"Oh, we'll do that," answered Mary Frances. "All we ask you to do, Billy, is to open the freezer and dish the ice-cream."

"Believe me, you may count on me, ladies," said Billy, bowing. "Count on me for a large share in the ice-cream work, although I can't see that there will be much work, for I ordered it in the form of bricks."

"Billy, you're a brick!" laughed Eleanor.

By twelve o'clock Wednesday, the refreshments were ready, and the girls went to the big house to "doll up," as Billy said.

Mary Frances' Garden Party 317

Mary Frances glanced out of the window just as she fastened the last button of Eleanor's dress.

"Here comes Aunt Maria!" she cried and bounded down-stairs and out on the porch to meet her. While she was hugging her, Eleanor's father and Bob appeared on the scene, and you can imagine how happy the little girls were.

"Where can Grandma be?" Mary Frances asked, after her mother and father had welcomed everybody. "Oh, there comes the station auto-bus. It's going to stop here!" Surely enough it stopped, and out stepped the dear old lady, whom everybody tried to greet at once.

In the midst of the confusion, Mary Frances and Eleanor slipped away to the play house, and a little later Billy and Bob piloted the guests to the play house garden.

> "Mistress Mary, never contrary,
>   Will show how her garden grows,"

announced Bob, leading the way up the path, where Mary Frances shook hands with each one in a most grown-up, dignified fashion introducing them to "My

friend, Miss Eleanor," just as Mother Paper Doll had done in the Housekeeper story.

"So this is you children's garden surprise, dear! Isn't it beautiful!" There were tears of joy in their mother's eyes.

"Were there ever such children!" exclaimed their grandmother.

"If there are any more wonderful, I have yet to see them!" Aunt Maria's nose went up into the air with pride.

"Jolly good gardener, Bill!" Bob slapped his friend on the back.

"What you'll be next year," Billy retorted.

"Father hasn't said a word!" Mary Frances suddenly discovered.

"I've been speechless with surprise, dear," he said. "It certainly paid to wait to see such a garden. The flowers are wonderful!"

"Why, haven't you seen the garden before this?" everybody asked, and he told the whole story.

As he finished, Bob and Eleanor's father spoke. "I'm gladder than ever that Bob's to go away to Billy's school!"

Then nearly everybody began to talk at once, saying how much more sensible the ideals of education were to-day than when they were young, and more of such grown-up talk, which gave the boys and girls a chance to slip away to get the refreshments.

"How did you guess we were hungry?" asked Bob's father as Mary Frances served the salad, and Eleanor passed the sandwiches in a dainty basket, trimmed with pink bows.

"Where did you find such beautiful lettuce and tomatoes, dear?" asked Grandma, showing her enjoyment of the treat.

"That's part of the secret," laughed Mary Frances. "After you've tested our vegetables, we'll show you our vegetable garden."

"Gee!" exclaimed Bob, "you don't mean to say you raised these?"

"Everything's from this garden except the ice-cream!" Eleanor asserted proudly.

"Some farmers!" Bob started to say, but his father interposed.

"You forget, son, that you're in a formal social gathering—at a garden party, if you please."

"Please pardon me," Bob begged, bowing to the company.

"Let them talk—it's the youngsters' party," somebody whispered so loud that everybody heard, and everybody laughed.

After the ice-cream and coffee had been served, and the bonbon dish of candy was passed, "What delicious mints!" so many people praised, that Mary Frances said she would carry the candy dish with them to the vegetable garden, and all could see the bed of mint where she gathered the leaves for the flavor.

It would be impossible to tell you how happy and proud the children were as they showed their vegetable garden, with its beautiful neat beds bordered with nasturtiums.

You can imagine how they looked, for if you read the garden lists in early chapters of this story, you know what they had growing.

"Everybody may pick a bouquet," said Mary Frances, seizing Eleanor's hand and leading the party to the flower garden. Just as they started, Doctor Hopewell drove up with his son and two daughters.

"We couldn't help stopping," he declared. "You made such a beautiful picture."

They were welcomed with delight, and the girls insisted upon their having some salad and ice-cream.

"Isn't this the most charming thing you ever heard of!" sighed Marjorie Hopewell.

"It's just like a girl's dream come true!" her sister Helen agreed.

"The girls will never get over this. To have peace I'll have to turn farmer yet! Bill and Bob will have to give me pointers!" their brother Harry laughed.

"Indeed, I'd like to see you all doing what these young people have done," their father told them.

The doctor and his family left in about an hour, with flowers for Mrs. Hopewell, but the other guests stayed until five o'clock, sitting on the easy chairs which Billy had placed along the walk in front of the play house.

The day was so beautiful—not too warm, not too cool; not a rain cloud in the sky, but scattered about with little white fleecy "flocks of lambs" clouds, as Mary Frances said. Perhaps that and the beauty of

the garden made them linger, but they seemed sorry to leave.

"You will all come again! Soon!" Mary Frances and Billy made them promise. "And you'll come to our garden party next year! We'll have both Bob and Eleanor for partners then!"

CHAPTER LIV

FEATHER FLOP'S CONCEIT

"OH, Feather Flop! Feather Flop!" called Mary Frances, as she carried a pan of the "left overs" of the garden party out to the rooster the next morning.

Feather Flop made some queer gurgling noise in his throat.

"Why, what's the matter, old fellow?" she asked in alarm.

"Matter?" cawed Feather Flop hoarsely. "Matter? Why, this: I've nearly crowed my bill off trying to call you. I'm so hoarse I can scarcely whisper! I grew so weak, finally I had to lean up against the fence to crow!"

"Mercy! Was it as bad as that?" asked Mary Frances. "Why, I must have been so tired out from our garden party that I slept so soundly I didn't hear. I'm sorry—you must have wanted to see me very particularly, too!"

"'Our garden party!'" echoed Feather Flop.

"'Our garden party!' As though any mention had been made of me!"

"Oh! oh! oh!" cried Mary Frances. "Oh, was that it, Feather Flop? I never thought—really! I supposed I must keep you a secret just as I've been accustomed with other fairy folks."

"Fairy folks!" exclaimed Feather Flop. "Fairy folks! I'm not a fairy! I'm a farmer! and even if you don't remember, it doesn't change the fact that if it hadn't been for me, you wouldn't have had any garden at all."

"Why, you conceited old fellow!" cried Mary Frances. "How do you make that out? But," seeing the disappointment on his face, "of course, I appreciate your help. Indeed I do, Feather Flop," she added.

"Don't you recollect?" asked Feather Flop. "Don't you recollect that day when you couldn't understand the seed catalogue? Who was it that helped you then? Who was it, little Miss?"

He cocked his head and looked up at her expectantly.

"Why, it was you, Feather Flop!" Mary Frances exclaimed. "It certainly was you, my old friend!"

Feather Flop blinked. "I'm glad you can call it to mind!" he remarked. "If you had only just mentioned my name at the garden party, I wouldn't have felt so bad."

"Oh!" said Mary Frances.

"Even if you'd just said to me, if you'd just said, 'Feather Flop, old chap, you can't come to the garden party, of course, but you're invited,' I wouldn't have felt as I did."

"Oh, dear!" said Mary Frances.

"If you'd said at the party, 'Now, if my old friend, Feather Flop, hadn't helped me,' or something like that, I'd have been so proud and glad."

"How do you know I didn't?" Mary Frances parleyed under sudden inspiration.

"How do I know? I was there. I was there even uninvited!" declared Feather Flop.

"Why, where in the world were you?" asked Mary Frances in astonishment. "You couldn't have been in the garden, for we were everywhere."

"It's a riddle!" Feather Flop's voice sounded as though he was laughing. "I was in the garden! You can't guess where!"

"Indeed, I can't." Mary Frances shook her head. "Unless you were under something inside the play house."

"No, I wasn't inside the play house," said Feather Flop, in a voice which still sounded like laughter. "Guess again! One more guess!"

"Give it up." Mary Frances acknowledged her defeat.

"Why, I was outside the play house on the roof!" declared the rooster triumphantly.

"Oh!" cried Mary Frances, delighted. "So that is where you were! You really were at the party, after all! Now I shall feel better. If I'd only realized how you felt, I'd loved to have invited you and to have had you there!"

"That makes it all right," said Feather Flop brightly. "I only thought you'd forgotten me and maybe didn't want me! That's what made me so sad!"

"Not want you!" exclaimed Mary Frances. "Not want you! I think you are the most wonderful rooster in the whole wide world, and the smartest——"

"Farmer?" asked Feather Flop anxiously.

"Yes, indeed, farmer!" declared the little girl, picking him up and tenderly smoothing him. "If it hadn't been for you, I doubt if I'd have had a garden!"

"Oh, I'm the happiest rooster in the wide world!" sighed Feather Flop, "and if I weren't just a plain farmer rooster, I'd turn into a fairy prince, dressed in blue satin trimmed with gold and diamonds, but as it is—I'm hungry!"

"Come!" laughed Mary Frances. "Come, eat," she said. "I like you far better than any fairy prince, for you're my own dear friend—my farmer, Feather Flop."

And Feather Flop looked so proud you might have imagined him in tiny overalls and sun hat.

CHAPTER LV

Bob and Billy's Vacation

THE boys had been at school several weeks, and Mary Frances and Eleanor were well started in their studies, when one golden-leafed day in October, each girl received a letter from her brother as they stopped at the post office on their way from school.

"We're coming home on Friday," both letters read alike, "to plant the bulbs, and we'll expect your help after school, and all day Saturday, if necessary; and we'll hope—just hope—for some play house cooking."

"Isn't it comical for them to say just the same thing!" exclaimed Eleanor.

"Won't we have fun!" Mary Frances answered. "Let's see, this is Wednesday. I wonder if Billy wrote to Mother." And away they flew to find out.

"Mother, you've known for several days, I just believe," declared Mary Frances, whereat her mother laughed and confessed that she had known, but that

Bob and Billy's Vacation

it was her turn to keep a surprise in store for them. Then all three fell to making plans for the visit.

"We'll give a dinner in the play house," decided Mary Frances, "and invite you and Father."

"Oh, you children would have more pleasure without grown-ups," protested her mother.

"Not a bit of fun without *our* kind of 'grown-ups,' you mean," Mary Frances contradicted lovingly. "Doesn't she, Eleanor?"

"Yes, indeed!" Eleanor answered emphatically.

"You dear children!" was all the mother said, but the girls knew that their invitation was accepted.

When the boys came, there was so much to talk about that they didn't get to work until Saturday. There were stories of the jokes which the second year fellows played on the "Freshies," and of the winning of the big football game, and of the rigid training in athletics, and a volume of other talk new to the girls; at least, new to Eleanor, and equally entertaining to Mary Frances and her parents.

"I wrote 'the governor' all about that," said Bob as he finished relating one particularly amusing incident.

The girls looked puzzled.

"He means his 'old man,' " explained Billy.

"Oh, Billy! How you talk!" cried Mary Frances. "Do you mean his father?"

"Sure guess!" nodded Billy.

"Well, Father, if that's the way they learn to talk, I shouldn't think you'd let them go back." Mary Frances pretended to be indignant.

But he only laughed, saying, "Oh, they'll outgrow it" And the boys took up anew the threads of their stories.

It was quite late before they got to bed, but they were up bright and early Saturday morning.

"We fellows haven't time now to explain why bulbous plants bloom so readily in the Spring."

"We know; don't we, Mary Frances?" Eleanor exclaimed without thinking.

Mary Frances pursed her lips to look like "Hush!" and shook her head, which made Eleanor remember that Jack-in-the-Pulpit and Bouncing Bet's lessons were to be a secret.

"If you know so much, Nell," Bob replied mockingly, "perhaps you can tell the difference

between a corm, a rhizome, a tuber, and a fleshy root."

"Well! Well!" cried Mary Frances, "I guess we better not lay claim to any more knowledge," and she winked at Eleanor, who nodded understandingly.

"But," said Billy, opening his note-book, "we will tell you a little something about—

The Planting of Bulbs

Anyone can have flowers which grow from bulbs.

They require so little care that everybody can be cheered in the early Spring with the sunshine of daffodils, and the fragrance of hyacinths, and the gay color of tulips; which, after the dullness of winter, are appreciated more, perhaps, than any other flowers.

Their leaves and flowers being wrapped with their food supply, in the storage bulbs, it takes only the call of a few days of warmth and sunshine to bring them into bloom.
So every one should—

Plant Spring-Flowering Bulbs in Autumn

In October or November is the best time of the year for planting Spring-flowering bulbs; in localities where the Winters are not severe, December is perfectly safe.

The bulbs should have time to make some roots before the ground freezes.

How to Plant Bulbs

Bulbs do not like clayey soil, nor do they like dampness; neither do they thrive on fresh manure.

Remembering this, you already know just about what kind of soil they need—well-drained, loamy soil, full of humus or well-rotted manure, and some sand; for sandy soil is needed by all bulbs.

If you do not have such garden soil, dig quite large holes with your trowel, and fill them with such a mixture. If you do not have well-rotted manure, use a sprinkling of bone meal.

Depth to Plant

A good rule for the depth to plant bulbs is twice their length; but sometimes it pays to plant them deeper to protect them.

If planted deeper they come into bloom a little later, but the protection of the depth may save them from destructive freezing.

Where to Plant Bulbs

Blooms of bulbs look beautiful anywhere. One need not hesitate to place them in masses (a number near each other) in the garden borders, for after they bloom and die down, there will be no bare spots if some annuals, with short roots, are grown over them; such as alyssum, ageratum, violas, verbenas.

Plant the low-growing sorts of bulbs in the front, and the taller kinds in the back of the garden.

Cover, when the ground begins to freeze, with several inches of dry leaves or grass.

Most bulbs do best if not lifted after blooming; that is, let them be in the ground for several years. Then the new bulbs which have grown on the old ones will need to be separated and planted.

Narcissus and daffodils may remain many years without disturbing.

Hyacinths do not do as well as other out-door hardy bulbs, becoming less vigorous each year. They do a little better if the bulbs are lifted and dried in the Summer and replaced in the Fall.

If you plant—

Bulbs in the Grass

One caution is necessary: after they are through blooming, wait until the green leaves turn yellow before cutting the grass. If the leaves are cut before they turn, the bulbs will die.

Nowhere else do such flowers look so beautiful as in the grass.

To plant small bulbs, such as crocus, dig holes in the turf with an apple-corer, or with a "dibble," which is a pointed stick. Throw in a tiny bit of bone meal and some sand. After placing the bulb, being certain to put the root end down, and the pointed top up, cover with sand and pack the turf firmly back in place.

A better way is to lift the turf with a spade. Dig, to loosen up the soil; add a little bone meal; plant bulbs, replace sod.

To place them in an artistic position, throw down a handful and plant where they fall.

CHAPTER LVI

Daffodil and Other Bulbs

"GOOD!" Bob approved as Billy paused, "that's a splendid lecture, Bill."

"Isn't it?" cried Eleanor. "I believe we know almost everything now about planting bulbs."

"What kinds are we going to plant?" asked Mary Frances, looking at the large package the boys had brought with them.

They opened it and Bob began to speak: "Young ladies," he commenced; then, "Oh, I say, Bill, I can't come this 'professor act.' You'd better do the lecturing!"

"No, sir-ee!" declared Billy. "It's your turn now. Go ahead."

"Oh, go on, Bob," cried Eleanor.

"Please do!" begged Mary Frances.

"All right, then," replied Bob, laughing, "only don't expect much erudite stuff from humble me— even when I read my notes."

Daffodil and Other Bulbs

Then, opening his book, and clearing his throat, he started once more: "Listen, young ladies, and you will hear of—

Bulbs to Plant in the Fall

Snowdrops

The earliest Spring garden flower, sometimes coming literally out of the snow as early as February; but usually blooming in March. The blossoms are small, white, bell-shaped, not in the least showy. Only one who has come upon them unexpectedly blooming in his garden knows the thrill of pleasure which they bring. As they are small and inexpensive, plant a number of bulbs about two inches apart, to cover an irregular circle. Once planted they take care of themselves.

Squills (Scilla)

Near the Snowdrops, plant in the same way, a dozen Siberian Squills. Beautiful blue flowers, which will bloom perhaps while some of the Snowdrops are in blossom. Once planted, do not disturb.

Grape Hyacinths (Muscari)

Little stalks of tiny tight blue bells, or white, somewhat the shape of tiny fairy-folks' grapes. Everyone should have a dozen or so of these pretty early Spring-flowering bulbs.

Narcissus or Daffodils

Everybody knows a daffodil, for breathes there a human being with soul so dead as not to feel warmth of heart at the sunshine glow of its yellow petals?

But not everybody knows the difference between daffodils and jonquils and narcissus.

The fact is, they are all sold by dealers under the name Narcissus.

Every Narcissus has a "cup and saucer" form. In some, the cup, or *trumpet*, is tall; in some, it is short; in others, it is double: and according to the shape of the cup, each Narcissus is named.

All dealers agree that the type with the double cup is called *daffodil*. It is not generally thought so attractive as the single sorts.

The single sorts are of the following different varieties of Narcissus:

Narcissus
- *Giant Trumpet.* Very showy, with large cups and saucers. Buy "Emperor," and "Empress."
- *Medium Trumpet.* ("Star" Narcissus.) Not so large nor attractive, but very graceful. Buy "Barii Conspicuus."
- *Poet's Narcissus.* Old-fashioned favorite. Charming fragrant white flowers, with cups edged with red. Buy "Poeticus" (Pheasant's Eye) or "King Edward VII." Very easily grown.

Jonquils are the small-flowering type of Narcissus. They are easily grown, and many have a charming fragrance.

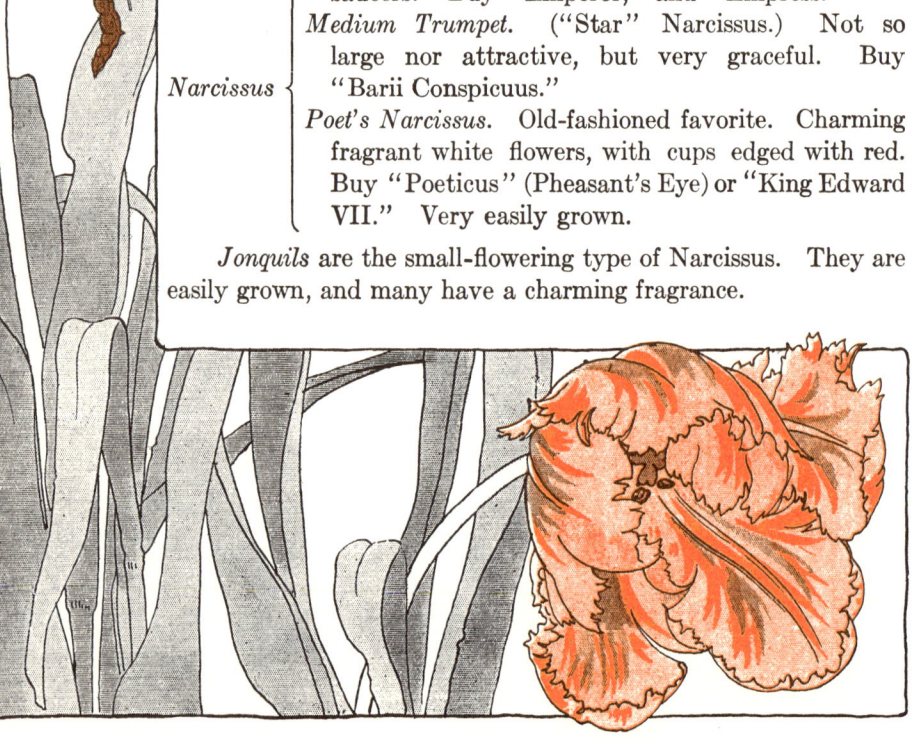

Daffodil and Other Bulbs

Polyanthus Narcissus or Nosegay Daffodils are the little clustered kind grown indoors.

All these distinctions, and many others, are made by the dealers, but almost everyone of us thinks of all the yellow Narcissus as Daffodils. They grow so readily, with almost no care, that everyone, with only the tiniest garden, should plant at least a half dozen bulbs of the "Giant Emperor."

Within a few years after planting, the Spring will bring dozens of blossoms of—

> "Daffodown-dilly,
>   Come up to town,
>   In a green petticoat
>   And a gold gown."

Hyacinths

Single sorts do better than double. As a rule, hyacinths do not improve from being kept in the ground all Winter; they may be taken up and stored in a cool cellar over Winter to be planted in the early Spring; but a better plan is to let the old bulbs gradually "run out," and plant a few new bulbs each Fall. These are sent to dealers every Autumn from Holland, because the climate of Holland is nearly perfect for bulb growing. Sometimes hyacinths do quite well for a number of years kept in the ground out-of-doors.

Their charming fragrance, color and form, make them a most attractive flower. They come in white, pinks and purples.

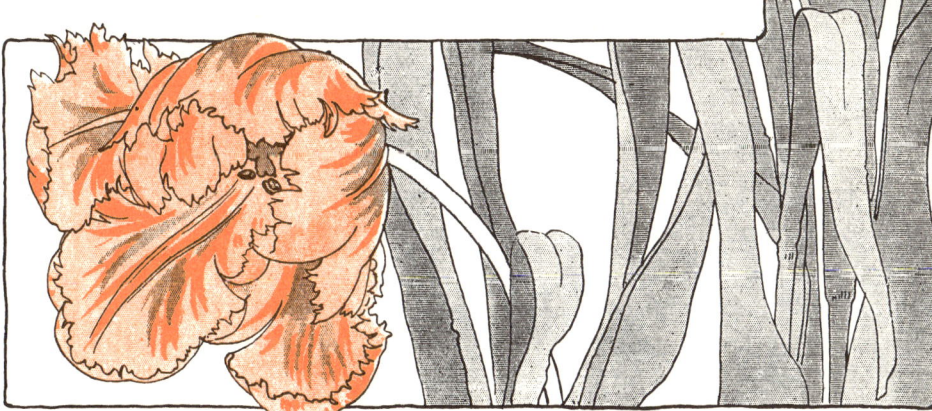

Tulips

The most gorgeous of all Spring-flowering bulbs.

Tulips
- *Early Single.* Grow about eight inches high; come in pinks, reds, yellows, white.
- *Early Double.* These are not so beautiful as the single varieties.
- *Cottage Garden* (May flowering). A tall variety, growing about eighteen inches high, blooming much later than the Early Single.
- *Darwin.* The most desirable of all tulips, but not very early. The tallest grow nearly thirty inches high. Globe-shaped flowers of most brilliant shades of reds, purples, pinks and white. If yellow is desired, buy one of the Cottage Garden, for there are no yellow Darwins.
- *Parrot.* Showy; of variegated shading and irregular petals. Not so artistic as single sorts, but very odd and interesting. Buy only a *few* bulbs.

While tulips are most effective if planted in groups or masses, an edging of the stiff blooms of the Early Single is delightful, especially if a red is alternated with a white. They look almost like "candles in bloom."

Lilies

Lilies dislike sour soil, so sprinkle some lime over the ground before digging it deeply. A little powdered charcoal in each hole

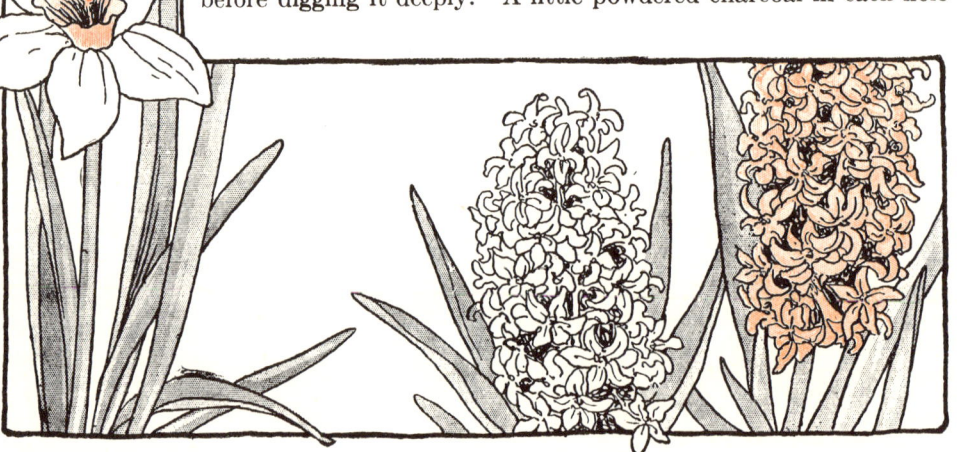

Daffodil and Other Bulbs

helps, too, and it is well to dust each bulb with flowers of sulphur to protect from worms and mildew.

Lilies love shade, and do best among other perennials because they will shade their roots, which spread out near the surface of the ground. By the way, since they spread near the surface, do not "cultivate" lilies. Do not disturb the bulbs, which will bloom for years if planted right in the first place. Most lilies bloom in Mid-summer.

Hardy Lilies
- *Plantain Lily* (Funkia). The most easily grown, with spikes of blooms about eighteen inches high, in white, blue or lavender.
- *Yellow Day Lily* (Hemerocallis). Grows anywhere, sometimes killing out other flowers. Blooms on stems about thirty inches high.
- *Madonna Lily* (Candidum). Beautiful, stately, tall white lilies with delightful fragrance. They resemble "Easter Lilies." Cover bulbs with only two inches of soil.
- *Red Spotted Lily* (Lilium Speciosum Rubrum). A tall Japanese lily, easily grown. Large white flowers dotted with red, borne on a tall stem.
- *Tiger Lily* (Tigrinum). Orange spotted with black. Very easily grown.
- *Lilies-of-the-Valley*. Grown from "pips," or tiny bulbs. Plant in the Spring in rich earth. They like some shade.

Iris (Flags)

Spanish Iris. Exquisite orchid-like blooms, in white and rich shades of blue, yellow, bronze.

German Iris. Very easily grown and very desirable.

Bulbs to Plant in Early Spring

Among these are:

Tuberoses

Plant in May, and again in June and July, in order to have a continuation of bloom of these powerfully fragrant and beautiful white flowers.

Gladiolus

These bulbs are planted in May and June at two weeks intervals, in order to have blooms from July to October. They like rich soil; and powdered sheep manure, which is sold by the pound, is a good substitute for rotted stable manure. They like the sunny places.

The bulbs of both tuberoses and gladiolus should be taken out of the ground in the Fall after the foliage becomes yellow. The stems are cut off and the bulbs dried on an airy shelf, or any place which is neither very warm nor very cold. They are set in the ground again in the Spring.

Cannas and dahlias grow from fleshy roots and are planted in the Spring also. They are lifted and dried in the Fall.

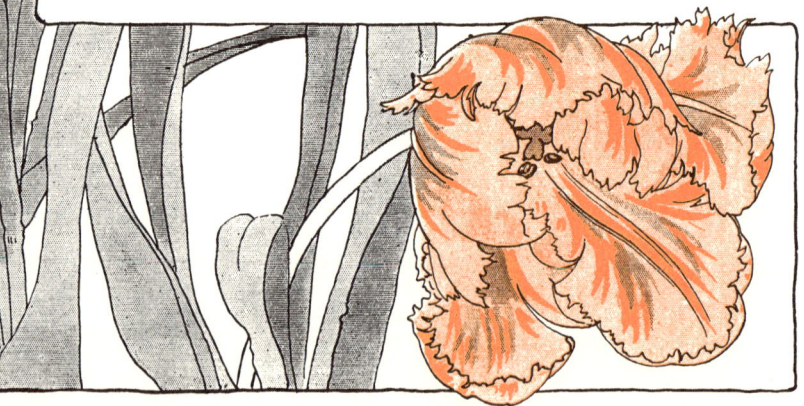

Daffodil and Other Bulbs

If your garden space is small, the following selection of bulbous plants will give a great deal of enjoyment:

Hardy Bulbs for a Small Garden

6 Snowdrops
6 Grape Hyacinths (2 white, 4 blue)
6 Emperor Daffodils
6 Poet's Narcissus (Pheasant's Eye)
6 Early Single Tulips
12 Darwin Tulips (3 each, of four different colors)
3 Spanish Iris
6 German Iris

Growing Bulbs Indoors

It is very interesting and delightful to grow bulbs indoors, where the warmth "forces" them into bloom in the cold winter months. If they are managed in the right way, you may have blooms from Christmas on. Do not attempt to have over a half dozen pots the first year.

Bulbs may be grown indoors in pots or in prepared fibre, which may be bought of a dealer.

If grown in pots, prepare a rich soil of sand and leaf mold. If impossible to get leaf mold, use a sprinkling of bone meal. Place some pieces of broken flower pots or pebbles in the bottom of the pots to drain the water off, or the bulbs will mold.

If grown in prepared fibre, moisten the fibre before putting

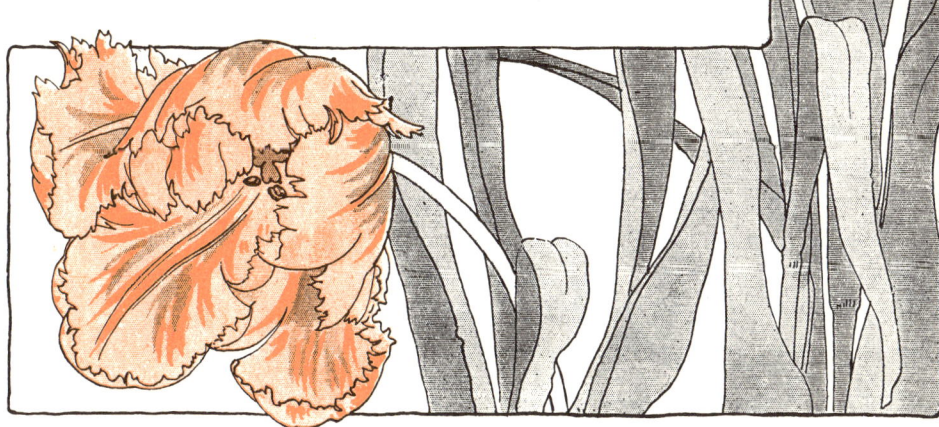

in the pot, but do not make it wet enough to wring. Plant bulbs as in soil, but do not pack in tight. After watering, turn pot on the side to drain off the water. A piece of charcoal in the bottom of the pan or pot keeps the fibre sweet.

Hyacinths do well when grown in glass vases. The glass vases used are made for the purpose, and hold the bulb just above the water—not touching.

The main point in growing bulbs indoors is to arrange to keep them growing in a *dark, cool* place until the roots have formed and the leaves show about three inches.

This is accomplished in several different ways. Perhaps the simplest of all is to place the pots on a cool cellar floor and cover them with ashes, which will assure their being kept in the dark. Keep them damp by watering the ashes once or twice a week. (The same idea is better carried out by the use of a *cold frame*, the making of which is described in the next chapter.)

Place the pots on ashes in the frame, throwing three or four inches of ashes over them; or use dried peat moss instead of ashes. This is sold by dealers in seeds and plants.

Place glass cover on the cold frame when the weather becomes severe.

About three weeks before you wish them to bloom bring some of the potted bulbs into the warmth of the house. Do not place them immediately in a very warm place or in the sunlight. Give them as much fresh air as possible.

After planting bulbs in prepared fibre, or hyacinths in glasses,

Daffodil and Other Bulbs

keep them in a dark, airy closet until the roots have formed, which will be in about six weeks. Then bring them into warmth and light. The roots of the hyacinth should reach the bottom of the glasses before bringing them into the light.

Daffodils and single tulips, crocuses, polyanthus narcissus (often grown in pebbles in water) all are easily forced into bloom indoors.

"But," added Billy as Bob drew a long breath, "growing bulbs indoors is a rather tedious experiment, and better not be attempted by young children," as he pulled Mary Frances' hair ribbon untied.

"Well, neither of you would have known much, Mr. Superior Knowledge," laughed Eleanor, "if you hadn't studied this all within a week or so."

"Let's begin to plant," was Billy's answer.

CHAPTER LVII

Billy Builds a Hotbed

DURING the Christmas holidays the children made wonderful plans for their gardens.

"Everything should be started very early," said Bob, airing his newly acquired knowledge, "and the best place to start seeds is in a hotbed."

"I tell you what we'll do, Bob," Billy suggested. "Let's come home in March and build one!"

"Won't that be grand!" cried the girls with enthusiasm. "We'll help all we can."

"Ah! You can't——" began Billy, then stopped.

. . . .

So one sunny day in the early part of March, just the very day Eleanor discovered some of the snowdrops blooming, the boys surprised them. About an hour after they came, the lumber and sashes for the hotbed arrived.

"We bought the frames ready to set up," Billy said, "but a fellow could make one quite well. Even a grocery box, if cut in the right shape and covered with glass, makes a good substitute."

"Yes, we made that kind at school for practice," added Bob, and to show how well he had learned his lesson, he started to dig where they had decided to place the hotbed.

Meanwhile Billy referred to his useful note book, and explained what they were about to do. "The situation is very important," he said, "for we learned at school that a—

Hotbed

should be sheltered from the north winds; so, if possible, place it on the south side of a large building.

Let it slant toward the sunny south, where the glass sash will catch the sun's rays.

You see, a hotbed is a tiny greenhouse. In both a greenhouse and a hotbed, artificial heat is supplied.

Greenhouses are heated by steam or hot water pipes: ordinary hotbeds are heated by fresh manure, which, in the process of decomposing, gives off a great amount of heat.

Heat, air and sunlight are essential for plants' growth.

The slanting glass sash catches the sunshine, and holds in the heat which the manure gives off. The sashes are raised a little in the warmest part of each day, which gives the plants air.

The frame is generally about eighteen inches high in back and twelve inches in front.

Dig nearly two feet deep, in a space a foot wider and longer than the frame.

Get ready a pile of fresh horse manure which has been mixed with one-third as much bedding straw or litter.

If very dry, sprinkle with water. When, in a day or two, it begins to steam, turn it well over, and in a day or so more, fill the dug-out space to within six inches of the top.

Place the frame on this, and bank up the *outside* with more manure. Cover the manure with earth.

Fill the inside with earth six or eight inches deep, and water with a sprinkler.

Put on the sash, and place a thermometer inside. It may go up to 120 degrees, but in a few days will come down to 90 degrees, when the bed is ready for planting.

Seeds may be planted direct in the soil, but a more convenient plan is to fill shallow boxes, called "flats," with soil, and plant the seeds in them, placing them in the hotbed. They are easily lifted if a slat is nailed across the middle, when the young plants are ready for transplanting into the—

Cold Frame

The frame and glass sash of a cold frame are just like those of a hotbed, but the cold frame is placed on the ground without fresh manure, sometimes without any manure.

Usually, the earth is dug up to the depth of a foot and mixed with well-rotted manure and the frame placed on *top* of it. Soil is also banked up on the outside for protection from cold winds.

Billy Builds a Hotbed

An old cooled off hotbed is really a cold frame.

A cold frame is always useful for—

1. "Wintering over" plants a little too tender to leave unprotected.

2. Transplanting seedlings (young plants) from the hotbed, where they will gradually become accustomed to a cooler atmosphere before they are placed in the outside ground.

Young lettuce plants may be placed in the cold frame in the Autumn, and will supply salad nearly all winter.

Parsley and herbs will stay green the winter through if placed in the cold frame.

Some hardier seeds may be started in the cold frame instead of the hotbed; such as cucumber or melons.

Always cover the sash with burlap or old carpet on very cold nights, to prevent young plants from freezing.

Before the boys returned to school, the children had sowed in their new hotbed the seeds of the following flowers and vegetables:

Ageratum	Lettuce
Alyssum	Radishes
Corn flowers	Parsley
Snapdragons	Tomatoes
Peppers	

CHAPTER LVIII

Some Hints on Growing Vegetables

MARY FRANCES repeated to Eleanor some of the lessons which Billy had given her on growing vegetables.

She had a little book in which she had taken notes.

"Billy told me," she said, "that when he was little, he used to wonder why things wouldn't grow if they were just 'stuck down' in the ground. You see, he didn't know that the making of the beds was the most important matter of all."

"Why, I've heard people say that anything would grow if planted by certain people—that they 'had luck,'" Eleanor stated.

"If you had watched those very people," Mary Frances replied wisely, "you would probably have seen that they loosened up the soil before they 'stuck' the plant down."

"I imagine that's true," agreed Eleanor.

"Well," Mary Frances continued, opening her book, "as you know, in getting the outdoor beds ready, you—

Some Hints on Growing Vegetables

(1) Dig deep to loosen the soil;
(2) Spread over it well-rotted manure;
(3) Dig and turn the soil over again;
(4) Rake the top soil fine and level.

It is a good plan to spread leaves and manure over the ground in the Fall and dig them in in the Spring to make the soil rich and crumbly, or friable.

Did you ever think how many different parts of plants are used for food?

We eat the *roots* of some vegetables; such as beets, carrots, radishes, turnips.

Of others we use the *leaves;* such as lettuce, celery, cabbage, spinach, parsley.

Of others, the seeds; as beans, peas, corn.

Of others, the fruit; as peppers, melons, tomatoes.

The Earliest Vegetables to Plant

The following vegetable seeds are not very delicate, and can stand a good deal of frost.

Plant as soon as the ground is warm, about the first of April.

Peas

Plant seeds 2 inches apart, 2 inches deep, 1½ feet between rows.

The new early "Lactonia" peas are to be recommended, because it is not necessary to use brush for them to climb upon. Buy one pint. Sow peas every week for a month to have them ripen from time to time ("successively").

Lettuce
Plant seeds ½ inch deep, broadcast, or 3 inches apart, in rows 1 foot apart.

"All Heart" is very delicious. Remember that lettuce will be much more tender and crisp if grown very quickly in beds rich in manure. Over it, a shade frame should be used in mid-summer and hot weather.

In transplanting to rows from the hotbed, put plants 6 inches apart.

Cos, or Romaine, or Celery Lettuce is very easily grown. The heavy ribs of the leaves are crisp and good. It grows quite well in hot weather.

Onions
Cover the onion with soil. Leave 2 inches between onions; 6 inches between rows.

Buy yellow onion sets—one pint. It takes two years to raise onions from seeds. When ready to pull, take every other one or so, leaving the smallest to grow larger.

Radishes
½ inch deep, about 2 inches apart. Rows 1 foot apart, or broadcast.

The best are the little red globe shape. Sow some in early Spring in hotbed. Sow every week to have "successive," crops. They will be ready in about four weeks. Radishes like a sprinkling of lime in the soil.

Beets
Seeds 1 inch deep, 2 inches apart, in rows 1 foot apart.

Buy five-cent package of Crosby's "Egyptian." Seeds may be sowed thick, or not all germinate. Thin the rows by pulling the weakest plants. The young leaves may be cooked as "greens." Never cut the tops off of beets when cooking. Cut off only the leaves. Beets may be sowed again in June for a late crop.

Some Hints on Growing Vegetables

The Second Early Vegetables to Plant
(About ten days after the first)

Carrots
　Sow ½ inch deep, 3 inches apart, in rows 1½ feet apart.

　　Buy one package "Sutton's Red Intermediate." Carrots do not like new rich soil.
　　Radishes may be sowed between the rows; for they will be pulled before the carrots need much room. Sow carrots rather thick, and thin out weak plants.

Leeks
　Sow seeds 1 inch deep, 2 inches apart, in rows 1 foot apart.

　　Buy one package "Prizetaker Leeks." Sow in March or April, and when they are about half a foot high, transplant to deep, rich soil, 6 inches apart, in rows 1 foot apart. Plant deep, to "blanch," or whiten the tops.
　　Leeks may be sowed in September and transplanted in the Spring.

Parsley
　Sow ½ inch deep, about 4 inches apart, in rows 1 foot apart.

　　Buy one package "Dwarf Perfection" or "Moss Curly." Soak seed over night in water. Parsley may be broadcast if space is limited. Add an equal quantity of sand to the seeds to help sowing. Throw sand and seeds over the seed bed. Cover by using a toy rake. When 4 inches high, it may be transplanted to rows. "Winters over" in cold frame, and in some localities outdoors, if covered with leaves.

Thyme and *Sweet Basil*
　Broadcast.

　　Buy one package each. Broadcast and rake in the seeds. Sweet Basil grows tall. Thyme only about four inches high.

Peppers

Sow broadcast in March in flats (shallow boxes) in hotbed, or under glass. When 2 or 3 inches high, thin out. When ground is really warm, set out 15 inches apart in rows 2 feet apart. Children will not need more than half a dozen plants of large sweet peppers. Buy "Chinese Giant."

Little red peppers are particularly pretty in the garden, and are useful for flavoring soup—use only a half or a quarter of one, though. Buy "Small Chili" or "Red Cherry."

Cucumbers

Sow about a dozen seeds in late March or early April in strawberry box filled with rich soil, and place under glass. Some warm day in May, make a hill about eight inches high, and after tearing off the bottom of the box, plant it in the hill. After a few days, thin out the weakest plants, leaving three or four standing. Two or three moth balls in the ground, when the leaves come through, will keep bugs away.

Corn

Sugar Corn takes up so much room in the garden that only a very few hills should be planted by a child. When the weather is very warm, make little hills 3 feet apart. Drop 6 corn kernels a little distance apart into the hole. Cover with about an inch of soil. Shallow cultivation helps. Buy one package "Stabler's Early" for early corn; one package "Stowell's Evergreen" for later crops.

Some Hints on Growing Vegetables

Beans
2 inches deep, 6 inches apart, in rows 18 inches apart

Lima Beans. Buy "Bush Limas," because it will not be necessary to set poles for them to climb upon. Wood ashes mixed with the soil helps them grow. They do not like damp, heavy soil. Do not plant before warm weather, because beans are tender. Plant in *warm* weather, edgewise, with the "eye" down.

String Beans. Buy "Stringless Green Pod." Plant every week after all danger of frost is past, 2 inches deep, 6 inches apart, in rows 18 inches or 2 feet apart.

Tomatoes
Plants, 2 feet apart, in rows 3 feet apart

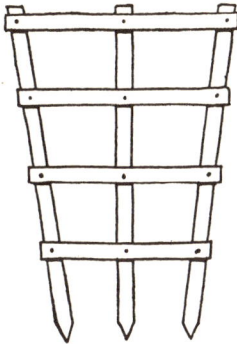

TOMATO TRELLIS OR SUPPORT

It is best for the small gardener to buy the plants and set them out in rows when the weather is really warm. "Earliana" is the best early variety.

"Ponderosa" is the best later variety. If you sow seeds, start them under glass in March or even earlier. When plants are about 3 inches high, transplant to strawberry boxes. Break bottom of box and transplant box into the open ground when it is really warm. Tomatoes need supports to rest or climb upon. The simplest support is a stake driven down near them, to which the stems are tied as they grow. Stakes driven at intervals with heavy cords running from one to the other make another good support; but the best is a slat frame.

If grown from seeds, they will not be ready for about 18 weeks.

Potatoes

> *White Potatoes.* It is best for children not to attempt to grow more than one plant of potatoes, but they may be interested to know that white potatoes are grown from the "eye," cut in a large square-shaped piece of the potatoes. The potatoes form on the roots of the bush, and are dug and stored in the Fall.
>
> *Sweet Potatoes* grow on the roots of a very pretty vine which trails over the ground. To get the young plants, some sweet potatoes are grown in hotbeds, and the vines are transplanted in hot weather to open ground.

In transplanting, always press with your fingers the soil firmly down around the roots.

Fertilizers

As you know, in order to make good and rapid growth, plants need the right kind of food. Manure is the best fertilizer. In manure almost every kind of plant food is supplied, but there are chemical foods which stimulate growth and are easily applied. If it is impossible to obtain manure, use decayed vegetables and leaves, and *Commercial Fertilizer*, which is made up of the mineral or chemical food needed by plants. Do not use too much, for it is very heating and may burn the roots of young plants. Never let the roots come into direct contact with the powder—always sprinkle some earth over it after throwing a small quantity (about two tablespoonfuls) in a hole.

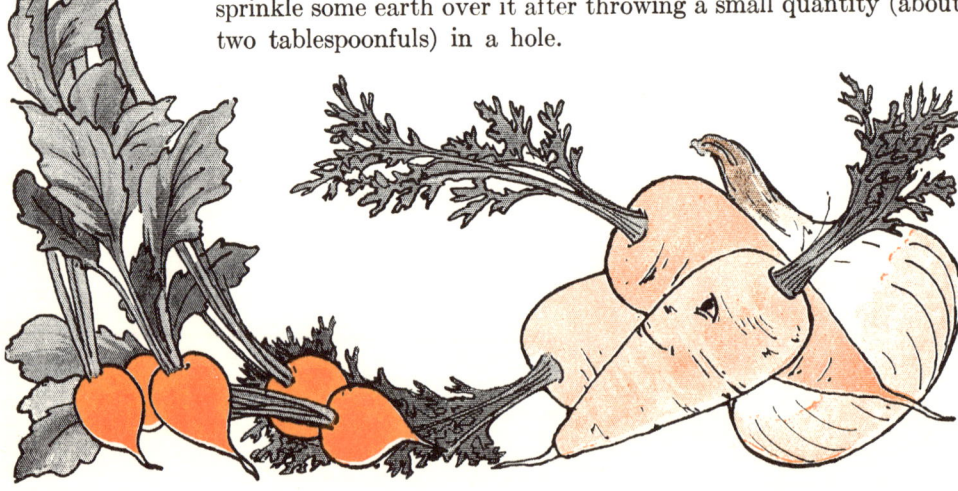

Some Hints on Growing Vegetables

Bone meal or Ground Bone is another excellent food. If sprinkled on the ground and dug in around the roots of roses, it will give them a good food supply.

Nitrate of Soda is a very stimulating food for *vegetables*. Use 1 tablespoonful in 4 quarts of water in the sprinkler. Do not use until the plants are at least 3 inches high, and only once in two weeks. Sprinkle ground near roots—do not sprinkle leaves.

Cow Manure and *Sheep Manure* may be purchased in powdered form for use in a small garden, and in this form are most easily managed by little folks.

Powdered Sheep Manure dug in around the roots of roses once a month assures a wealth of bloom.

Insecticides

All plants will be attacked by insects.

One of the best insecticides for children to use, because it is not poisonous to human beings, is Slug Shot, a patent preparation, which will kill worms and many other biting insects. It is inexpensive and need be dusted but lightly on foliage which is bitten.

Tobacco tea made by throwing boiling water over tobacco stems, and letting it cool, is used for aphides (Plant lice).

For other insecticides, see Chapter XXIX.

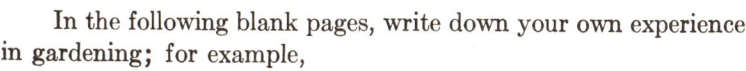

In the following blank pages, write down your own experience in gardening; for example,

356　The Mary Frances Garden Book

Name.	Dates.	Remarks.
Sweet Peas. (Improved Early Spencer.) Pink, lavender, white.	Plant in the *Autumn*, or early Spring.	Plant in deep drills, in rich earth. Give them a wire frame to climb upon. Never water at night, as the dampness causes them to mildew. Pick blossoms daily.

Some Hints on Growing Vegetables 357

Name.	Dates	Remarks.

Name.	Dates.	Remarks.

Some Hints on Growing Vegetables

Name.	Dates.	Remarks.

CHAPTER LIX

The City Garden

CHILDREN who live in the city usually have so little ground that they are not often encouraged to attempt gardening.

Even in the tiny 9 x 12 foot city yard, provided it has sunshine during some part of the day, a surprising variety of plants may be grown.

In the new style of building, happily the old-fashioned boarded-up fence is disappearing, being replaced by iron fencing, which gives an open appearance and admits air to the rear of the dwelling; but if one lives where the garden is "walled in," a great deal of pleasure may be gained from—

Hanging Gardens

Along the sunniest wall of the garden, hang boxes on iron brackets as shown in the picture on this page.

The lower garden should be placed high enough to let the sunlight into the small hotbed which is placed on the ground.

In the upper garden, annual flowers and vines may be grown.

In the lower garden, plan to have—

A Soup and Sauce Garden

containing mint, parsley, chives, onions, little red peppers.

In the ground near the hotbed, you may grow tomatoes, carrots, and—

Okra or *Gumbo*

Plant seeds in May. You will probably need only two plants, one foot apart. Use the pods while young. "White Velvet" is a good variety. The plants grow three feet tall. In chicken or tomato soup the beautiful green odd-shaped slices give a richness of flavor.

In using fresh thyme in soup, add it a few moments before serving instead of cooking it from the first, and notice the improvement of flavor.

In the hotbed garden you may have radishes and lettuce at the time they come with their tempting freshness and their high prices in the Spring markets.

In the city, many flowering plants are grown in sunny windows. The following named will be found among the best for the—

Indoor Garden

Hyacinths	Bermuda Buttercup Oxalis
Chinese Lilies	English Ivy
Tulips	Impatiens Sultana
Tuberous-rooted Begonias	Spirea
Ferns	Geraniums

Bermuda Buttercup Oxalis blooms all winter in clusters of golden yellow flowers. The foliage is beautiful, resembling that of clover.

Grand Duchess Oxalis, in pink, is another charming house plant. It comes in white and lavender also.

The other types of Oxalis are pretty in hanging baskets.

The bulbs of Oxalis cost from three to five cents each. Plant six in a pot, and be certain to give them good soil, partly leaf loam. Keep them in a dark, cool place for a short time. Water them as they dry out. Bring to the light gradually. They will sometimes bloom in six weeks. Oxalis, already started, may be had of a florist.

Another pretty house plant is a vine grown from a sweet potato placed in a hyacinth glass or bottle of water.

SWEET POTATO VINE

For the dining table center piece, the next time you have grapefruit for breakfast, save the seeds, and plant them quite thick, about one-half inch deep, in a shallow earthen flower pot. Keep well watered. It may take six weeks for the leaves to peep through, but they make a beautiful green decoration for the house in winter.

The City Garden

Do not forget your strawflowers which you dried in the Summer. They look pretty with the Japanese air plant, which stays green so long without water.

Watering House Plants

Immerse the pot in a bucket of water, and leave it until it stops bubbling. This done twice a week is far better than daily sprinkling. Neither is it good to keep water in a saucer under a plant; the roots do not like a constant soaking. Wash the leaves from time to time, and when the weather is warm enough, give them some fresh air.

Tobacco dust will keep away green lice (aphides); so, also, will Persian insect powder. Blow either on with little bellows, or "air guns."

There is a plant food for house plants which is sold by dealers. One teaspoonful dug into the earth once in two weeks is very beneficial to their growth.

CHAPTER LX

Garden Color-Pictures

MOTHER NATURE never makes a mistake if left to her own choice of colors.

Indeed, she is a real color artist. What could be lovelier than the purple of the New England aster, near the lavender of the Joe Pye weed, with an interlacing of wild carrot and yarrow; then, not too near, the dangling orange jewel weed, and a little farther away, the brown cat-tail—all set in a green frame, in the soft light of the dove blue of the sky?

That is just one of Mother Nature's color-pictures. If you watch her many pictures, you will learn that—

Flowers in masses are more beautiful than in design.

That many white flowers are needed to divide the severe contrast of colors.

That—

Yellow combines well with { purple and lavender / blue / scarlet / browns

but that yellow does not combine well with crimson or magenta.

Blue combines well with $\begin{cases} \text{yellow} \\ \text{crimson, magenta} \\ \text{pink} \end{cases}$

Light pink and yellow are good together, depending upon the shades.

It is difficult to describe the beauty of Mary Frances' garden. Peeping over the green velvet of the lawn is a border of low-growing white flowers which look like ribbons of snow. They are sweet alyssum—"Little Gem."

Just back of them come pink Baby Rambler roses; next, a large mass of charming blue-lavender eupatorium; and "locking arms" with the eupatorium, on the other side, is a rudbeckia, a bush bearing little "brown-eyed" flowers.

Between the pink of the Baby Rambler and the blue of the eupatorium is a bush of feverfew; and between the blue of the eupatorium and the yellow of the rudbeckia is the white of achillea.

Mary Frances says that she thinks that these

flowers form the most perfect color-picture in her garden.

On the other side of the garden are perennial sunflowers which are so much more desirable than golden glow, and beneath them are brilliant nasturtiums.

One must remember that the various shades of one color always combine well together.

For instance, in the Spring, Mary Frances has pink tulips blooming just beneath a bush of flowering almond; and daffodils beneath golden bell or forsythia.

The flowering almond and forsythia shrubs that Mary Frances has, she grew from little sprigs which a neighbor gave her. She simply put them down into the ground and kept them well watered!

All the flowers mentioned except nasturtiums are hardy perennials, and have never had but the slightest care since planting two years ago, except thinning out where they became too thick.

CHAPTER LXI

Patterns for Paper Flowers

DEAR Girls and Boys:
   Don't you want to make a flower, now that you begin to know how wonderful they are?

To Make a Wild Rose

Materials required:

Pink, green, yellow tissue paper; white tracing paper; very *fine* wire; heavy wire for stem; yellow beads; small piece beeswax; pair small pincers; scissors; glue.

1. To make the *corolla*,—

(*a*) Lay a piece of pink tissue paper over the pattern of the *corolla* shown in the picture on the next page.

(*b*) Cut out; and curl the tips of the petals, by drawing them through between the thumb and blade of the scissors, just as your mother does ostrich feathers.

2. Trace, through a piece of tracing paper, the *calyx*, and *foliage*, as shown in the picture. Cut out, and use for patterns in cutting green tissue paper calyx and leaves.

3. To make the *stamens*,—

(*a*) Cut three pieces of fine wire, two and a half inches long, for the *filaments*. (See picture of stamens.)

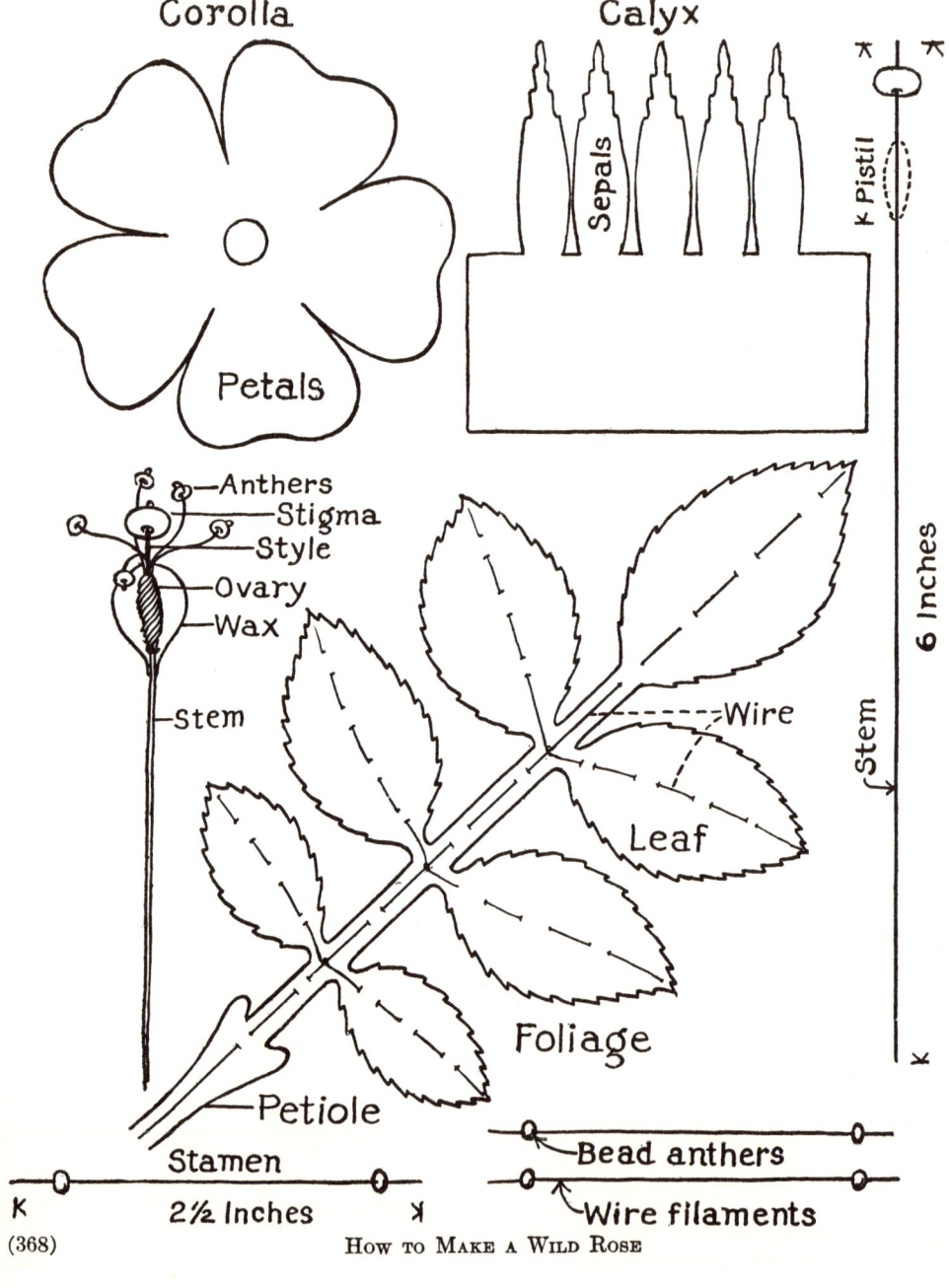

How to Make a Wild Rose

(b) Fasten a small yellow bead *anther* on each end of the wire *filaments*, by bending the end of the wire over the bead with pincers. Fold the filament wires in half.

4. To make the *pistil* and *stem*,—

(a) Cut a piece of heavy wire six inches long—to form the stem.

(b) On one end, fasten a large yellow bead to form the *stigma*. Cut a piece of fine wire eight inches long. One inch below the *stigma* bead, hold the folded *filament* wires in a little bundle around the stem wire, and wind with the fine eight inch wire—to form the *ovary*. The heavy wire between the *stigma* and the *ovary* represents the *style*.

5. Cut a piece of beeswax a little less than a half-inch square. Mould it with the fingers under hot water until you have a soft ball.

6. Slip the pink *corolla* up the wire stem until over the wound wire. Spread the *stamens* out to prevent the corolla from slipping off.

7. Fit the beeswax over the wound wire to form the *calyx* cup; and pack a tiny bit of yellow tissue paper into the opening of the corolla *under the stamens.*

8. Wind the *calyx cup* with the green tissue paper calyx which you cut by the pattern, and fasten the end with a tip of glue.

9. Run a fine wire in and out through the stems of the foliage.

10. Cut a piece of green tissue paper eleven inches long and one inch wide. Commencing at the green *calyx* cup, wind the

stem of the rose with this green strip of paper. Half way down, insert the *petiole* of the foliage, or leaves, under the strip, and continue winding to the end of the stem. Fasten the end by winding with fine wire.

There! you have the flower, and you know the names of the parts as well as Billy and Mary Frances know them.

CHAPTER LXII

The Mary Frances Garden Cut-Outs

EVERY boy or girl who will carefully make up the Mary Frances Garden Cut-Outs, and will study the lists of flowers printed on the reverse side of each garden, will very soon become familiar with the name, season of bloom, and appearance of the best-known perennials. Notice the artistic effect of "massing," or grouping the same kind of plants close together.

In order to recognize the flowers mentioned in the lists, turn to Chapters VII, VIII, IX, and X, to read descriptions.

Directions for Making
THE MARY FRANCES GARDEN CUT-OUTS

1. Turn to the picture of Mary Frances' Play House before the Children Planted the Gardens.

Cut along the red lines A, B, C, on the edge of the picture; and D in center of grass plot.

2. Turn to Mary Frances' Garden Cut-Out No. 1—Early Spring Hardy Garden.

372   THE MARY FRANCES GARDEN BOOK

Detach or cut out the page.
Cut along the edges of each colored portion.
3. Insert the little flaps A, B, C, D, of the cut-out portions into the openings A, B, C, D.
4. Follow the same directions in
Garden No. 2—Early Summer Hardy Garden.
Garden No. 3—Mid-Summer Hardy Garden.
Garden No. 4—Late Summer or Early Fall Hardy Garden.

You will be delighted with the fairy-like way in which you have changed the landscape in front of the picture of Mary Frances' Play House; but the pictures give only a slight idea of the beauty of the real gardens which Billy and Mary Frances made. In order to see how beautiful the flowers are, you will have to plant your own real gardens.

May they give you as much pleasure as they did Billy and Mary Frances.

CHAPTER LXIII

LITTLE GARDENERS' CALENDAR

THE following plan was given to Mary Frances and Eleanor by the boys.
They called it—

THE LITTLE GARDENERS' CALENDAR

In *Mid-Winter* or *January*, plan out your garden, drawing a map and filling in space.

A little later, in *February*, get the hotbed ready, and spray roses with Bordeaux Arsenate of Lead, remembering it is a violent poison. Use one tablespoon to a quart of water. This will help prevent mildews and fungi.

In *March*, or even in *February*, study seed catalogue and order seeds.

Plant some seeds in the hotbed.

Prepare some of the out-door seed beds by spading and manuring.

In *April*, transplant hardier plants to cold frame, or open ground.

Spray everything again.

If weather is warm enough, sow seeds out of doors.

In *May*, sow seeds of some annuals and vegetables out-of-doors.

Look out for weeds: kill them while young.

In *June*, plant seeds and seedlings in open ground.

In *July*, plant late seeds; carrots, turnips, etc.

In *August*, start perennials for next year. Weed!

In *September*, order bulbs needed.

Move flowering plants which are not in right place.

In *October*, save seeds of annual flowers, labeling each envelope carefully.

Set out bulbs, unless you live below or near the Mason and Dixon line; *November* is a better time in that case.

In *November*, rake up leaves and make into compost heap. Throw a little lime among them. Never burn them. They make humus.

Take up summer bulbs and store them carefully.

Spread manure over the ground to be spaded in the Spring.

Hill earth about six inches high over rose bush roots.

Spread litter and leaves over bulbs and perennials to protect them during winter.

In *December*, trim dead wood from rose bushes.

Destroy nests of cocoons, burning them, and read the MARY FRANCES GARDEN BOOK.

CHAPTER LXIV

Budding and Grafting

TO most boys and girls, the marvelous method of getting new varieties of fruit is a matter of great interest.

In budding, as you know, a bud is set under the bark of a growing plant.

In grafting, the top of the plant is cut off and a branch of another plant is inserted. These branches are usually cut in the Autumn and kept in sand all winter.

In the Spring, the tree to be grafted is cut and the branch (or, scion) is inserted and held in place by raffia and grafting wax, as shown in the accompanying drawing.

GRAFTING

It was not until the boys' second winter at the garden school that they experimented with grafting peach trees and budding rose bushes, and it was a year later before they knew the result of their work.

If you are particularly interested in the subject, send to the United States Department of Agriculture for Bulletin No. 157, on "The Propagation of Plants."

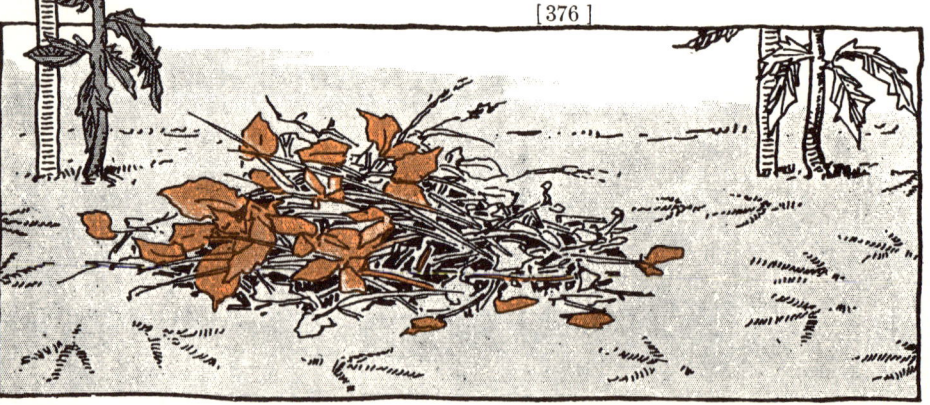

CHAPTER LXV

Prizes at the County Fair

"REMEMBER in all gardening, that experience is your best teacher. Do not become discouraged if you fail. Do not undertake too much. Remember that most people fail to get good plants because they do not prepare deep good beds, and do not 'cultivate,' or stir the ground. Watering is nothing like so necessary."

This is what Mary Frances was telling a number of children in the garden one day as Billy came upon her unawares.

"You couldn't have better advice, children," he said.

"Than Billy gave me," Mary Frances added. "He taught two friends and me so well, that next year we are each to have our own garden plot, and 'race' with Billy to see who can raise the finest vegetables."

"Some of the very finest are to be sent to the County Fair," stated Billy.

"And they'll be 'winners,' you may be sure," Bob prophesied as he and Eleanor joined the group.

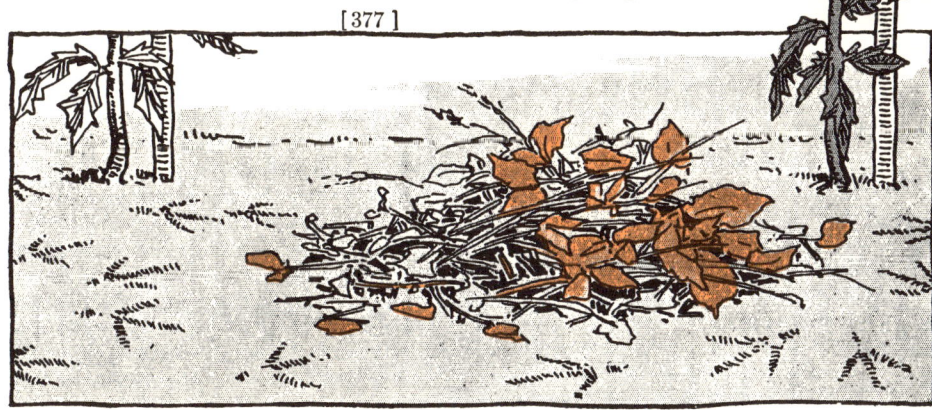

"So will some of our flowers, won't they, Nell?"

Before Eleanor could answer Mary Frances, there sounded the joyous shrill crow of Feather Flop.

"I'm sure they will!" it meant to the little girl, but none of the others seemed to hear the rooster.

Perhaps he did know—for one year from that day, each of the children received some premiums at the County Fair; but, to Mary Frances' surprise, she had three more than Eleanor; two more than Bob, and one more than Billy!

"I wonder why your garden did better than all the rest," said Bob. "You didn't seem to work any harder than we did."

"Oh, it was just a 'happen so,'" answered Mary Frances, but she remembered that many a morning she had seen prints of the claws of Feather Flop in her garden, and a little pile of weeds at

THE END

The Mary Frances Books
For Teaching Useful Things in an Entertaining Way
by Jane Eayre Fryer

These are not mere story books to be read through and cast aside. They are instruction books in story form which the youthful readers joyfully study because they think it is play. But in this play they learn principles of usefulness which fascinate because of the manner in which these principles are presented.

The MARY FRANCES SEWING BOOK
or Adventures Among the Thimble People

It tells, in as quaint and delightful a story as ever appealed to a child's imagination, how the fairy Thimble People teach Mary Frances to sew. It teaches the reader how to sew—how to use patterns—how to cut and fold the material—how to piece it together. The book includes a complete set of patterns for doll clothes—undergarments—street clothes—coats—hats—even a wedding dress. Illustrated with 300 colored drawings that for interest and instruction are absolutely inimitable. Colored illustrations by Jane Allen Boyer on every page.

The MARY FRANCES KNITTING and CROCHETING BOOK
or Adventures Among the Knitting People

Here is the fascinating story of how little Mary Frances took her first lessons in crocheting and knitting, and from this advanced to deserve recognition as an expert. The first steps were making things for dollies, but after a girl has learned to crochet and knit for the dollies it is "as easy as A-B-C" to crochet and knit for real people.

The MARY FRANCES HOUSEKEEPER
or Adventures Among the Doll People

It is doubtful whether any story more captivating than The Mary Frances Housekeeper has ever been written for girls. In the most skillful manner, it takes advantage of the natural childish instinct to "play house," and the opportunity to instill the fundamental principles of good housekeeping is improved through the medium of the delightful story of Mary Frances' experience in teaching her dolls to keep house.

The MARY FRANCES COOK BOOK
or Adventures Among the Kitchen People

This winsome book so happily combines fact and fancy that any girl who reads it will unconsciously absorb the principles of cookery while devouring the most fascinating sort of story. It throws a glamour around the processes of baking and boiling and leads girls into pleasant habits of usefulness and industry. The book gives recipes in the simplest, plainest words. It describes every operation clearly—just what Mary Frances did, and how she learned to avoid mistakes. The book stimulates the imagination and creates a desire to follow Mary Frances' example.

[the above is from original promotional copy for these books]

Heirloom, cloth bound editions of these titles have been published by and are available from this publisher.

LACIS PUBLICATIONS
3163 Adeline Street
Berkeley, CA 94703

LACIS publishes and distributes books specifically related to the textile arts, focusing on the subjects of costume, lace and lace making, embroidery and hand sewing.

Also published by LACIS:

KNITTING: 19th CENTURY SOURCES, ed. by Jules & Kaethe Kliot
TATTED LACE OF BEADS, Nina Libin
THE CARE AND PRESERVATION OF TEXTILES, Karen Finch & Greta Putnam
THE ART OF HAIR WORK, Mark Campbell
THE COMPLETE BOOK OF TATTING, Rebecca Jones
NEW DIMENSIONS IN TATTING, To de Haan-van Beek
TATTING WITH VISUAL PATTERNS, Mary Konior
CLASSIC BEADED PURSE PATTERNS, Jong-Kramer
ILLUSTRATED DICTIONARY OF LACE, Judyth L. Gwynne
MILLINERY FOR EVERY WOMAN, Georgina Kerr Kaye
LADIES' TAILOR-MADE GARMENTS: 1908, S.S. Gordon
INTRODUCTION TO BOBBIN LACE MAKING, Rosemary Shepherd
CROCHET: NOVELTIES, ed by Jules & Kaethe Kliot
THE BARGELLO BOOK, Frances Salter
HAUTE COUTURE EMBROIDERY, Palmer White
TAMBOUR WORK, Yusai Fukuyama
BEADED ANIMALS IN JEWELRY, Latty Lammens & Els Scholte
MACRAMÉ, SOURCES OF FINE KNOTTING, ed by Jules & Kaethe Kliot
MOUNTMELLICK EMBROIDERY, ed by Jules & Kaethe Kliot
FLORENTINE EMBROIDERY, Barbara Muller
BERLIN WORK, SAMPLERS & EMBROIDERY OF THE NINETEENTH CENTURY, Raffaella Serena
THE MAGIC OF FREE MACHINE EMBROIDERY, Doreen Curran
DESIGNS FOR CHURCH EMBROIDERIES, Thomas Brown & Son
EMBROIDERY WITH BEADS, Angela Thompson
BEAD WORK, ed. by Jules & Kaethe Kliot
THE BEADING BOOK, Julia Jones
BEAD EMBROIDERY, Valerie Campbell-Harding and Pamela Watts
BEADED BAGS AND MORE, ed. by Jules & Kaethe Kliot

For a complete list of LACIS titles, write to:
LACIS
3163 Adeline Street
Berkeley, CA 94703
USA

PICTURE OF MARY FRANCES PLAY HOUSE BEFORE THE CHILDREN PLANTED THE GARDENS

For Directions for Garden Cut-Outs, see Chapter LXII